SAVAGE DRAGON

BY
ERIK
LARSEN

THIS SAVAGE WORLD

THIS SAVAGE WORLD

ERIK LARSEN	Creator • Writer • Penciller • Inker
CHRIS ELIOPOULOS	Letterer
I.H.O.C	Colors

**REUBEN RUDE, ABEL MOUTON
ANTONIO KOHL, BILL ZINDEL
STEPHANE KRIESHOK,
LEA RUDE & JOHN ZAIA**

JOSH EICHORN	The knave of comics

**Dedicated to the memory of
Jack Kirby**

IMAGE COMICS

Jim Valentino	Publisher
Brent Braun	Director of Production
Eric Stephenson	Director of Marketing
Traci Hale	Controller/Foreign Licensing
Brett Evans	Art Director
Allen Hui	Web Developer
Sean O'Brien	Inventory Controller
Cindie Espinoza	Accounting Assitant

INTRODUCTION
BY ERIK LARSEN

It's no secret that I'm a huge fan of the work of Jack Kirby. I've made that clear enough. The beginning of the Savage World saga was a tribute to the King of Comics.

But it didn't start out that way...

It all started with an image.

I'd created this time-traveling foe named Darklord to face off against my newly formed government super-team call Special Operations Strikeforce. Darklord was from an alternate world called Darkworld where things had pretty much gone to hell. Having been moved from its original location by cosmic beings, Darkworld was dying a premature death. Desperate to save his imperiled planet, Darklord began substituting the crust and inhabitants of his foul Earth with ours. In an effort to save their world, the Dragon and a select group of heroes headed over to Darkworld to shut down the machines and kick some cans. In the end, Darklord killed a woman Dragon had loved and then met his own end.

The good guys won.

Sort of.

You see, sometime earlier, Martians had attacked earth and experimented on SuperPatriot's daughter, Liberty, impregnating her. Staunchly pro-life, Liberty Farrell carried the child to its full term. Shortly after Darklord met his untimely demise, Liberty gave birth...

...To Darklord.

Which leads me to that image I'd mentioned earlier. The picture that popped into my head was that of SuperPatriot, pointing a gun at a baby Darklord with Dragon's son standing in the way attempting to protect him.

Pretty powerful stuff.

Once that visual had occurred to me I couldn't stop thinking about it and its ramifications. What if SuperPatriot DID kill Darklord BEFORE he could grow up and do the damage he did? What might be the result? What changes might result if Darklord never grew up--never traveled back in time to tamper with things?

It got me thinking.

I drew up my idea, turning it into a cover image and used it to solicit Savage Dragon #67. When it came time to actually draw the issue (the cover had been drawn for promotional purposes several months before I actually drew the comic book itself) I was sorely tempted to have SuperPatriot pull the trigger just to see what happened.

But then I thought...it's Dragon's book.

So I planted the seed. Let the idea sit out there. And I got top work.

I thought it through. I made copious notes and determined just what would have happened if the time-traveling foe had been taken out of the picture. And then I set out to tie up a lot of dangling plot lines and set things in motion. Darklord had set up this huge organization in preparation for his own arrival and getting all of my ducks in a row involved setting up a lot of little pieces so that the end result would be as dramatic as possible. I intended to make the world as messed up as possible after the big change took place.

I set things up. Made the necessary changes. Wrote the necessary dialogue. And then it was that time. It all built up to Savage Dragon #75, a double-sized anniversary issue. Getting Dragon in place and pissed off and all the rest was only the beginning--the next step was to follow...

The effect was, if nothing else, startling. Gone were full-bleed pages where drawings would extend to the edge of the paper--gone were panels that would take on nearly any shape conceivable, stories that ran into each other in a veritable jumble. The Savage World introduced, to Savage Dragon readers, titles and credits and captions and page numbers and ever (gasp) thought balloons! The entire style, look and presentation of the stories were completely foreign to what had come before and it threw a lot of readers completely for a loop!

Which brings me back to why I got interested in comics in the first place and the work of Jack Kirby.

When I first became aware of Kirby's work he was writing and drawing a book called Kamandi over at DC Comics. Kamandi was an odd one. A book set outside of the traditional DC Universe--one in which the title character roamed around in a post-apocalyptic world running into fantastic creatures, situations and talking animals.

Kamandi kicked ass!

If you're ever at a comic book convention with Bruce Timm and me be prepared to listen to two fanatical Kamandi buffs go on a Kamandi rant like nobody's business. If you can manage to wander off after listening to our enthusiastic exchange and NOT head directly in search of a sampling than you've got more willpower than most. Between the two of us we must have persuaded a good hundred guys to go pawing through back issue bins in search of Kamandi comics!

What was different about Kamandi? Everything. The entire approach was different from everything else at the time. In Kamandi's book, Kamandi was the focus. This may seem like a given but by that point in time readers had come to expect sub-plots where you'd get a glimpse at what various supporting characters were doing. Not in Kamandi. In Kamandi he was the focus. Sure, he'd run into other characters that he knew from time to time but unless they were interacting with Kamandi--they were nowhere to be seen.

Kamandi was a book for all ages. The hero was young and feisty and the adventures were imaginative and action-packed.

At this point you may be wondering why I'm going on and on about a book that was cancelled years ago from another company but I'll get to it.

In any case, Kamandi did things in a different way--it was a novel approach and once Jack Kirby decided to leave DC and return to Marvel, those that followed immediately blew it. The stories began to have sub-plots, Kamandi became a bit player in his own book, continued stories rambled on for months at a time and a bevy of artists and writers all with completely different styles and approaches took a stab at driving the book into the ground.

Still, after everything had been said and done, Kamandi was Jack Kirby's biggest success at DC comics. Yeah, the New Gods were revived a few times as were Mister Miracle and the Demon but Kamandi was not prematurely cancelled in mid-stream like all the others. Kamandi ran for well over a year after Jack had done his 40 issue run!

Here's where I came into the picture. I'm a comic book fan, to be sure, and a Jack Kirby enthusiast, like no other, but I'm also a father of two terrific kids. Part of being a dad is sharing my enthusiasm and reading stories to my kids. At this point in time there are precious few modern comics that I can read them. Superhero comics have become too dark, too brooding, too depressing and, frankly, too BORING for a young kid to really get hooked on. Needless to say, finding suitable reading material for the little ones has been no easy feat.

Thank god for reprints of old Marvel Comics, Tin Tin, Captain Marvel Adventures and Kamandi!

After having treated my son Christopher to Kamandi, I thought it would be a lot of fun to use a similar approach on Savage Dragon.

Like many comics, Savage Dragon had become mired in continuity. Supporting characters had taken on bigger roles, lessened Dragon's participation in his own title and while stories were engaging over a span of issues with plots weaving in and out and characters coming and going on an individual issue basis the stories seldom stood on their own. Heck, more often than not a casual reader would be completely baffled by who half of the characters were, much less what their relationship was with the Dragon. The Dragon had pushed the envelope over the years and was often downright raunchy. It had gotten to a point where I had gone as far as I wanted to go. I felt a certain pressure to have to continually top myself in terms of how outrageous I could get and there reached a point where I felt I was no longer enjoying that.

I also felt like somebody ought to be doing comics that could be enjoyed by readers of ALL ages and that if nobody else was going to produce comics that I could read to my kids-I would.

And so I did.

Man, what a gas! I'd never done a comic book where the lead character was on every single page before, much less every single panel! Using the straightforward panel layout was an eye-opening experience as well--rather than focussing on making a particular page be splashy and exciting my focus became on telling a story in the clearest, most exciting, most compelling way possible.

The reaction was, as you might expect, somewhat mixed. While new readers were compelled to try out the title for their first time and others welcomed the change and enjoyed seeing me try something new, some older readers found the new look to be too jarring and preferred things the way they had been. They missed all of the old supporting cast and art with full bleeds and varied panel shapes and borders. They found the inclusion of captions and thought balloons intrusive and excessive.

Christopher enjoyed it.

I enjoyed it.

And I can't help but think that Jack would have enjoyed it as well.

This Savage World was the start of an epic adventure. It set the stage for what was to come. The look, feel and tone set here was established in these tomes included here and over the course of the next few years more and more familiar characters, elements and styles gradually crept into the mix. The ultimate goal here was to create a better world--a world that was the best of all worlds where I was free to let my imagination run rampant.

This Savage World was the first step.

I think it was a step in the right direction.

I hope you think so as well.

-Erik Larsen

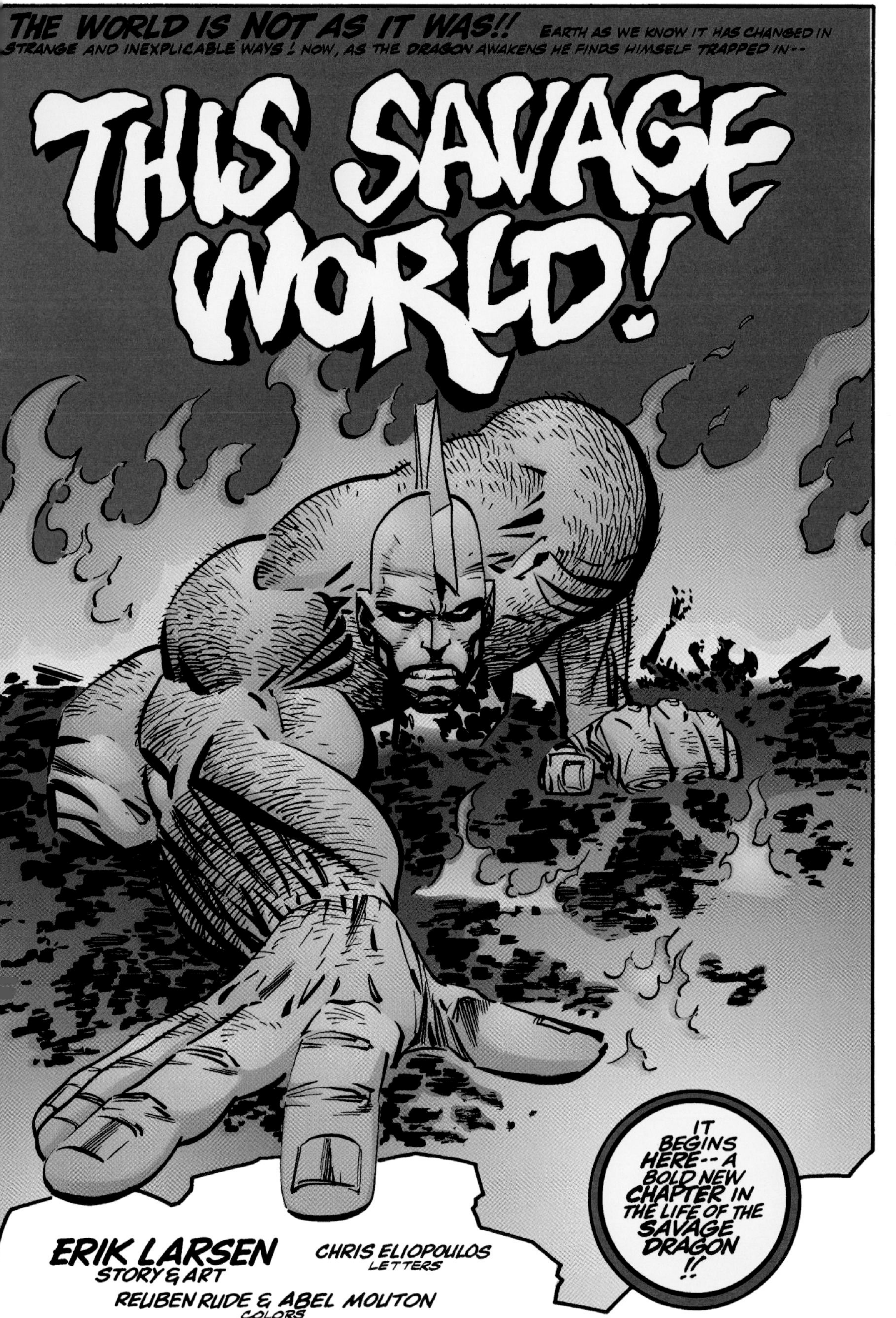

THE WORLD IS NOT AS IT WAS!! EARTH AS WE KNOW IT HAS CHANGED IN STRANGE AND INEXPLICABLE WAYS! NOW, AS THE DRAGON AWAKENS HE FINDS HIMSELF TRAPPED IN--
THIS SAVAGE WORLD!
IT BEGINS HERE-- A BOLD NEW CHAPTER IN THE LIFE OF THE SAVAGE DRAGON !!
ERIK LARSEN STORY & ART
CHRIS ELIOPOULOS LETTERS
REUBEN RUDE & ABEL MOUTON COLORS

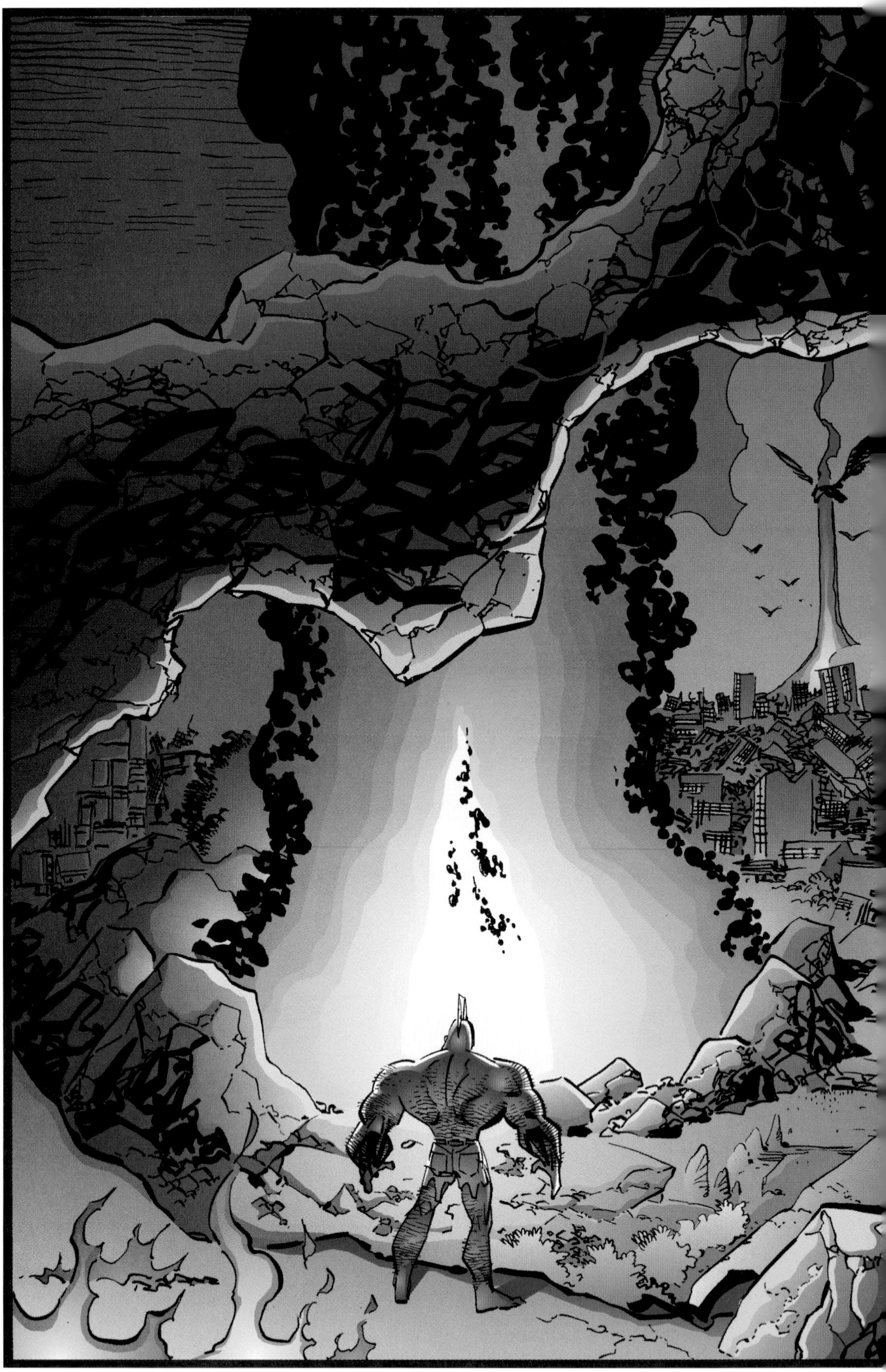

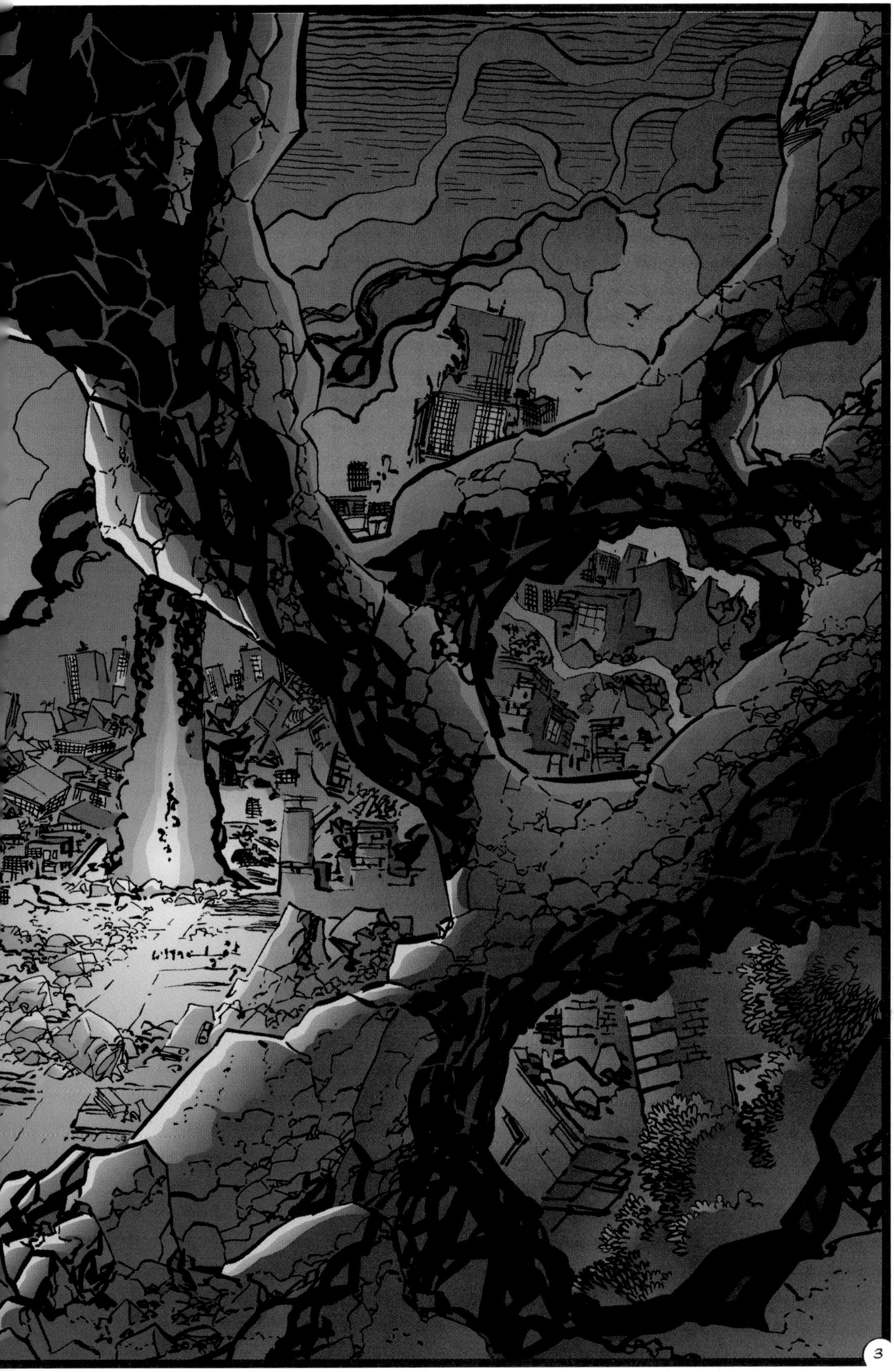

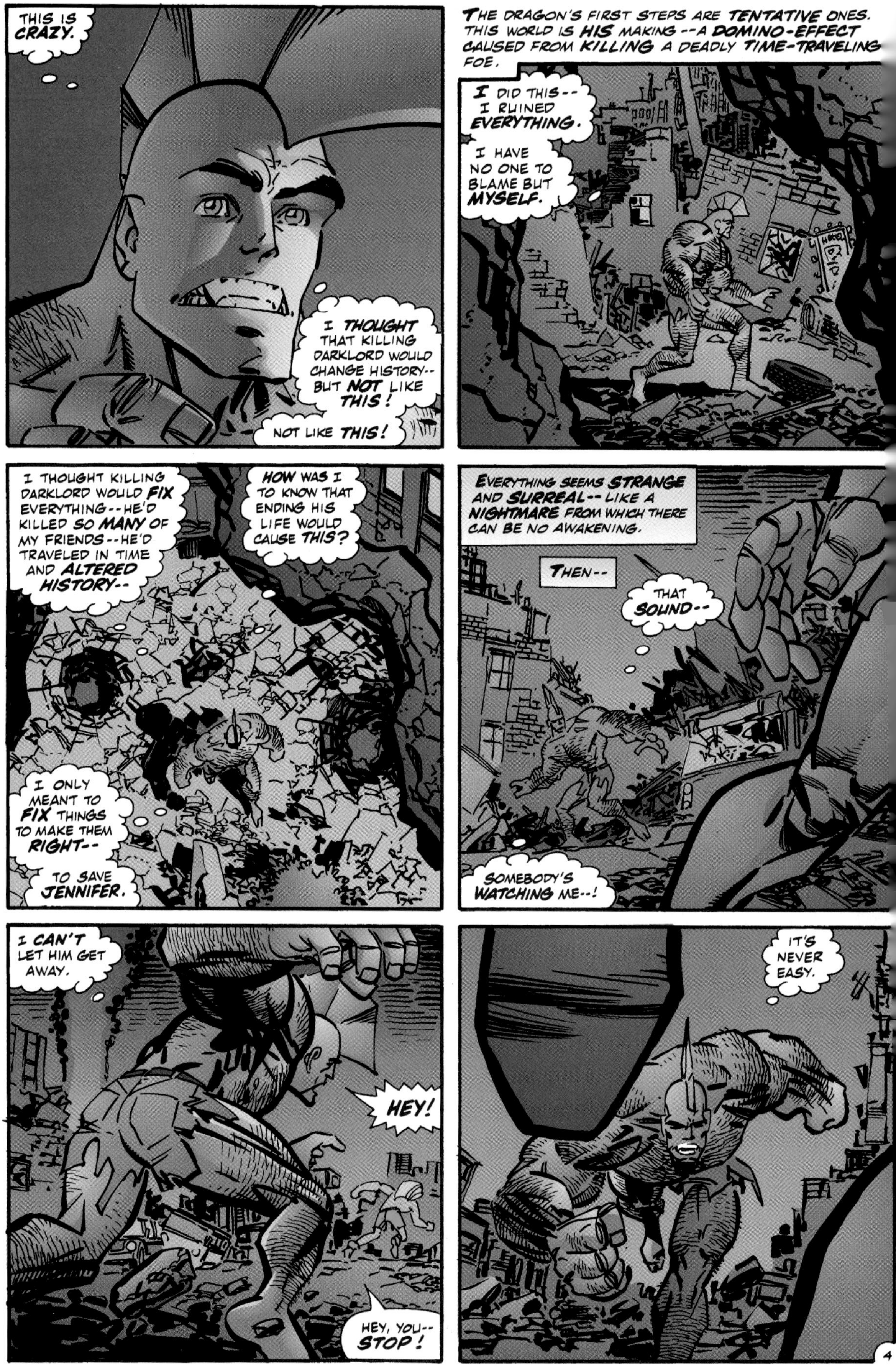

THIS IS CRAZY.
I THOUGHT THAT KILLING DARKLORD WOULD CHANGE HISTORY-- BUT NOT LIKE THIS!
NOT LIKE THIS!
THE DRAGON'S FIRST STEPS ARE TENTATIVE ONES. THIS WORLD IS HIS MAKING --A DOMINO-EFFECT CAUSED FROM KILLING A DEADLY TIME-TRAVELING FOE.
I DID THIS-- I RUINED EVERYTHING.
I HAVE NO ONE TO BLAME BUT MYSELF.
I THOUGHT KILLING DARKLORD WOULD FIX EVERYTHING--HE'D KILLED SO MANY OF MY FRIENDS--HE'D TRAVELED IN TIME AND ALTERED HISTORY--
HOW WAS I TO KNOW THAT ENDING HIS LIFE WOULD CAUSE THIS?
I ONLY MEANT TO FIX THINGS TO MAKE THEM RIGHT--
TO SAVE JENNIFER.
EVERYTHING SEEMS STRANGE AND SURREAL-- LIKE A NIGHTMARE FROM WHICH THERE CAN BE NO AWAKENING.
THEN--
THAT SOUND--
SOMEBODY'S WATCHING ME--!
I CAN'T LET HIM GET AWAY.
HEY!
HEY, YOU-- STOP!
IT'S NEVER EASY.

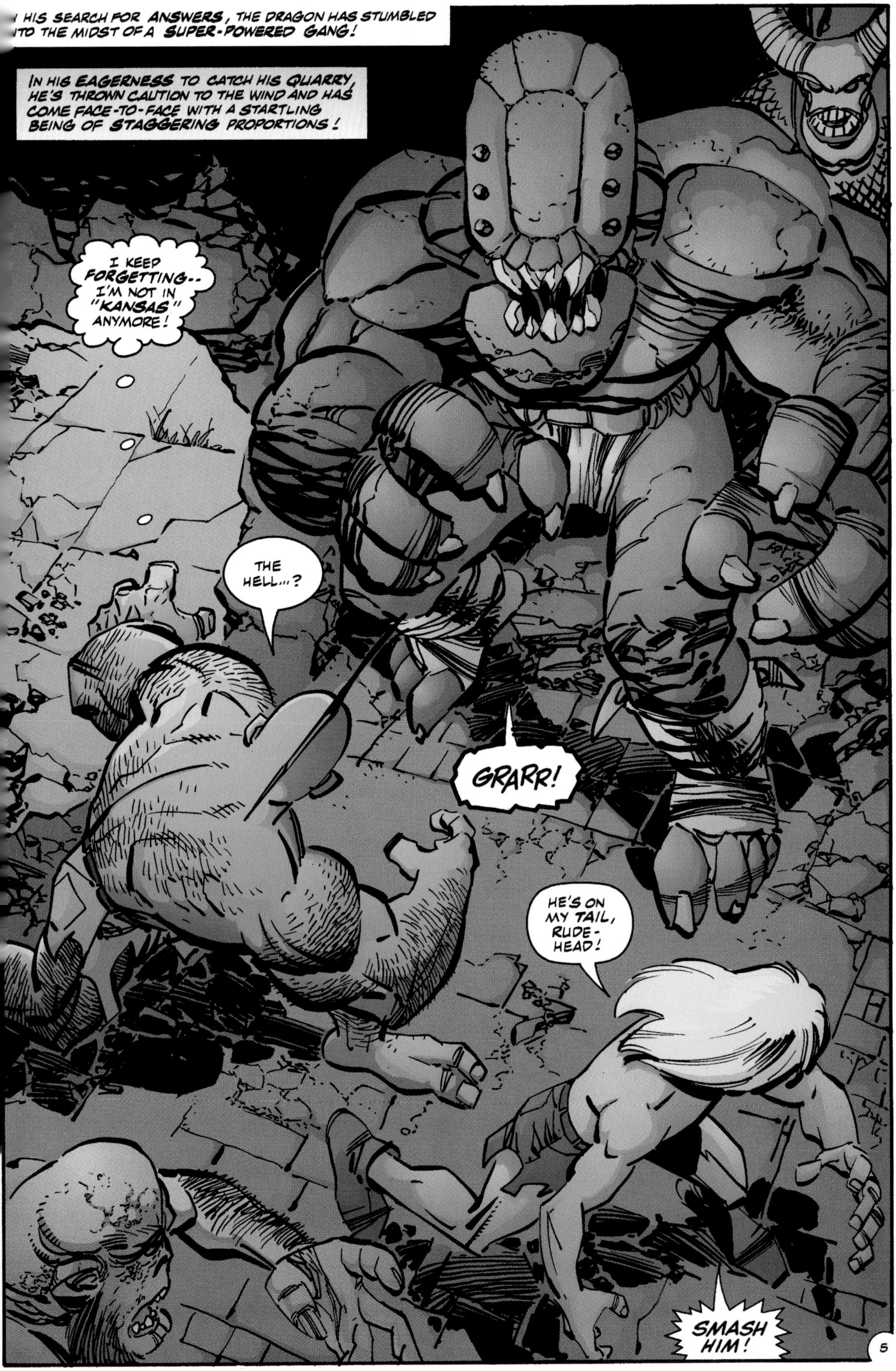

HIS SEARCH FOR ANSWERS, THE DRAGON HAS STUMBLED
TO THE MIDST OF A SUPER-POWERED GANG!
IN HIS EAGERNESS TO CATCH HIS QUARRY, HE'S THROWN CAUTION TO THE WIND AND HAS COME FACE-TO-FACE WITH A STARTLING BEING OF STAGGERING PROPORTIONS!
I KEEP FORGETTING-- I'M NOT IN "KANSAS" ANYMORE!
THE HELL...?
GRARR!
HE'S ON MY TAIL, RUDE-HEAD!
SMASH HIM!

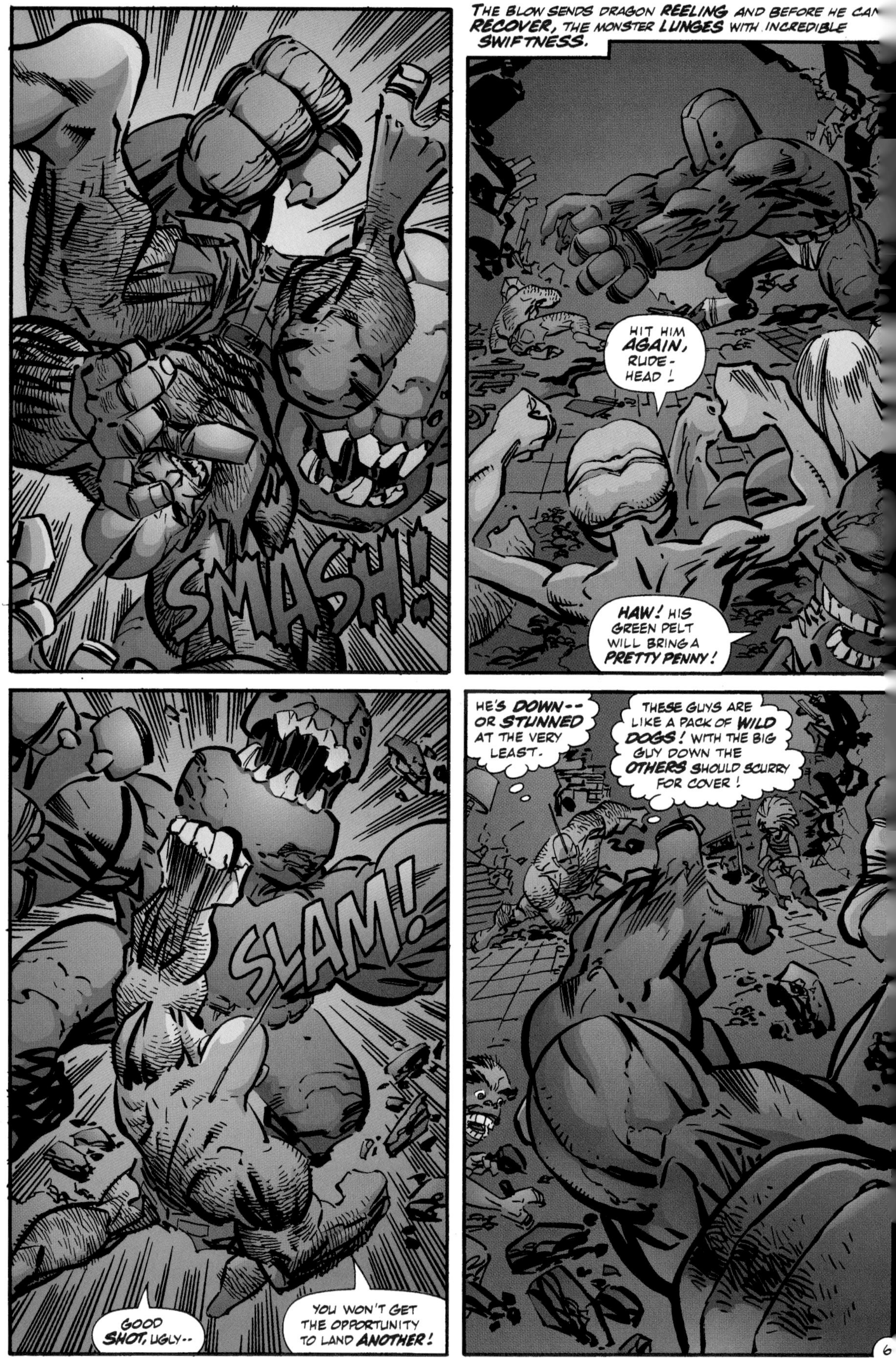
SMASH!
THE BLOW SENDS DRAGON REELING AND BEFORE HE CAN RECOVER, THE MONSTER LUNGES WITH INCREDIBLE SWIFTNESS.
HIT HIM AGAIN, RUDE-HEAD!
HAW! HIS GREEN PELT WILL BRING A PRETTY PENNY!
SLAM!
GOOD SHOT, UGLY--
YOU WON'T GET THE OPPORTUNITY TO LAND ANOTHER!
HE'S DOWN-- OR STUNNED AT THE VERY LEAST.
THESE GUYS ARE LIKE A PACK OF WILD DOGS! WITH THE BIG GUY DOWN THE OTHERS SHOULD SCURRY FOR COVER!

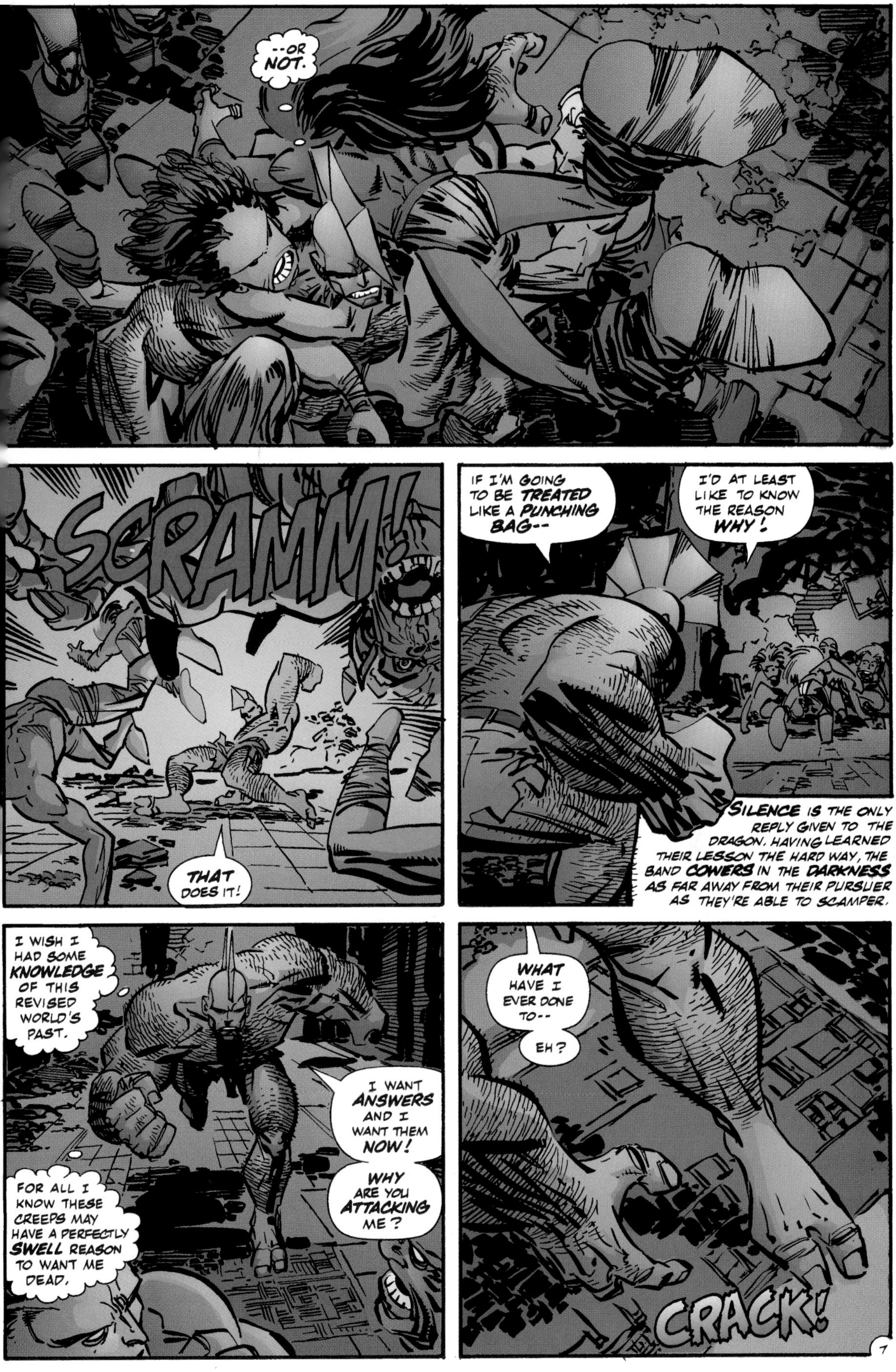
--OR NOT.
SCRAMM!
THAT DOES IT!
IF I'M GOING TO BE TREATED LIKE A PUNCHING BAG--
I'D AT LEAST LIKE TO KNOW THE REASON WHY!
SILENCE IS THE ONLY REPLY GIVEN TO THE DRAGON. HAVING LEARNED THEIR LESSON THE HARD WAY, THE BAND COWERS IN THE DARKNESS AS FAR AWAY FROM THEIR PURSUER AS THEY'RE ABLE TO SCAMPER.
I WISH I HAD SOME KNOWLEDGE OF THIS REVISED WORLD'S PAST.
FOR ALL I KNOW THESE CREEPS MAY HAVE A PERFECTLY SWELL REASON TO WANT ME DEAD.
I WANT ANSWERS AND I WANT THEM NOW!
WHY ARE YOU ATTACKING ME?
WHAT HAVE I EVER DONE TO--
EH?
CRACK!

THE GROUND BENEATH DRAGON'S FEET GIVES WAY.

DAMN!

AND A SIXTY-FOOT DROP FOLLOWS!

I'D WAGER THOSE CREEPS WEREN'T EXPECTING ME TO LAND ON MY FEET.

THAT MAY BE THE ONLY THING I'VE DONE RIGHT TODAY!

PAF!

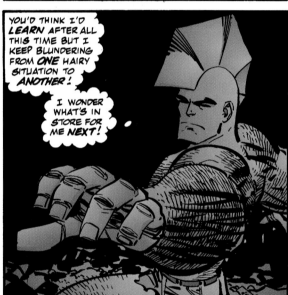

YOU'D THINK I'D LEARN AFTER ALL THIS TIME BUT I KEEP BLUNDERING FROM ONE HAIRY SITUATION TO ANOTHER!

I WONDER WHAT'S IN STORE FOR ME NEXT!

GHAA!

I HAD TO ASK!

THIS SUCKER'S THE SIZE OF A TRUCK AND TWICE AS FAST!

NO TELLING HOW POWERFUL OR DEADLY HE IS AND I'M NOT TOO ANXIOUS TO FIND OUT!

MY BEST BET IS TO STAY OUT OF HIS REACH AND MAKE EVERY EFFORT TO HEAD FOR THE HILLS!

8

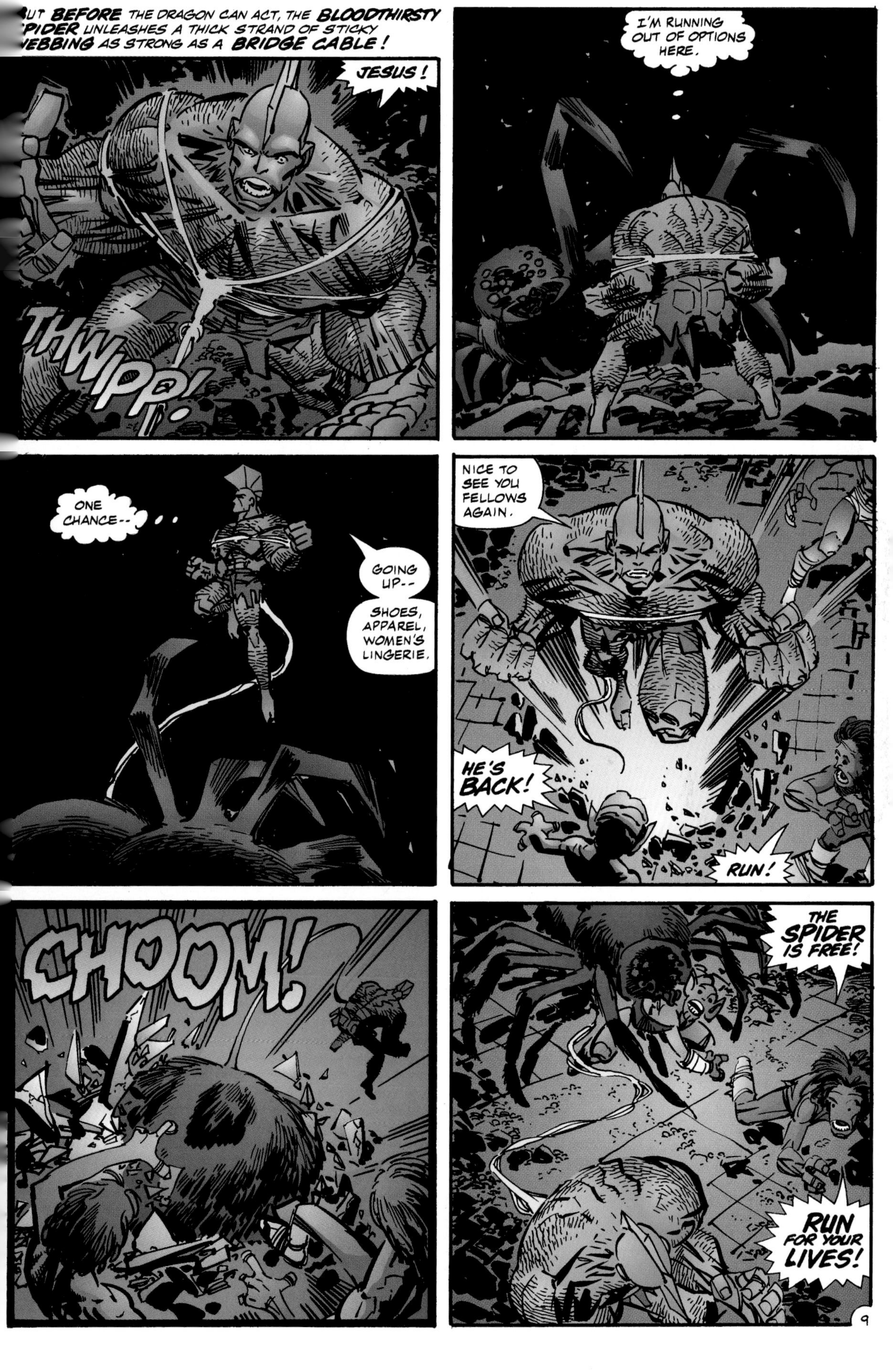
UT BEFORE THE DRAGON CAN ACT, THE BLOODTHIRSTY
PIDER UNLEASHES A THICK STRAND OF STICKY
EBBING AS STRONG AS A BRIDGE CABLE!
JESUS!
THWIPP!
I'M RUNNING OUT OF OPTIONS HERE.
ONE CHANCE--
GOING UP--
SHOES, APPAREL, WOMEN'S LINGERIE.
NICE TO SEE YOU FELLOWS AGAIN.
HE'S BACK!
RUN!
CHOOM!
THE SPIDER IS FREE!
RUN FOR YOUR LIVES!

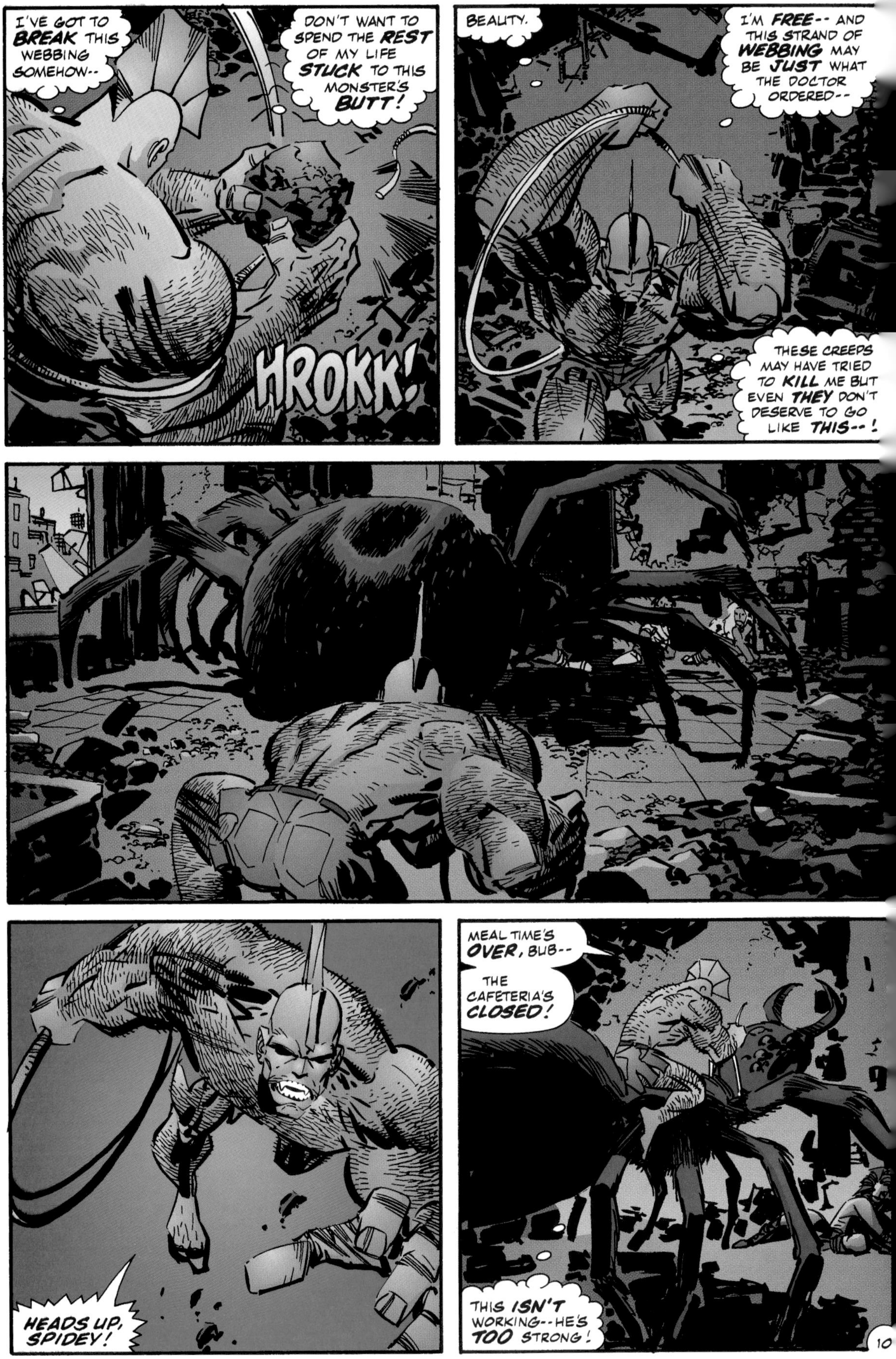

I'VE GOT TO BREAK THIS WEBBING SOMEHOW--
DON'T WANT TO SPEND THE REST OF MY LIFE STUCK TO THIS MONSTER'S BUTT!
HROKK!
BEAUTY.
I'M FREE-- AND THIS STRAND OF WEBBING MAY BE JUST WHAT THE DOCTOR ORDERED--
THESE CREEPS MAY HAVE TRIED TO KILL ME BUT EVEN THEY DON'T DESERVE TO GO LIKE THIS--!
HEADS UP, SPIDEY!
MEAL TIME'S OVER, BUB--
THE CAFETERIA'S CLOSED!
THIS ISN'T WORKING--HE'S TOO STRONG!

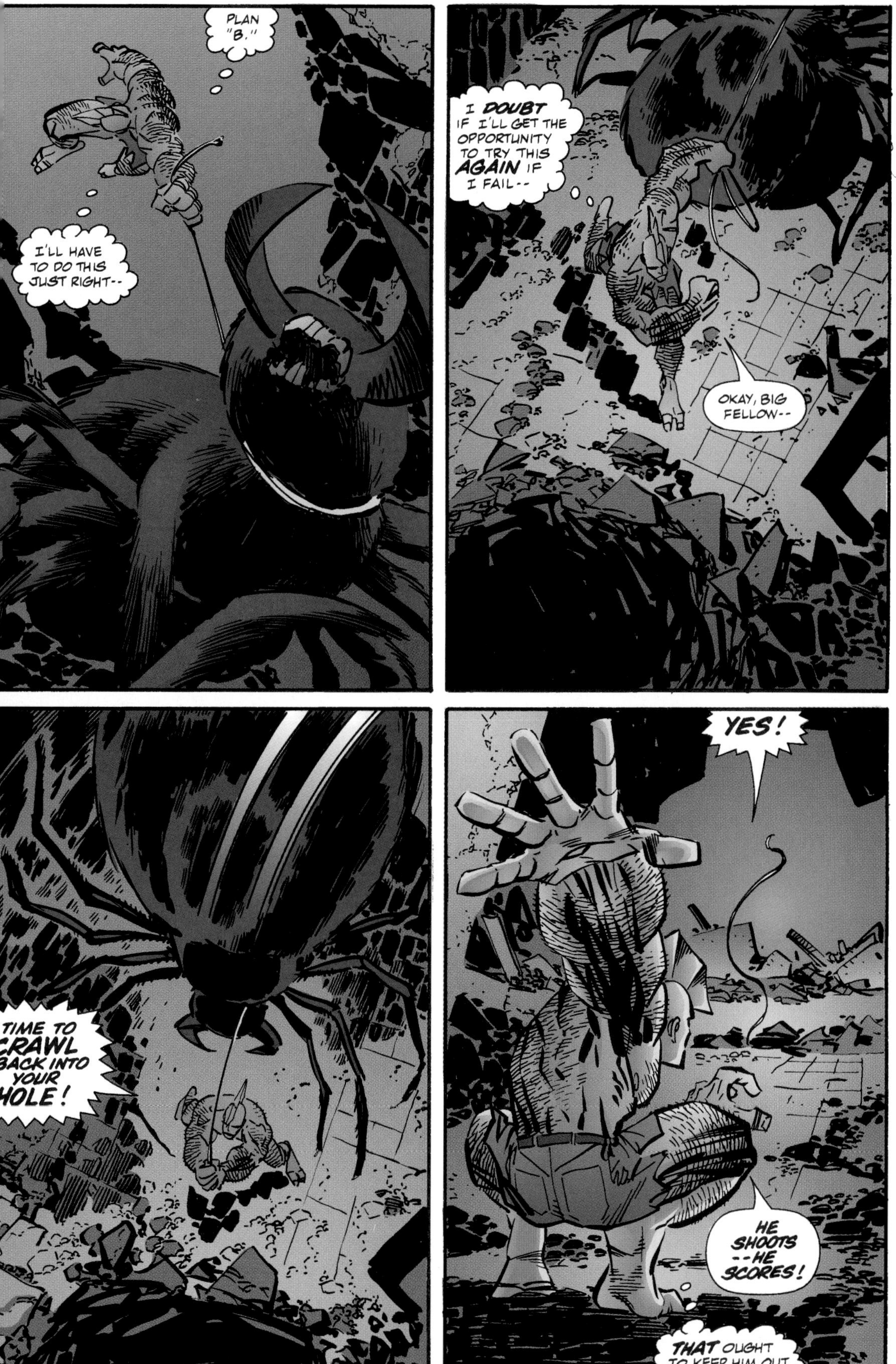
PLAN "B."
I'LL HAVE TO DO THIS JUST RIGHT--
I DOUBT IF I'LL GET THE OPPORTUNITY TO TRY THIS AGAIN IF I FAIL--
OKAY, BIG FELLOW--
TIME TO CRAWL BACK INTO YOUR HOLE!
YES!
HE SHOOTS --HE SCORES!
THAT OUGHT TO KEEP HIM OUT OF TROUBLE.

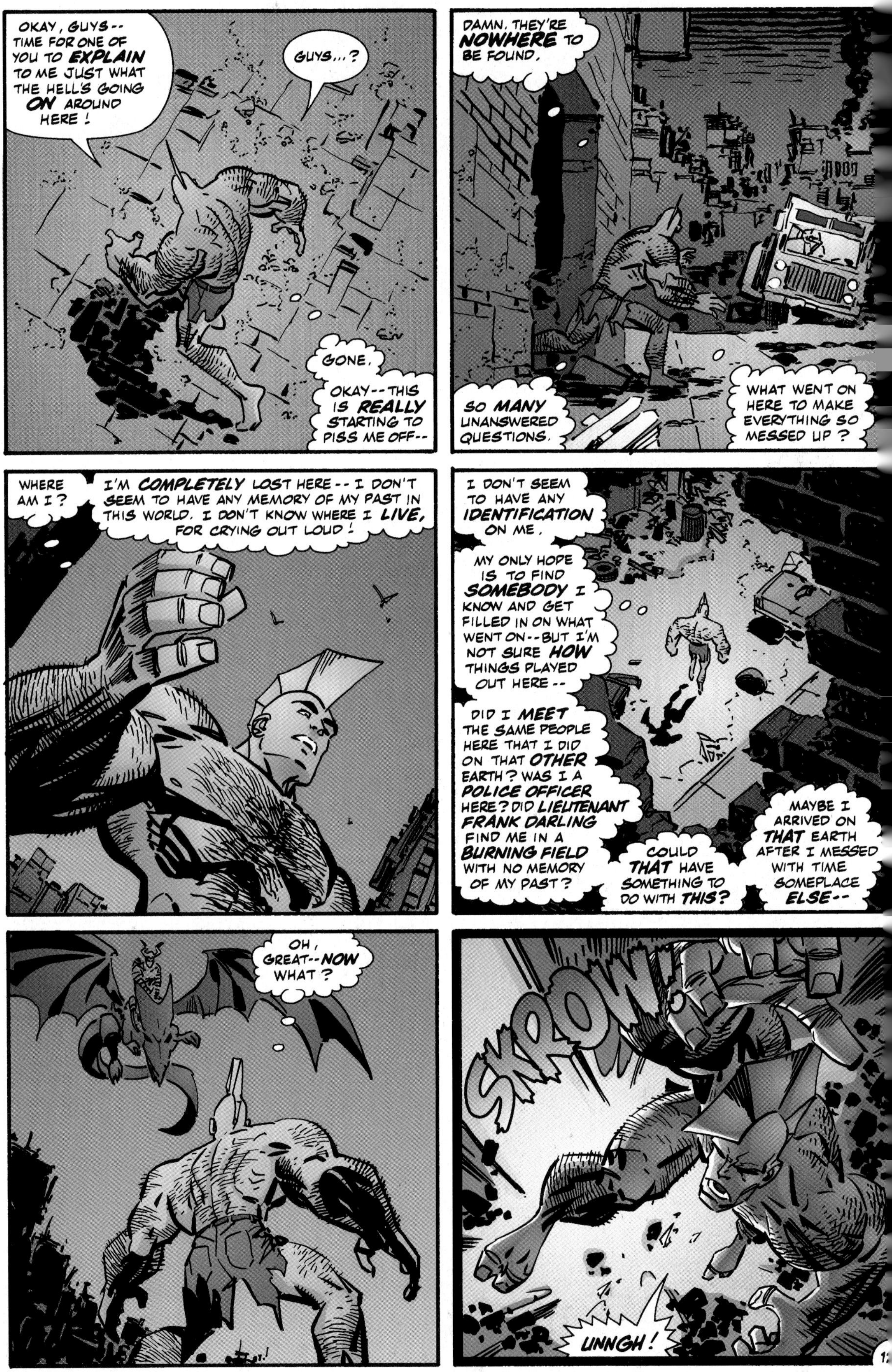

OKAY, GUYS-- TIME FOR ONE OF YOU TO EXPLAIN TO ME JUST WHAT THE HELL'S GOING ON AROUND HERE!
GUYS...?
GONE.
OKAY--THIS IS REALLY STARTING TO PISS ME OFF--
DAMN. THEY'RE NOWHERE TO BE FOUND.
SO MANY UNANSWERED QUESTIONS.
WHAT WENT ON HERE TO MAKE EVERYTHING SO MESSED UP?
WHERE AM I?
I'M COMPLETELY LOST HERE--I DON'T SEEM TO HAVE ANY MEMORY OF MY PAST IN THIS WORLD. I DON'T KNOW WHERE I LIVE, FOR CRYING OUT LOUD!
I DON'T SEEM TO HAVE ANY IDENTIFICATION ON ME.
MY ONLY HOPE IS TO FIND SOMEBODY I KNOW AND GET FILLED IN ON WHAT WENT ON--BUT I'M NOT SURE HOW THINGS PLAYED OUT HERE--
DID I MEET THE SAME PEOPLE HERE THAT I DID ON THAT OTHER EARTH? WAS I A POLICE OFFICER HERE? DID LIEUTENANT FRANK DARLING FIND ME IN A BURNING FIELD WITH NO MEMORY OF MY PAST?
COULD THAT HAVE SOMETHING TO DO WITH THIS?
MAYBE I ARRIVED ON THAT EARTH AFTER I MESSED WITH TIME SOMEPLACE ELSE--
OH, GREAT--NOW WHAT?
SKROW!
UNNGH!

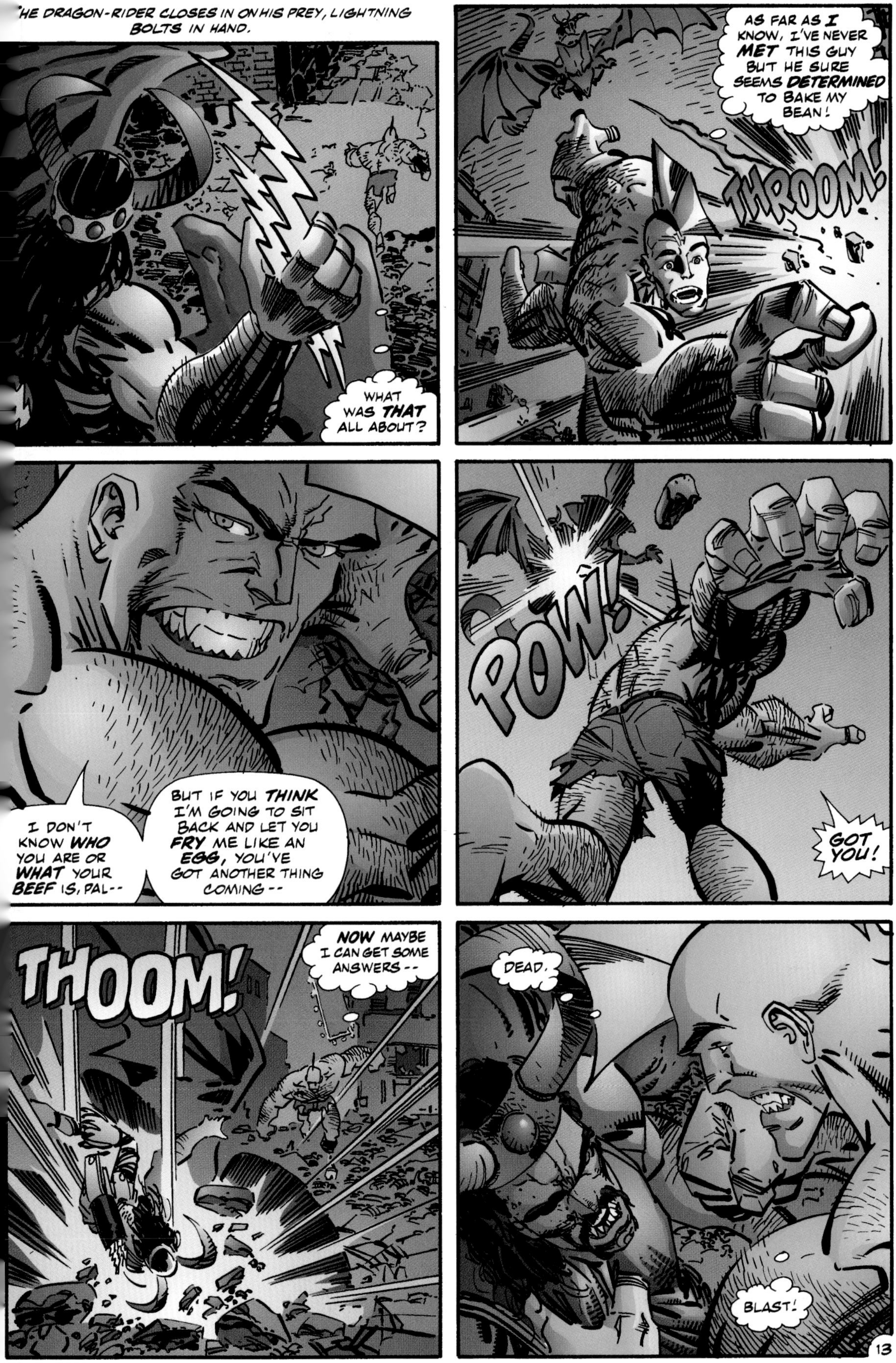

THE DRAGON-RIDER CLOSES IN ON HIS PREY, LIGHTNING BOLTS IN HAND.
WHAT WAS THAT ALL ABOUT?
AS FAR AS I KNOW, I'VE NEVER MET THIS GUY BUT HE SURE SEEMS DETERMINED TO BAKE MY BEAN!
THROOM!
I DON'T KNOW WHO YOU ARE OR WHAT YOUR BEEF IS, PAL--
BUT IF YOU THINK I'M GOING TO SIT BACK AND LET YOU FRY ME LIKE AN EGG, YOU'VE GOT ANOTHER THING COMING--
POW!
GOT YOU!
THOOM!
NOW MAYBE I CAN GET SOME ANSWERS--
DEAD.
BLAST!

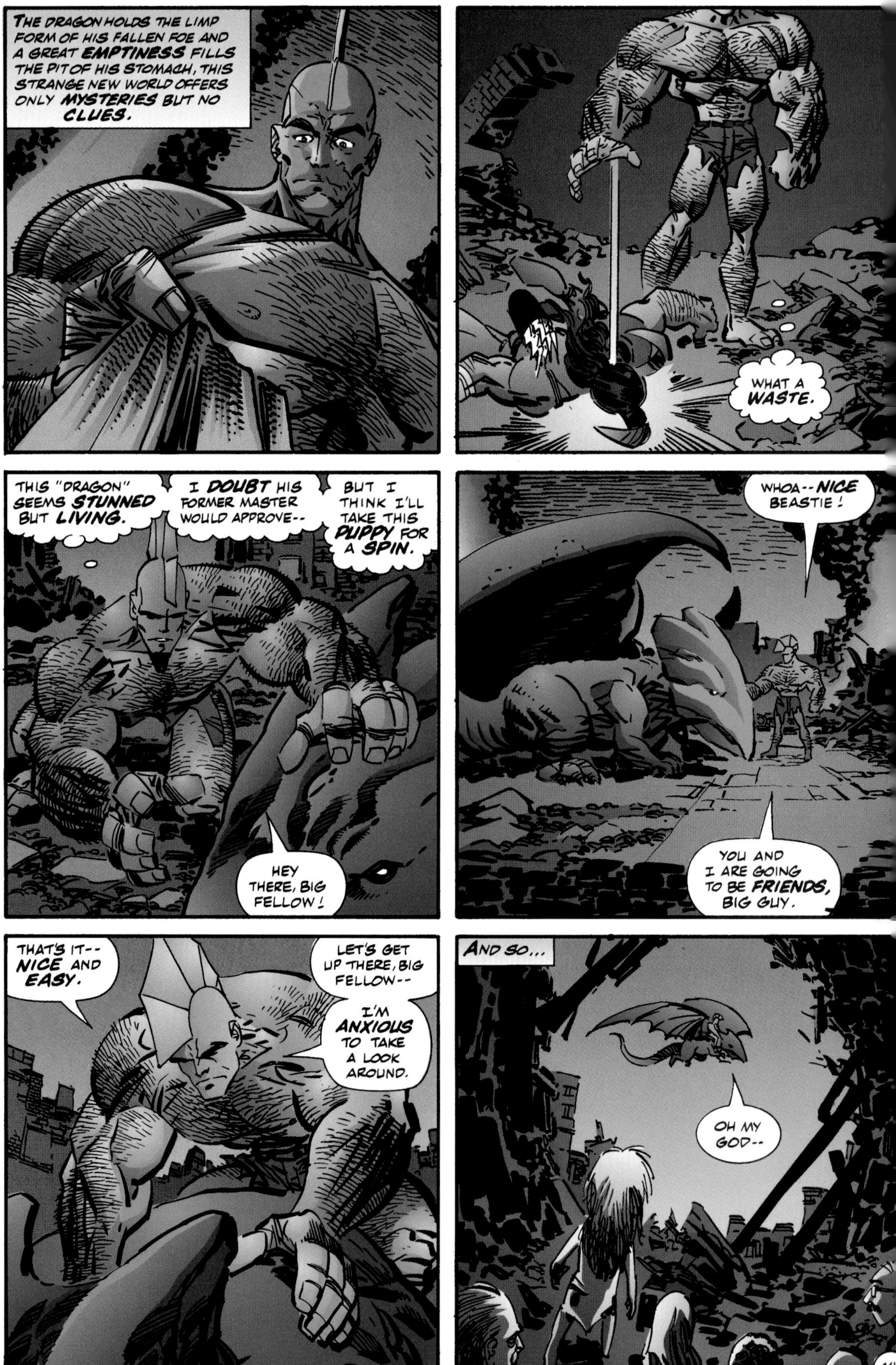
THE DRAGON HOLDS THE LIMP FORM OF HIS FALLEN FOE AND A GREAT EMPTINESS FILLS THE PIT OF HIS STOMACH. THIS STRANGE NEW WORLD OFFERS ONLY MYSTERIES BUT NO CLUES.
WHAT A WASTE.
THIS "DRAGON" SEEMS STUNNED BUT LIVING.
I DOUBT HIS FORMER MASTER WOULD APPROVE--
BUT I THINK I'LL TAKE THIS PUPPY FOR A SPIN.
HEY THERE, BIG FELLOW!
WHOA--NICE BEASTIE!
YOU AND I ARE GOING TO BE FRIENDS, BIG GUY.
THAT'S IT--NICE AND EASY.
LET'S GET UP THERE, BIG FELLOW--
I'M ANXIOUS TO TAKE A LOOK AROUND.
AND SO...
OH MY GOD--

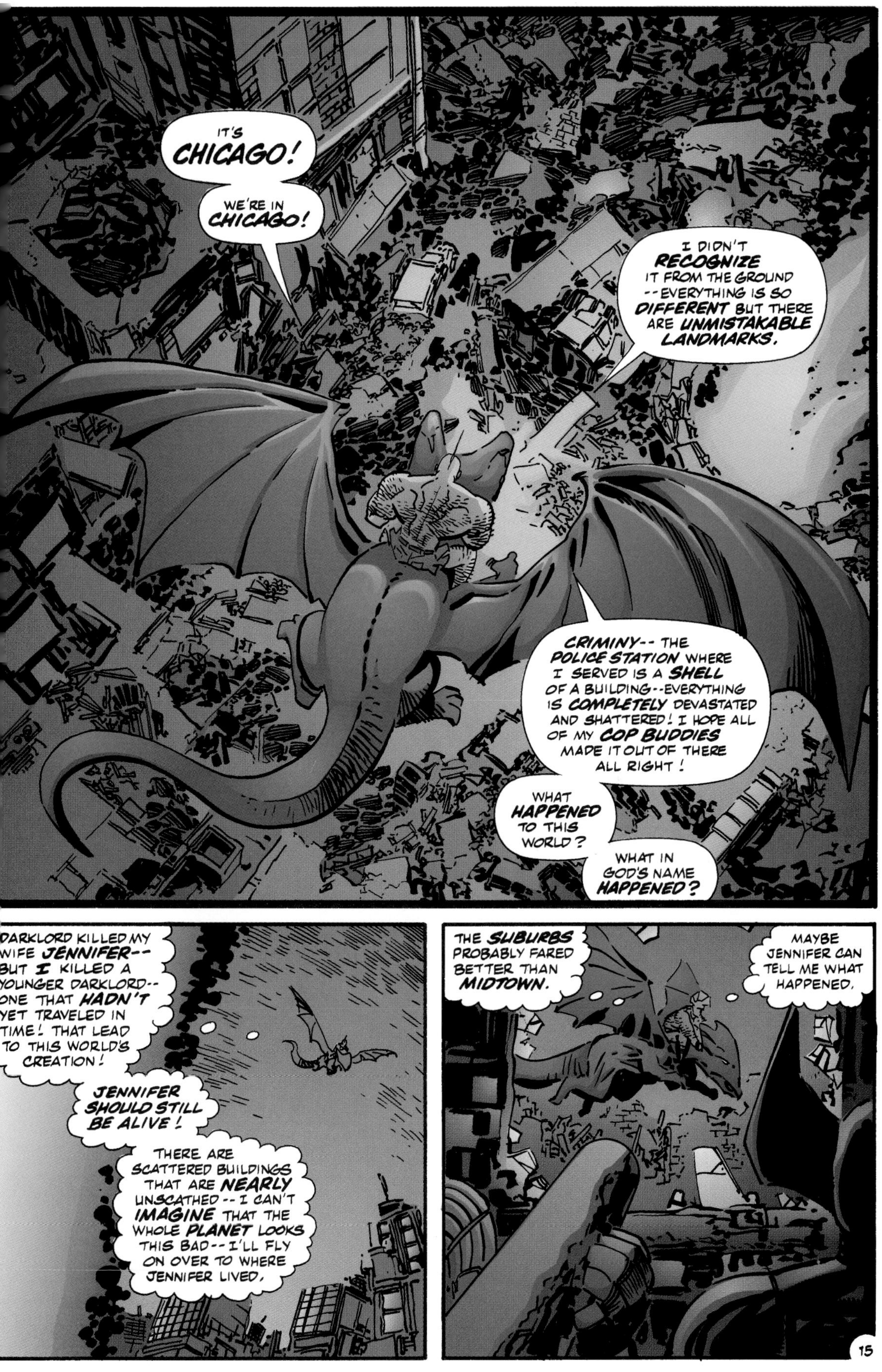
IT'S CHICAGO!
WE'RE IN CHICAGO!
I DIDN'T RECOGNIZE IT FROM THE GROUND --EVERYTHING IS SO DIFFERENT BUT THERE ARE UNMISTAKABLE LANDMARKS.
CRIMINY-- THE POLICE STATION WHERE I SERVED IS A SHELL OF A BUILDING--EVERYTHING IS COMPLETELY DEVASTATED AND SHATTERED! I HOPE ALL OF MY COP BUDDIES MADE IT OUT OF THERE ALL RIGHT!
WHAT HAPPENED TO THIS WORLD?
WHAT IN GOD'S NAME HAPPENED?
DARKLORD KILLED MY WIFE JENNIFER--BUT I KILLED A YOUNGER DARKLORD--ONE THAT HADN'T YET TRAVELED IN TIME! THAT LEAD TO THIS WORLD'S CREATION!
JENNIFER SHOULD STILL BE ALIVE!
THERE ARE SCATTERED BUILDINGS THAT ARE NEARLY UNSCATHED -- I CAN'T IMAGINE THAT THE WHOLE PLANET LOOKS THIS BAD--I'LL FLY ON OVER TO WHERE JENNIFER LIVED.
THE SUBURBS PROBABLY FARED BETTER THAN MIDTOWN.
MAYBE JENNIFER CAN TELL ME WHAT HAPPENED.

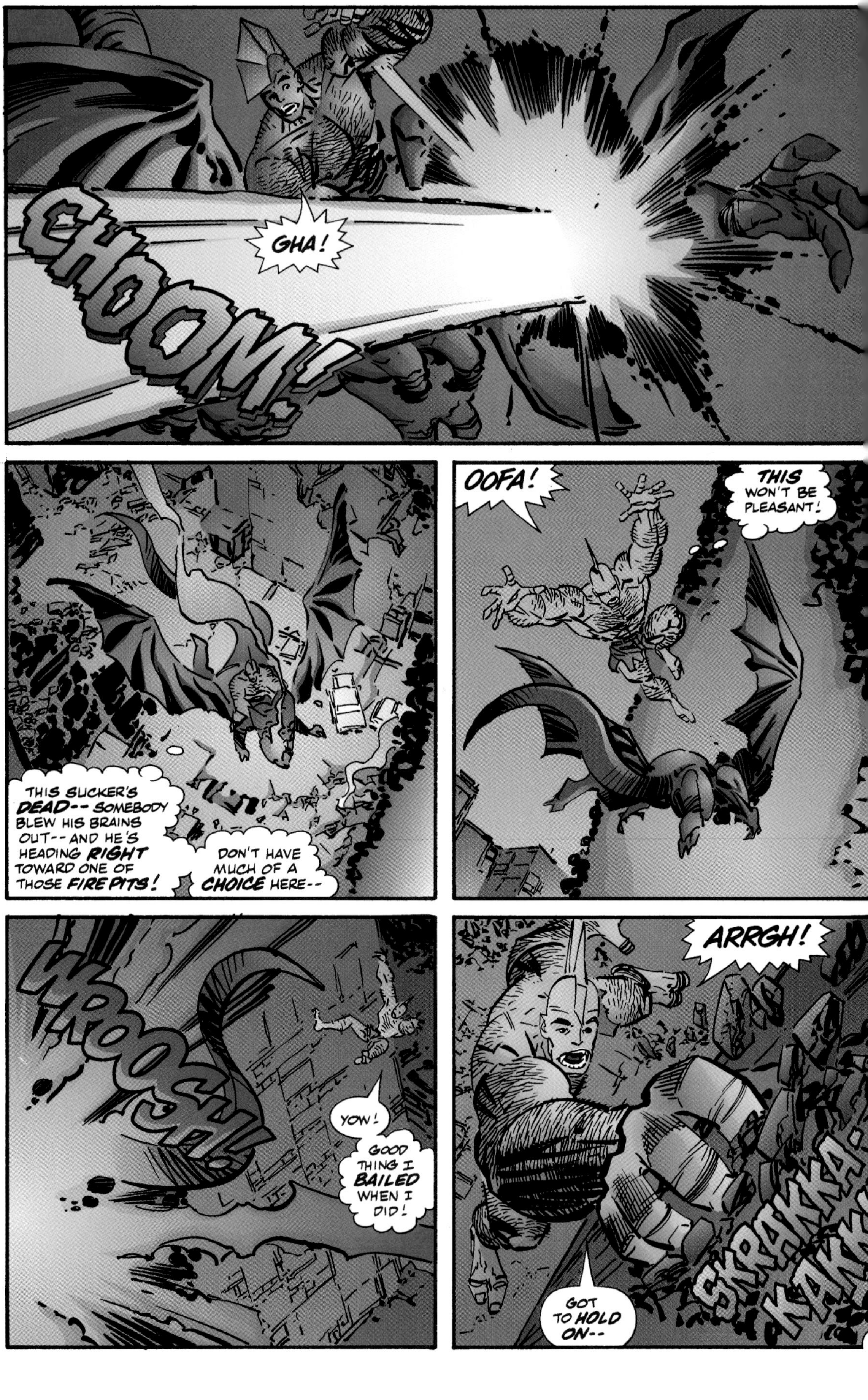
CHOOM!
GHA!
THIS SUCKER'S DEAD-- SOMEBODY BLEW HIS BRAINS OUT-- AND HE'S HEADING RIGHT TOWARD ONE OF THOSE FIRE PITS!
DON'T HAVE MUCH OF A CHOICE HERE--
OOFA!
THIS WON'T BE PLEASANT!
YOW!
GOOD THING I BAILED WHEN I DID!
ARRGH!
GOT TO HOLD ON--

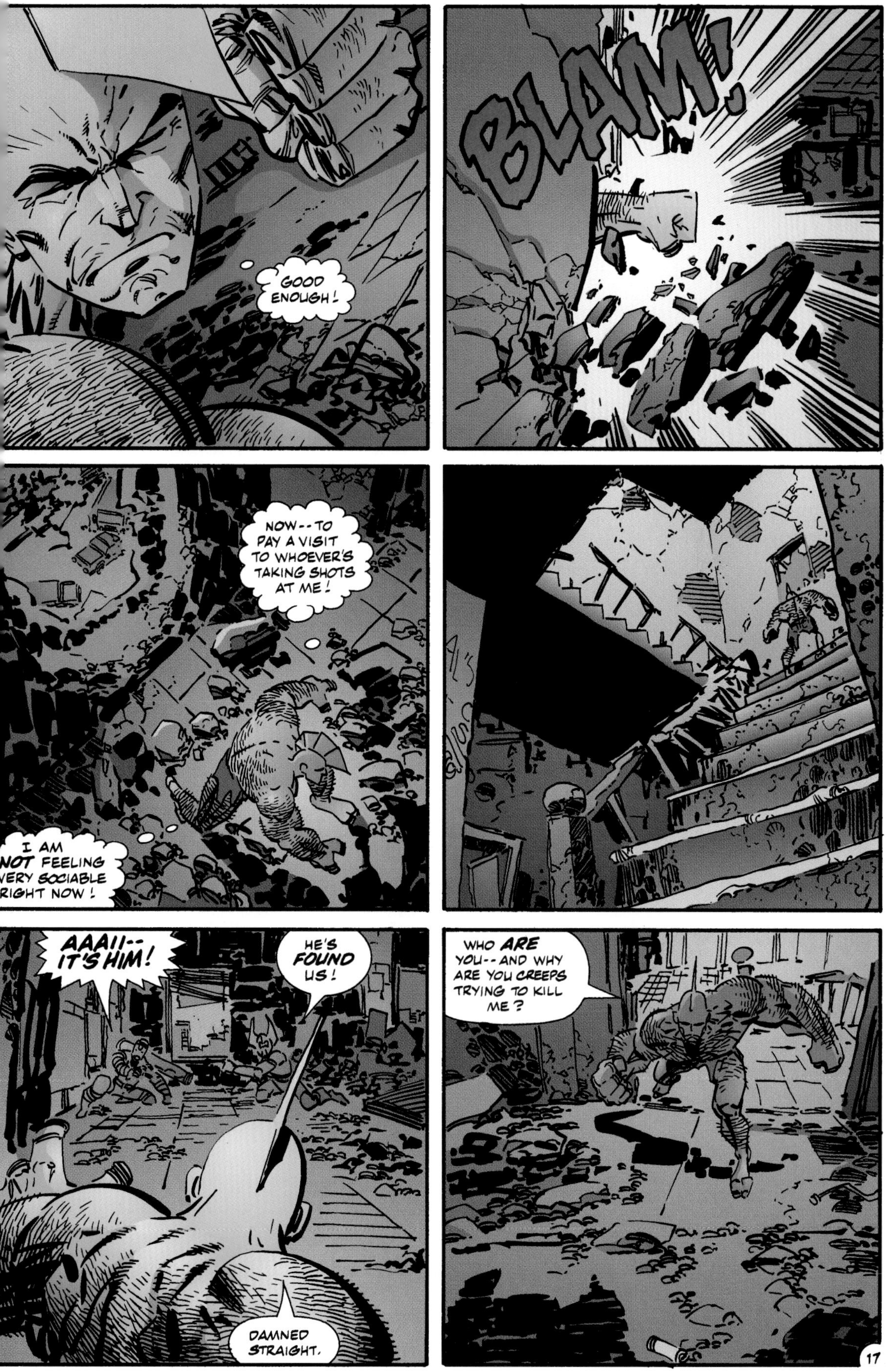
GOOD ENOUGH!
BLAM!
NOW--TO PAY A VISIT TO WHOEVER'S TAKING SHOTS AT ME!
I AM NOT FEELING VERY SOCIABLE RIGHT NOW!
AAAII-- IT'S HIM!
HE'S FOUND US!
DAMNED STRAIGHT.
WHO ARE YOU--AND WHY ARE YOU CREEPS TRYING TO KILL ME?

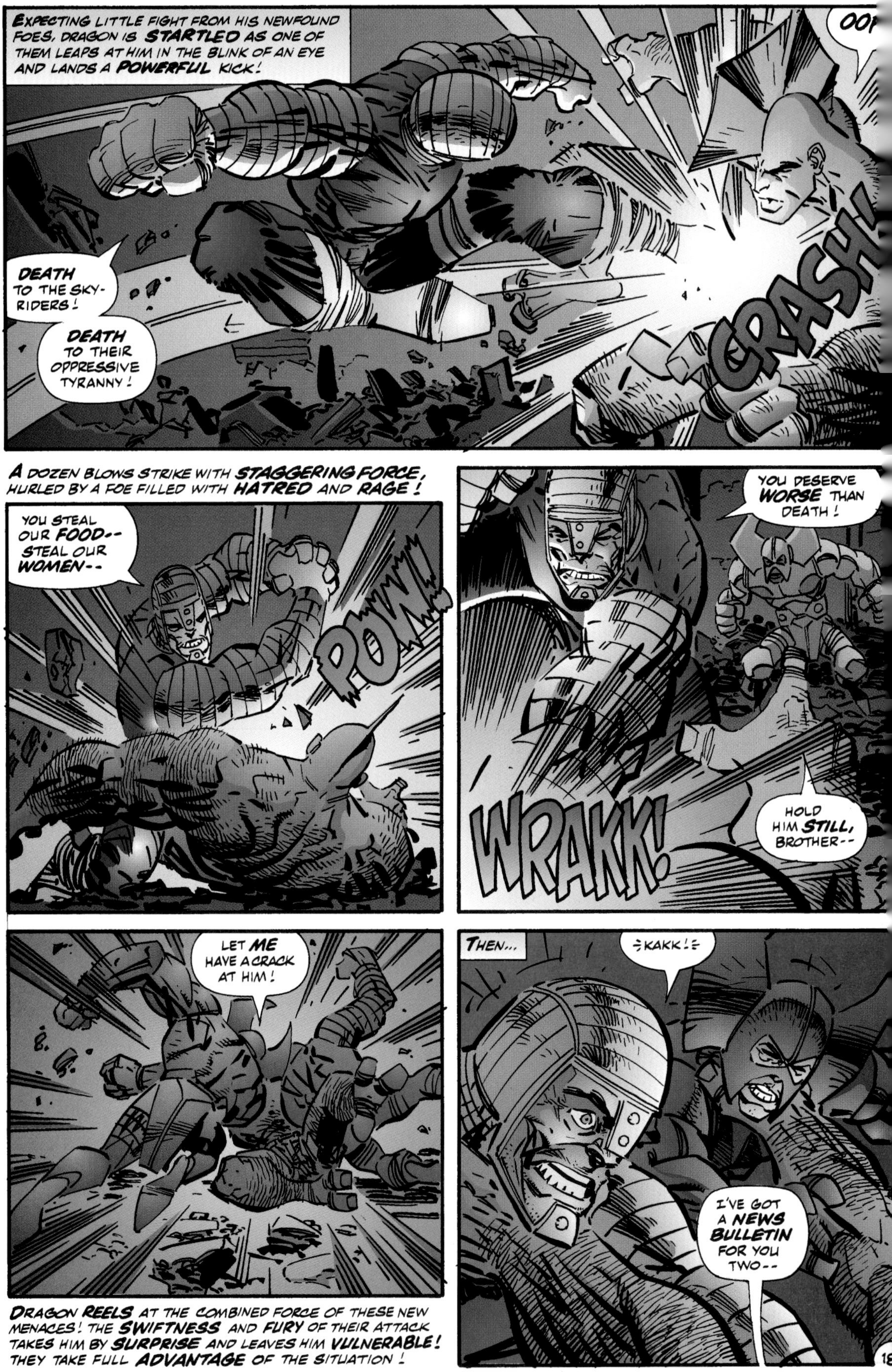
EXPECTING LITTLE FIGHT FROM HIS NEWFOUND FOES, DRAGON IS STARTLED AS ONE OF THEM LEAPS AT HIM IN THE BLINK OF AN EYE AND LANDS A POWERFUL KICK!
DEATH TO THE SKY-RIDERS!
DEATH TO THEIR OPPRESSIVE TYRANNY!
CRASH
A DOZEN BLOWS STRIKE WITH STAGGERING FORCE, HURLED BY A FOE FILLED WITH HATRED AND RAGE!
YOU STEAL OUR FOOD-- STEAL OUR WOMEN--
POW!
YOU DESERVE WORSE THAN DEATH!
WRAKK!
HOLD HIM STILL, BROTHER--
LET ME HAVE A CRACK AT HIM!
DRAGON REELS AT THE COMBINED FORCE OF THESE NEW MENACES! THE SWIFTNESS AND FURY OF THEIR ATTACK TAKES HIM BY SURPRISE AND LEAVES HIM VULNERABLE! THEY TAKE FULL ADVANTAGE OF THE SITUATION!
THEN...
KAKK!
I'VE GOT A NEWS BULLETIN FOR YOU TWO--

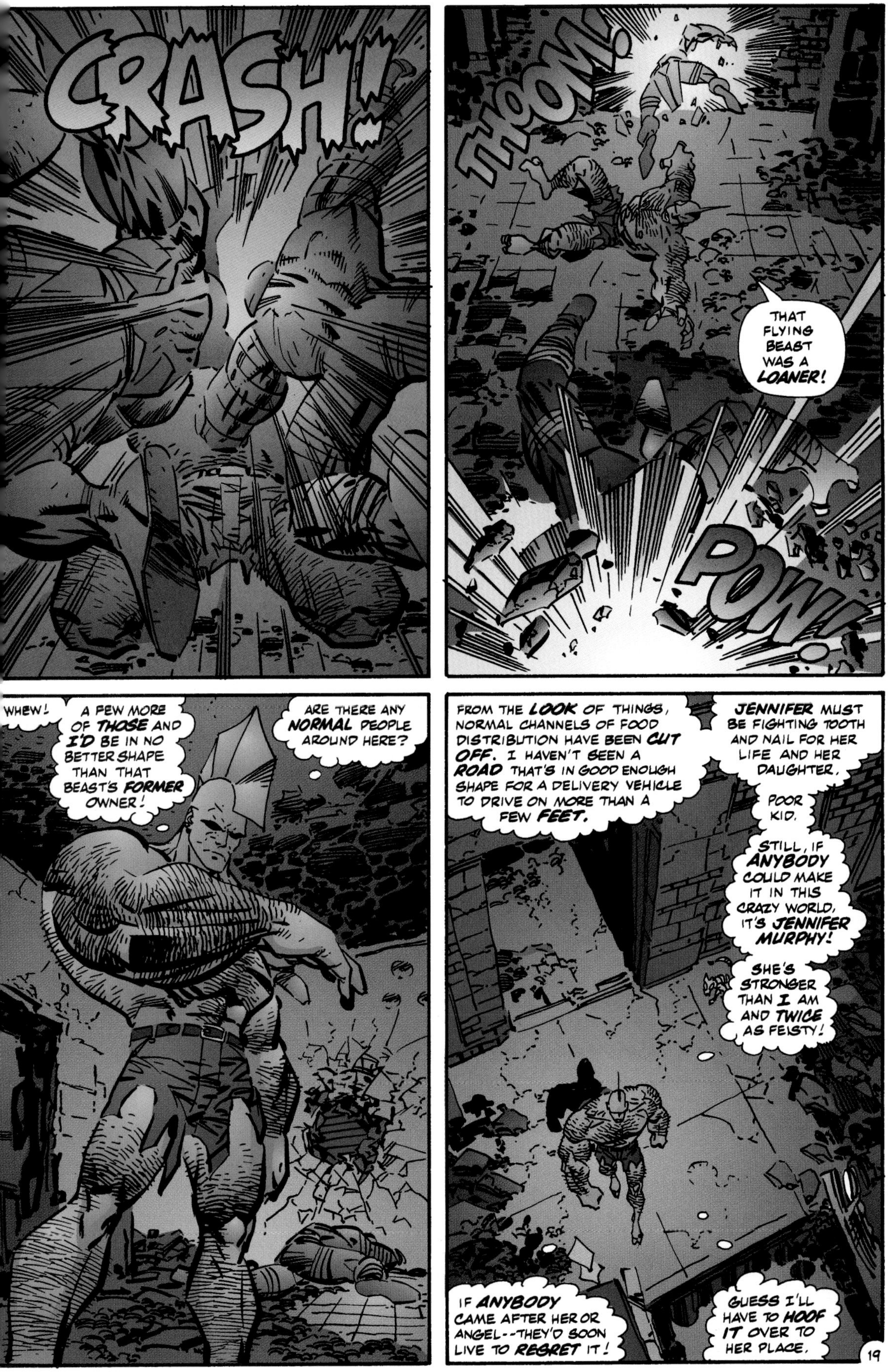
CRASH!
THOOOM!
THAT FLYING BEAST WAS A LOANER!
POW!
WHEW!
A FEW MORE OF THOSE AND I'D BE IN NO BETTER SHAPE THAN THAT BEAST'S FORMER OWNER!
ARE THERE ANY NORMAL PEOPLE AROUND HERE?
FROM THE LOOK OF THINGS, NORMAL CHANNELS OF FOOD DISTRIBUTION HAVE BEEN CUT OFF. I HAVEN'T SEEN A ROAD THAT'S IN GOOD ENOUGH SHAPE FOR A DELIVERY VEHICLE TO DRIVE ON MORE THAN A FEW FEET.
JENNIFER MUST BE FIGHTING TOOTH AND NAIL FOR HER LIFE AND HER DAUGHTER.
POOR KID.
STILL, IF ANYBODY COULD MAKE IT IN THIS CRAZY WORLD, IT'S JENNIFER MURPHY!
SHE'S STRONGER THAN I AM AND TWICE AS FEISTY!
IF ANYBODY CAME AFTER HER OR ANGEL--THEY'D SOON LIVE TO REGRET IT!
GUESS I'LL HAVE TO HOOF IT OVER TO HER PLACE.

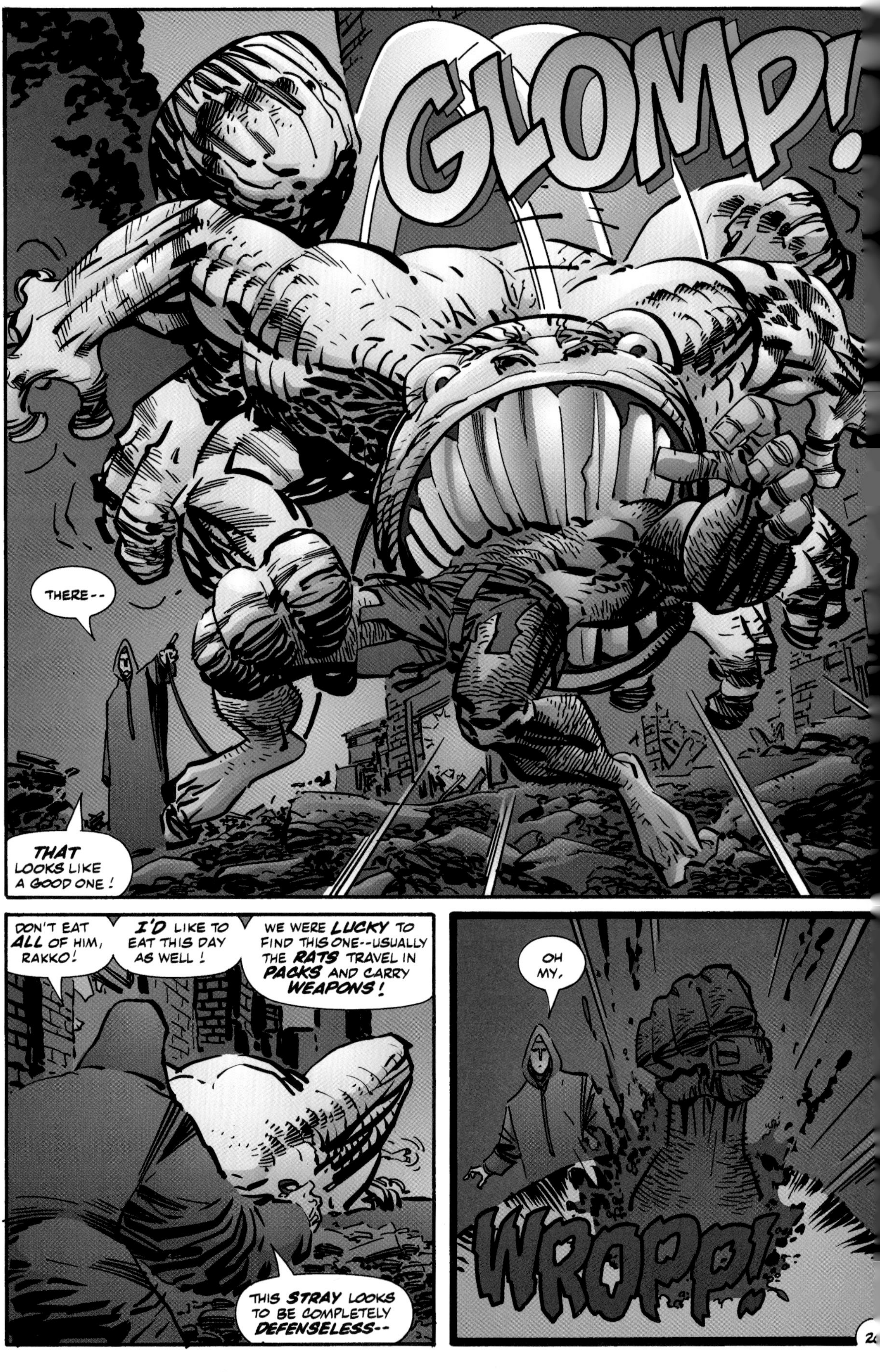
GLOMP!
THERE--
THAT LOOKS LIKE A GOOD ONE!
DON'T EAT ALL OF HIM, RAKKO!
I'D LIKE TO EAT THIS DAY AS WELL!
WE WERE LUCKY TO FIND THIS ONE--USUALLY THE RATS TRAVEL IN PACKS AND CARRY WEAPONS!
THIS STRAY LOOKS TO BE COMPLETELY DEFENSELESS--
OH MY.
WROPP!

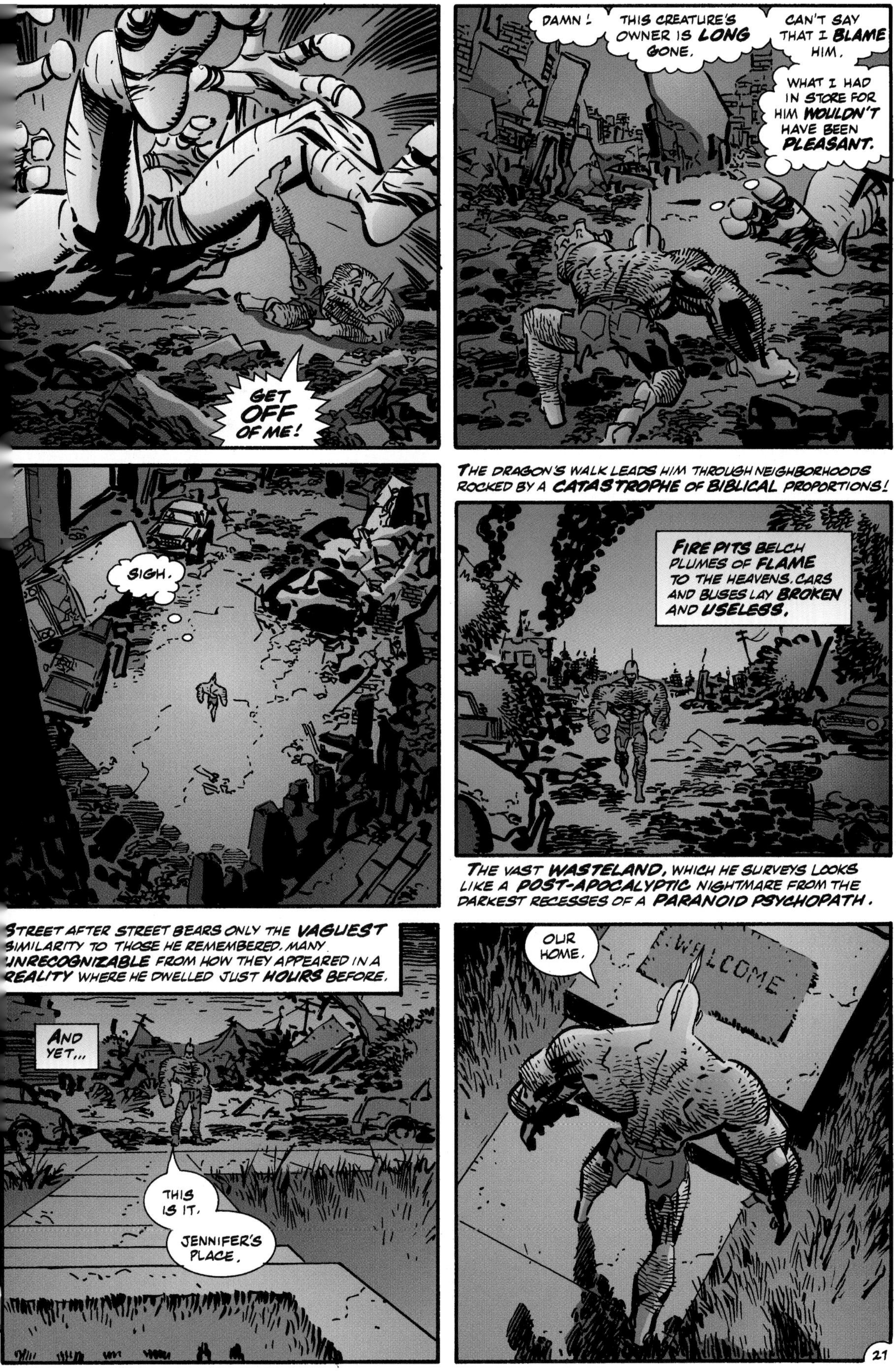
GET OFF OF ME!
DAMN!
THIS CREATURE'S OWNER IS LONG GONE.
CAN'T SAY THAT I BLAME HIM.
WHAT I HAD IN STORE FOR HIM WOULDN'T HAVE BEEN PLEASANT.
SIGH.
THE DRAGON'S WALK LEADS HIM THROUGH NEIGHBORHOODS ROCKED BY A CATASTROPHE OF BIBLICAL PROPORTIONS!
FIRE PITS BELCH PLUMES OF FLAME TO THE HEAVENS. CARS AND BUSES LAY BROKEN AND USELESS.
THE VAST WASTELAND, WHICH HE SURVEYS LOOKS LIKE A POST-APOCALYPTIC NIGHTMARE FROM THE DARKEST RECESSES OF A PARANOID PSYCHOPATH.
STREET AFTER STREET BEARS ONLY THE VAGUEST SIMILARITY TO THOSE HE REMEMBERED, MANY UNRECOGNIZABLE FROM HOW THEY APPEARED IN A REALITY WHERE HE DWELLED JUST HOURS BEFORE.
AND YET...
THIS IS IT.
JENNIFER'S PLACE.
OUR HOME.
WELCOME

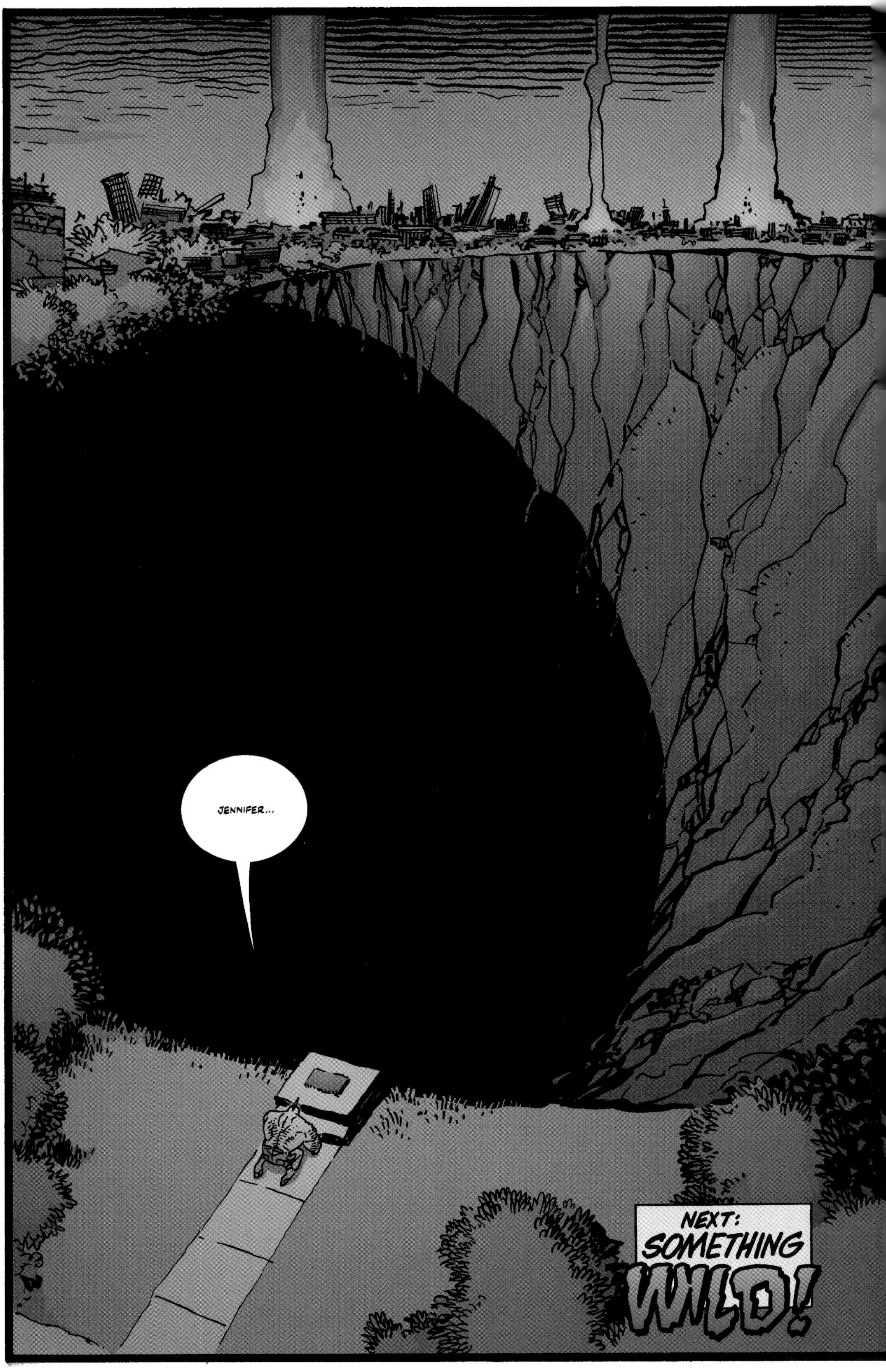
JENNIFER...
NEXT: SOMETHING WILD!

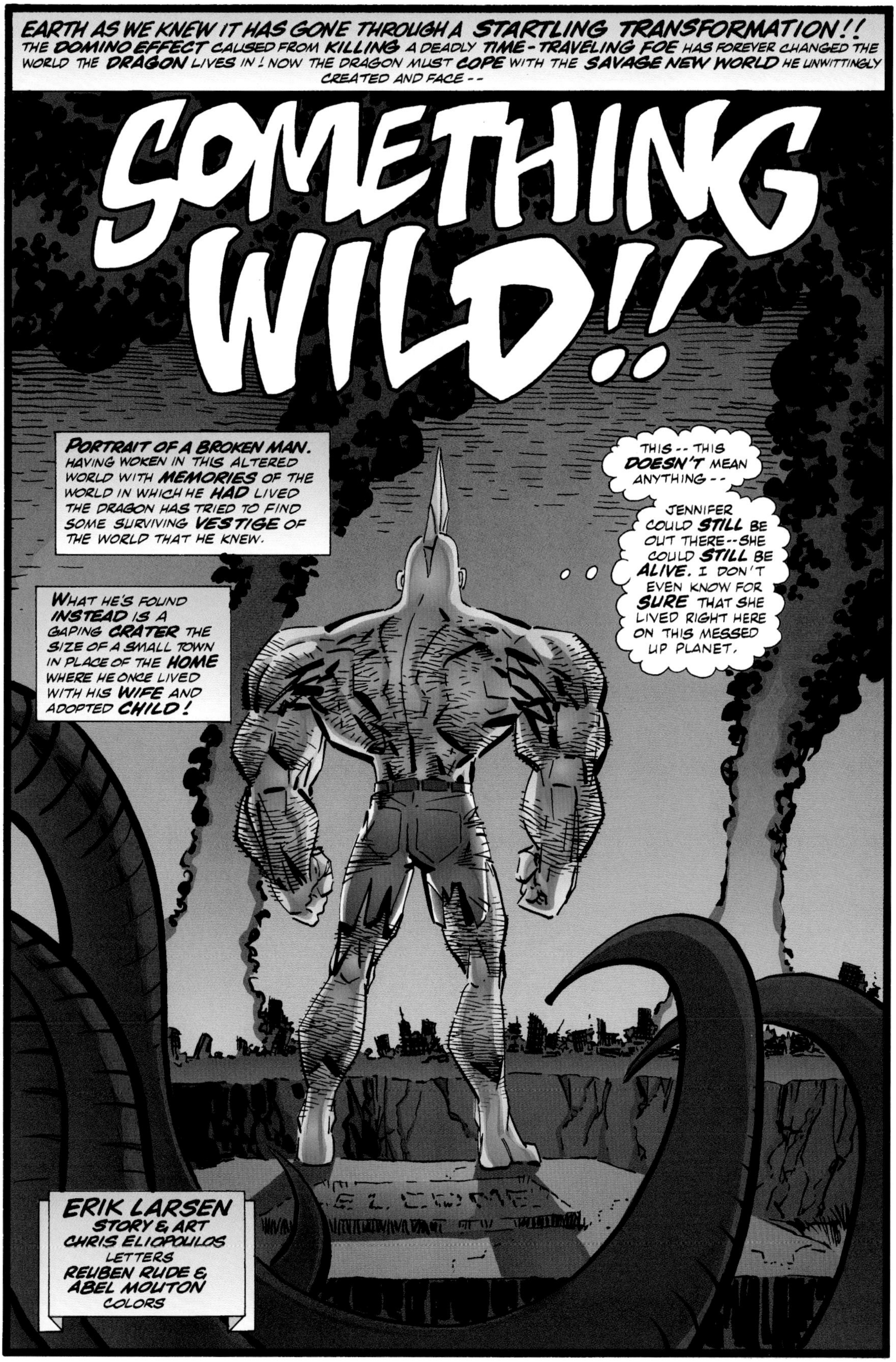
EARTH AS WE KNEW IT HAS GONE THROUGH A STARTLING TRANSFORMATION!! THE DOMINO EFFECT CAUSED FROM KILLING A DEADLY TIME-TRAVELING FOE HAS FOREVER CHANGED THE WORLD THE DRAGON LIVES IN! NOW THE DRAGON MUST COPE WITH THE SAVAGE NEW WORLD HE UNWITTINGLY CREATED AND FACE --
SOMETHING WILD!!
PORTRAIT OF A BROKEN MAN. HAVING WOKEN IN THIS ALTERED WORLD WITH MEMORIES OF THE WORLD IN WHICH HE HAD LIVED THE DRAGON HAS TRIED TO FIND SOME SURVIVING VESTIGE OF THE WORLD THAT HE KNEW.
WHAT HE'S FOUND INSTEAD IS A GAPING CRATER THE SIZE OF A SMALL TOWN IN PLACE OF THE HOME WHERE HE ONCE LIVED WITH HIS WIFE AND ADOPTED CHILD!
THIS -- THIS DOESN'T MEAN ANYTHING --
JENNIFER COULD STILL BE OUT THERE--SHE COULD STILL BE ALIVE. I DON'T EVEN KNOW FOR SURE THAT SHE LIVED RIGHT HERE ON THIS MESSED UP PLANET.
ERIK LARSEN STORY & ART
CHRIS ELIOPOULOS LETTERS
REUBEN RUDE & ABEL MOUTON COLORS

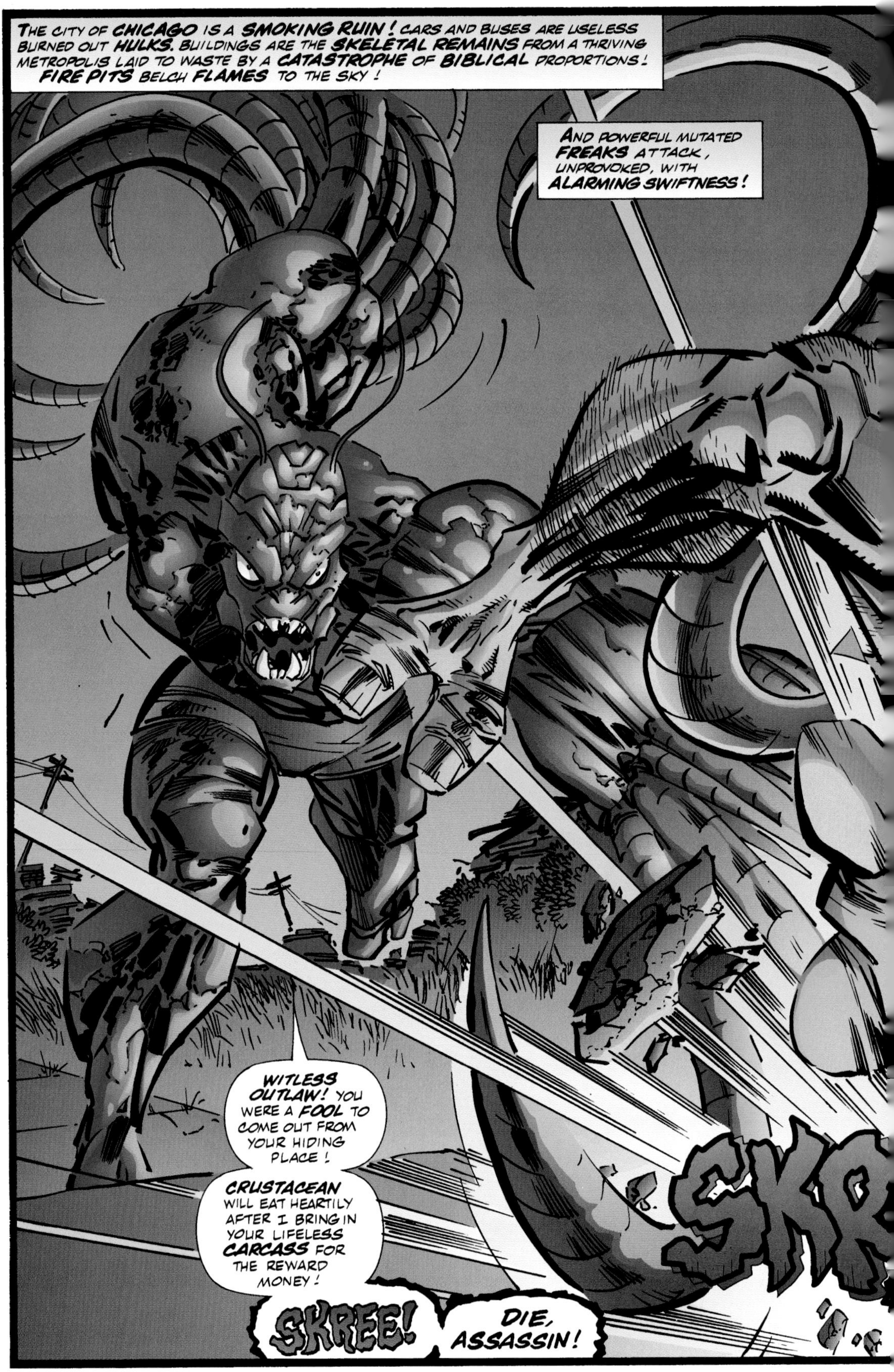

THE CITY OF CHICAGO IS A SMOKING RUIN! CARS AND BUSES ARE USELESS BURNED OUT HULKS. BUILDINGS ARE THE SKELETAL REMAINS FROM A THRIVING METROPOLIS LAID TO WASTE BY A CATASTROPHE OF BIBLICAL PROPORTIONS! FIRE PITS BELCH FLAMES TO THE SKY!
AND POWERFUL MUTATED FREAKS ATTACK, UNPROVOKED, WITH ALARMING SWIFTNESS!
WITLESS OUTLAW! YOU WERE A FOOL TO COME OUT FROM YOUR HIDING PLACE!
CRUSTACEAN WILL EAT HEARTILY AFTER I BRING IN YOUR LIFELESS CARCASS FOR THE REWARD MONEY!
SKREE!
DIE, ASSASSIN!

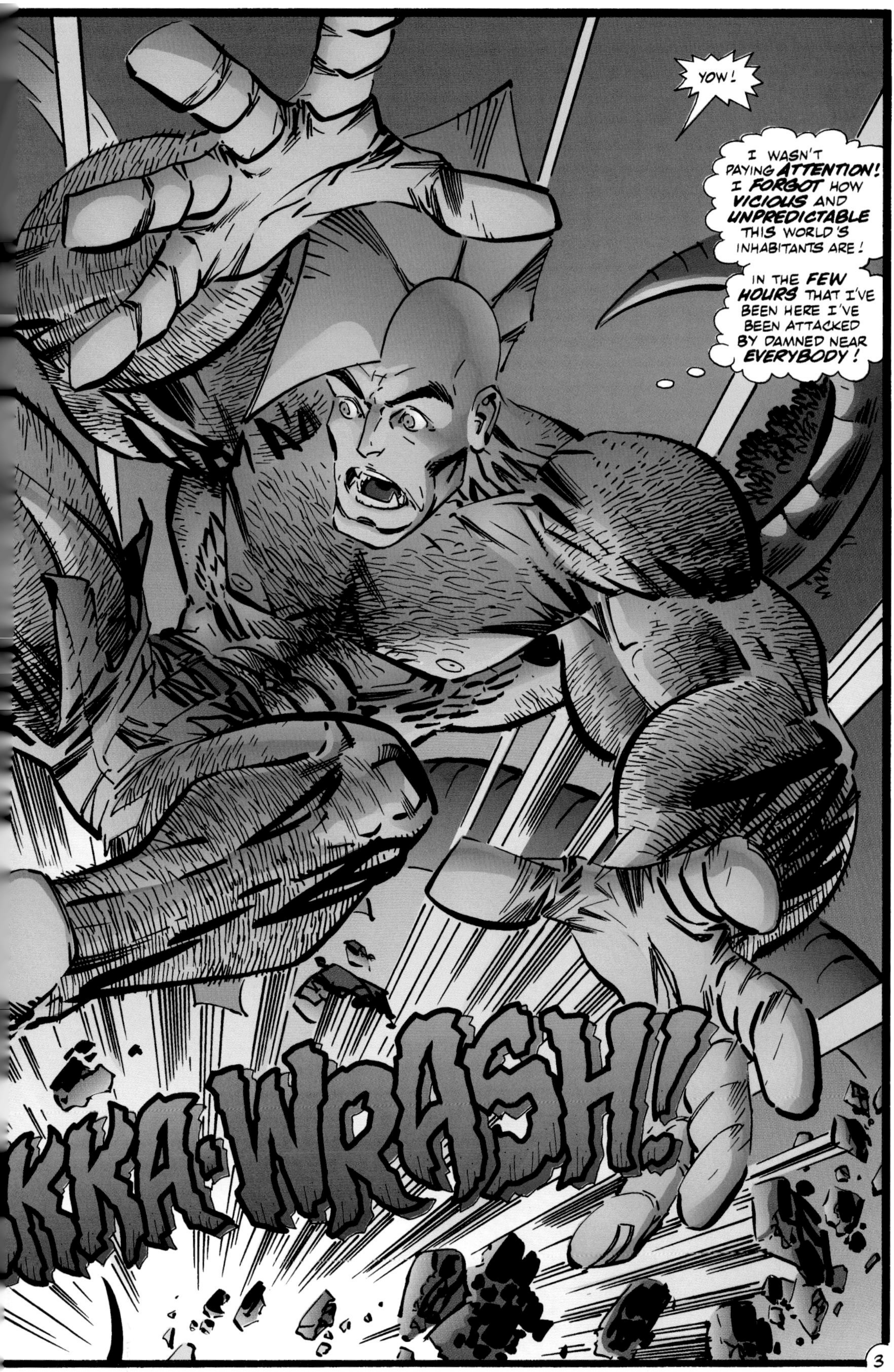
YOW!
I WASN'T PAYING ATTENTION! I FORGOT HOW VICIOUS AND UNPREDICTABLE THIS WORLD'S INHABITANTS ARE!
IN THE FEW HOURS THAT I'VE BEEN HERE I'VE BEEN ATTACKED BY DAMNED NEAR EVERYBODY!
KKA-WRASH!!

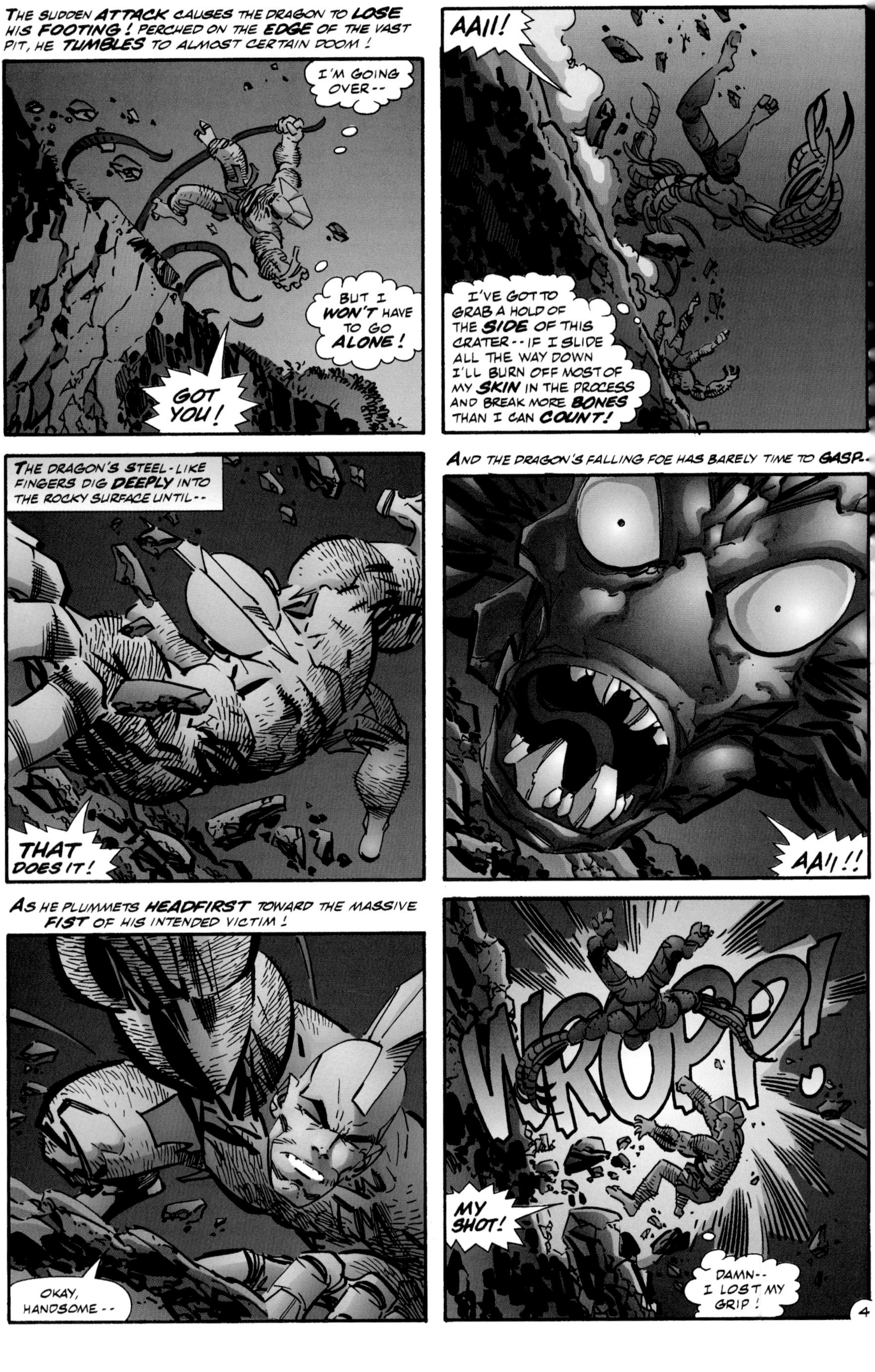
THE SUDDEN ATTACK CAUSES THE DRAGON TO LOSE HIS FOOTING! PERCHED ON THE EDGE OF THE VAST PIT, HE TUMBLES TO ALMOST CERTAIN DOOM!
I'M GOING OVER--
BUT I WON'T HAVE TO GO ALONE!
GOT YOU!
AAII!
I'VE GOT TO GRAB A HOLD OF THE SIDE OF THIS CRATER--IF I SLIDE ALL THE WAY DOWN I'LL BURN OFF MOST OF MY SKIN IN THE PROCESS AND BREAK MORE BONES THAN I CAN COUNT!
THE DRAGON'S STEEL-LIKE FINGERS DIG DEEPLY INTO THE ROCKY SURFACE UNTIL--
THAT DOES IT!
AND THE DRAGON'S FALLING FOE HAS BARELY TIME TO GASP--
AAII!!
AS HE PLUMMETS HEADFIRST TOWARD THE MASSIVE FIST OF HIS INTENDED VICTIM!
OKAY, HANDSOME--
WROOP!
MY SHOT!
DAMN--I LOST MY GRIP!

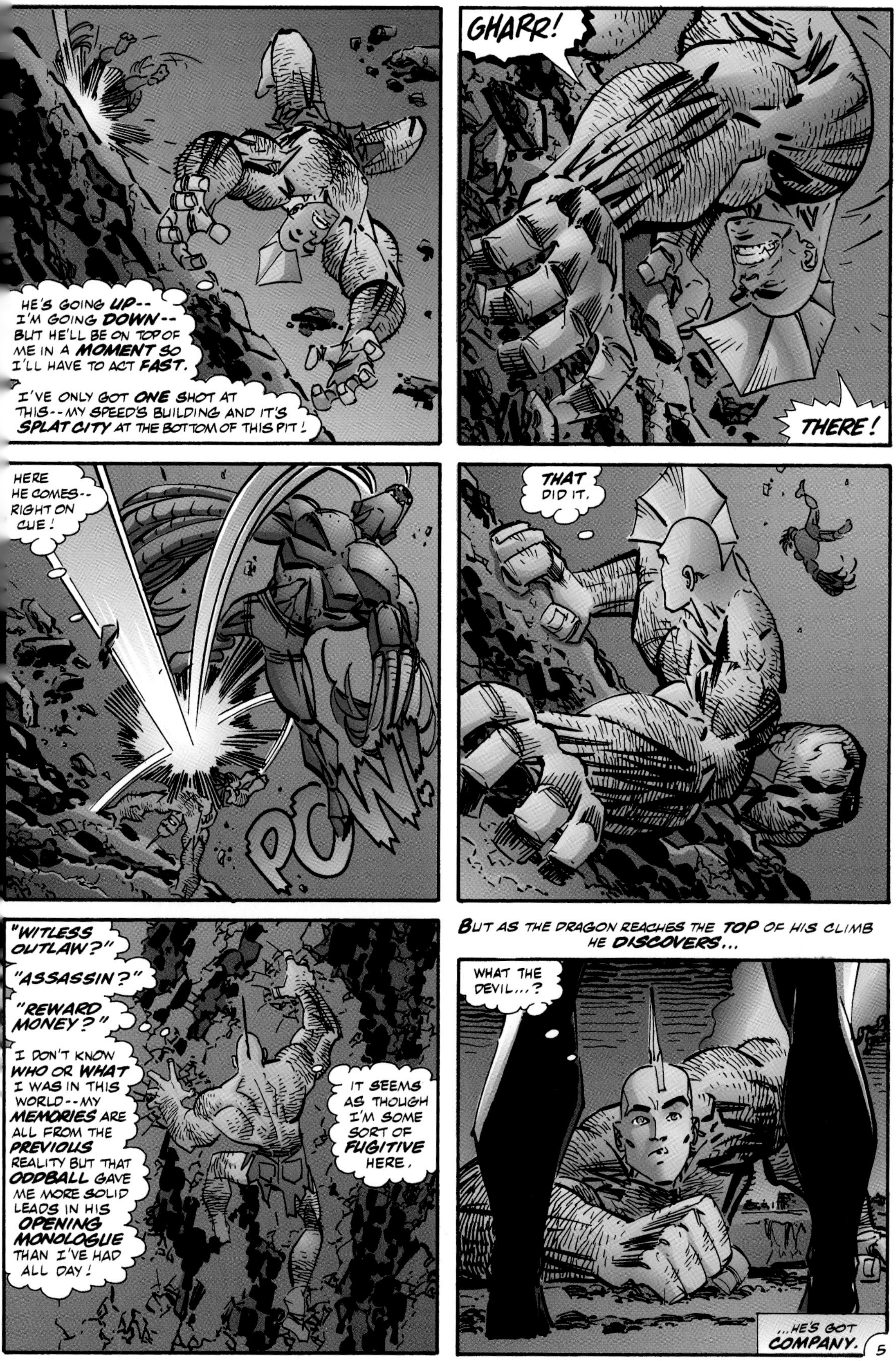
HE'S GOING UP-- I'M GOING DOWN-- BUT HE'LL BE ON TOP OF ME IN A MOMENT SO I'LL HAVE TO ACT FAST.
I'VE ONLY GOT ONE SHOT AT THIS--MY SPEED'S BUILDING AND IT'S SPLAT CITY AT THE BOTTOM OF THIS PIT!
GHARR!
THERE!
HERE HE COMES-- RIGHT ON CUE!
POW
THAT DID IT.
"WITLESS OUTLAW?"
"ASSASSIN?"
"REWARD MONEY?"
I DON'T KNOW WHO OR WHAT I WAS IN THIS WORLD--MY MEMORIES ARE ALL FROM THE PREVIOUS REALITY BUT THAT ODDBALL GAVE ME MORE SOLID LEADS IN HIS OPENING MONOLOGUE THAN I'VE HAD ALL DAY!
IT SEEMS AS THOUGH I'M SOME SORT OF FUGITIVE HERE.
BUT AS THE DRAGON REACHES THE TOP OF HIS CLIMB HE DISCOVERS...
WHAT THE DEVIL...?
...HE'S GOT COMPANY.

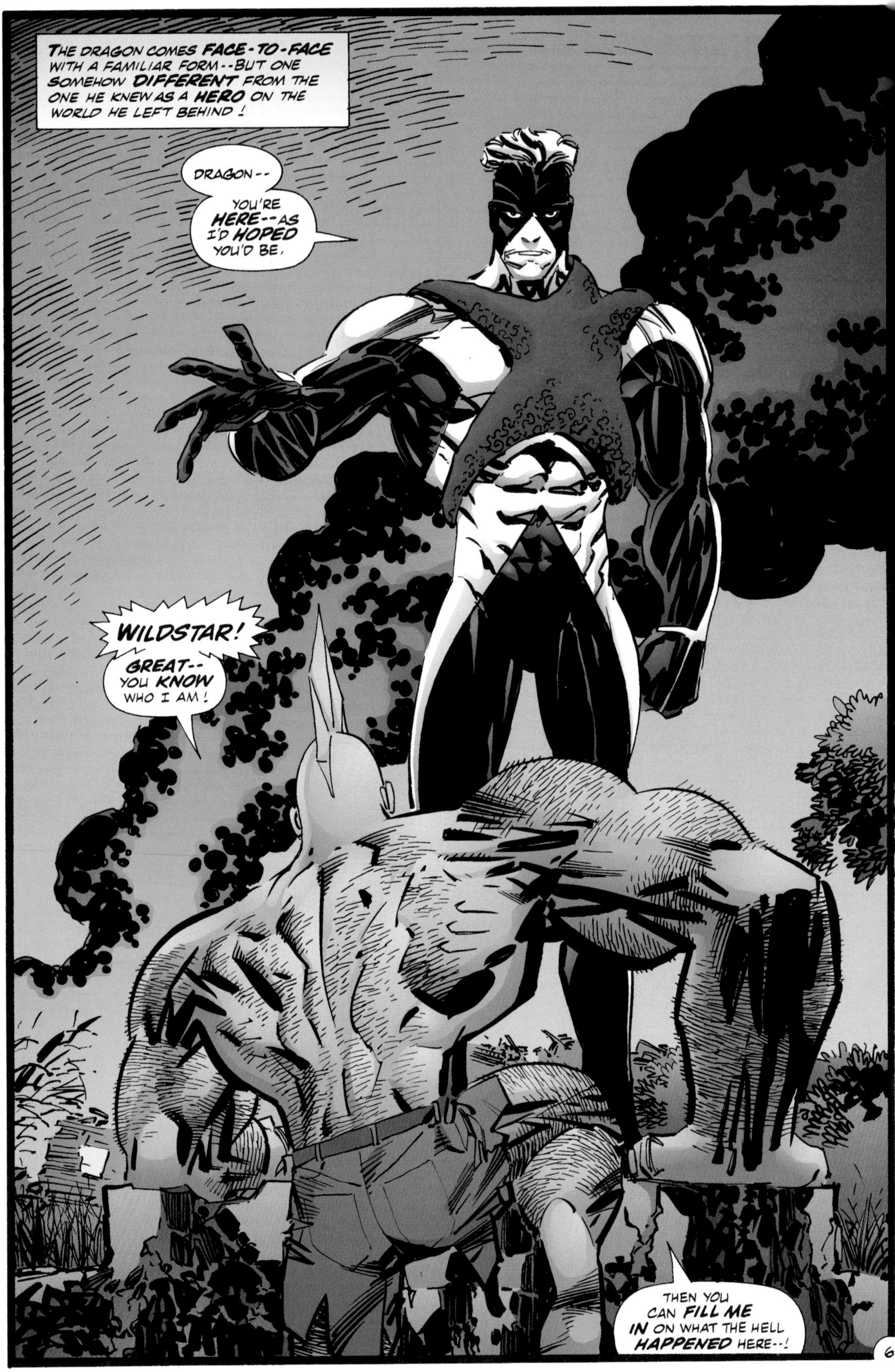

THE DRAGON COMES FACE-TO-FACE WITH A FAMILIAR FORM--BUT ONE SOMEHOW DIFFERENT FROM THE ONE HE KNEW AS A HERO ON THE WORLD HE LEFT BEHIND!
DRAGON--
YOU'RE HERE--AS I'D HOPED YOU'D BE.
WILDSTAR!
GREAT--YOU KNOW WHO I AM!
THEN YOU CAN FILL ME IN ON WHAT THE HELL HAPPENED HERE--!

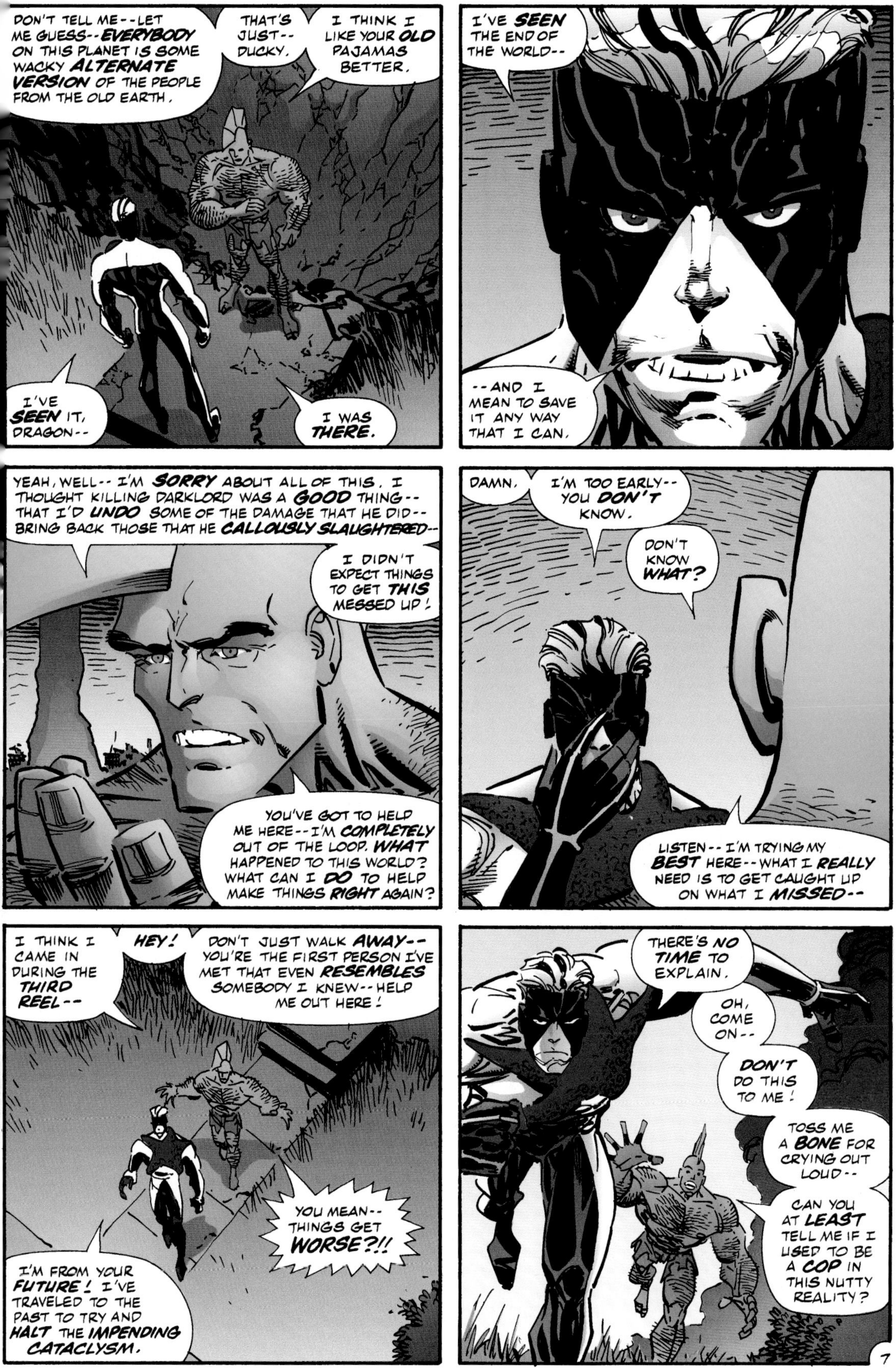
DON'T TELL ME--LET ME GUESS--EVERYBODY ON THIS PLANET IS SOME WACKY ALTERNATE VERSION OF THE PEOPLE FROM THE OLD EARTH.
THAT'S JUST--DUCKY.
I THINK I LIKE YOUR OLD PAJAMAS BETTER.
I'VE SEEN IT, DRAGON--
I WAS THERE.
I'VE SEEN THE END OF THE WORLD--
--AND I MEAN TO SAVE IT ANY WAY THAT I CAN.
YEAH, WELL-- I'M SORRY ABOUT ALL OF THIS. I THOUGHT KILLING DARKLORD WAS A GOOD THING--THAT I'D UNDO SOME OF THE DAMAGE THAT HE DID--BRING BACK THOSE THAT HE CALLOUSLY SLAUGHTERED--
I DIDN'T EXPECT THINGS TO GET THIS MESSED UP!
YOU'VE GOT TO HELP ME HERE--I'M COMPLETELY OUT OF THE LOOP. WHAT HAPPENED TO THIS WORLD? WHAT CAN I DO TO HELP MAKE THINGS RIGHT AGAIN?
DAMN.
I'M TOO EARLY--YOU DON'T KNOW.
DON'T KNOW WHAT?
LISTEN--I'M TRYING MY BEST HERE--WHAT I REALLY NEED IS TO GET CAUGHT UP ON WHAT I MISSED--
I THINK I CAME IN DURING THE THIRD REEL--
HEY!
DON'T JUST WALK AWAY--YOU'RE THE FIRST PERSON I'VE MET THAT EVEN RESEMBLES SOMEBODY I KNEW--HELP ME OUT HERE!
YOU MEAN--THINGS GET WORSE?!!
I'M FROM YOUR FUTURE! I'VE TRAVELED TO THE PAST TO TRY AND HALT THE IMPENDING CATACLYSM.
THERE'S NO TIME TO EXPLAIN.
OH, COME ON--
DON'T DO THIS TO ME!
TOSS ME A BONE FOR CRYING OUT LOUD--
CAN YOU AT LEAST TELL ME IF I USED TO BE A COP IN THIS NUTTY REALITY?

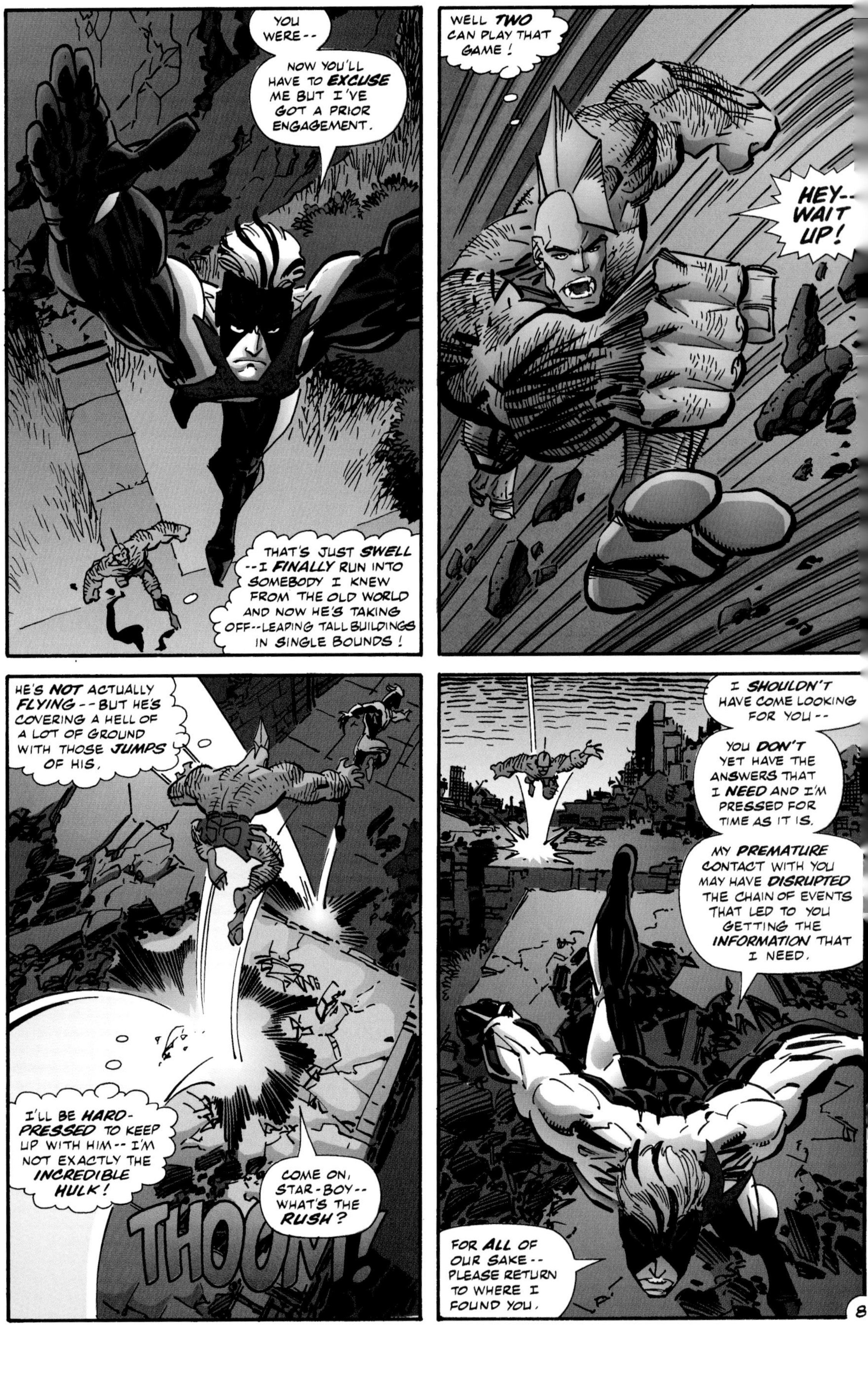

YOU WERE--
NOW YOU'LL HAVE TO EXCUSE ME BUT I'VE GOT A PRIOR ENGAGEMENT.
THAT'S JUST SWELL --I FINALLY RUN INTO SOMEBODY I KNEW FROM THE OLD WORLD AND NOW HE'S TAKING OFF--LEAPING TALL BUILDINGS IN SINGLE BOUNDS!
WELL TWO CAN PLAY THAT GAME!
HEY--WAIT UP!
HE'S NOT ACTUALLY FLYING--BUT HE'S COVERING A HELL OF A LOT OF GROUND WITH THOSE JUMPS OF HIS.
I'LL BE HARD-PRESSED TO KEEP UP WITH HIM--I'M NOT EXACTLY THE INCREDIBLE HULK!
COME ON, STAR-BOY--WHAT'S THE RUSH?
THOOM!
I SHOULDN'T HAVE COME LOOKING FOR YOU--
YOU DON'T YET HAVE THE ANSWERS THAT I NEED AND I'M PRESSED FOR TIME AS IT IS.
MY PREMATURE CONTACT WITH YOU MAY HAVE DISRUPTED THE CHAIN OF EVENTS THAT LED TO YOU GETTING THE INFORMATION THAT I NEED.
FOR ALL OF OUR SAKE--PLEASE RETURN TO WHERE I FOUND YOU.

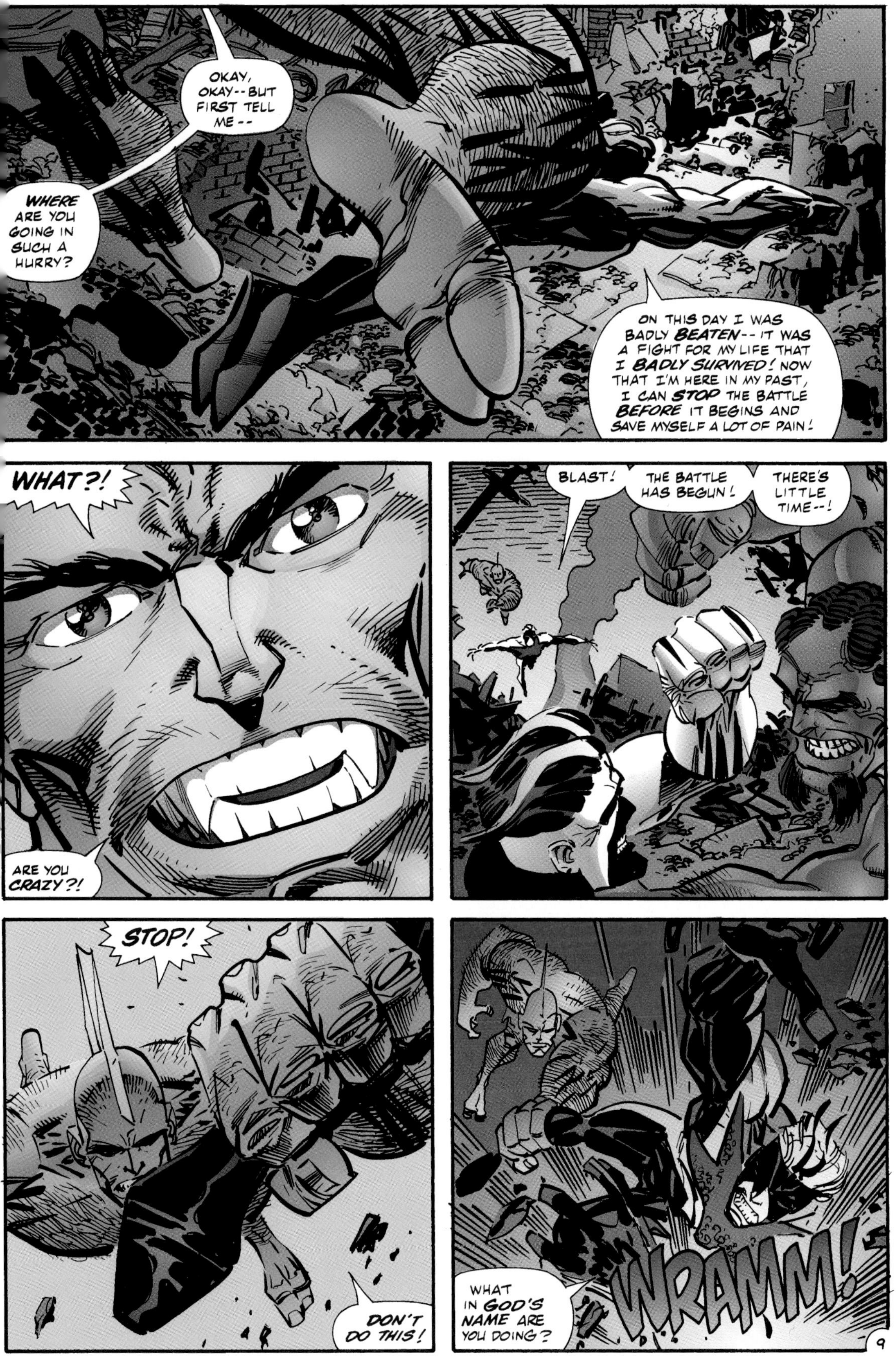
OKAY, OKAY-- BUT FIRST TELL ME --
WHERE ARE YOU GOING IN SUCH A HURRY?
ON THIS DAY I WAS BADLY BEATEN-- IT WAS A FIGHT FOR MY LIFE THAT I BADLY SURVIVED! NOW THAT I'M HERE IN MY PAST, I CAN STOP THE BATTLE BEFORE IT BEGINS AND SAVE MYSELF A LOT OF PAIN!
WHAT?!
ARE YOU CRAZY?!
BLAST!
THE BATTLE HAS BEGUN!
THERE'S LITTLE TIME--!
STOP!
DON'T DO THIS!
WHAT IN GOD'S NAME ARE YOU DOING?
WRAMM!

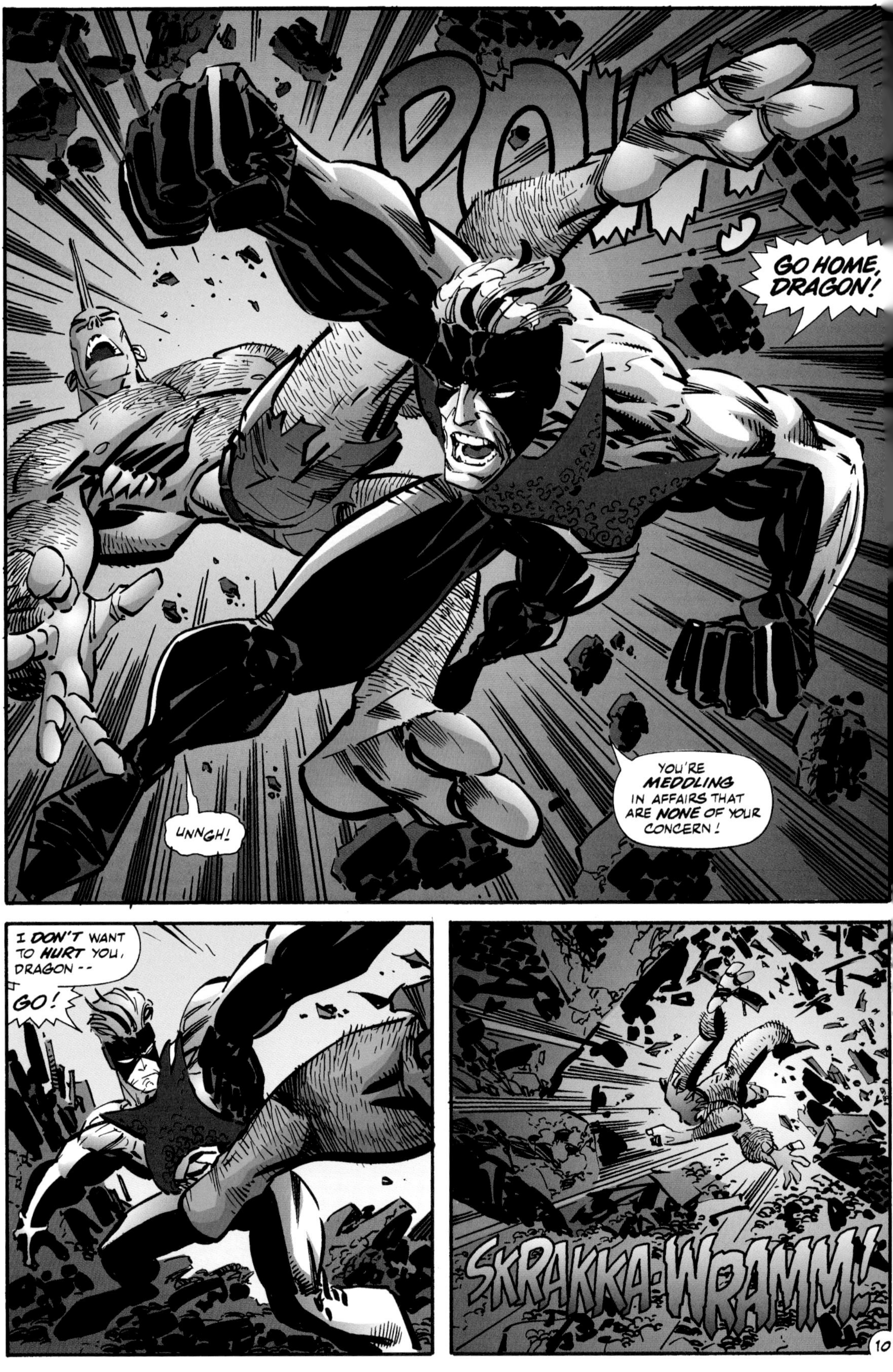
GO HOME, DRAGON!
YOU'RE **MEDDLING** IN AFFAIRS THAT ARE **NONE** OF YOUR CONCERN!
UNNGH!
I **DON'T** WANT TO **HURT** YOU, DRAGON --
GO!
SKRAKKA-WRAMM!

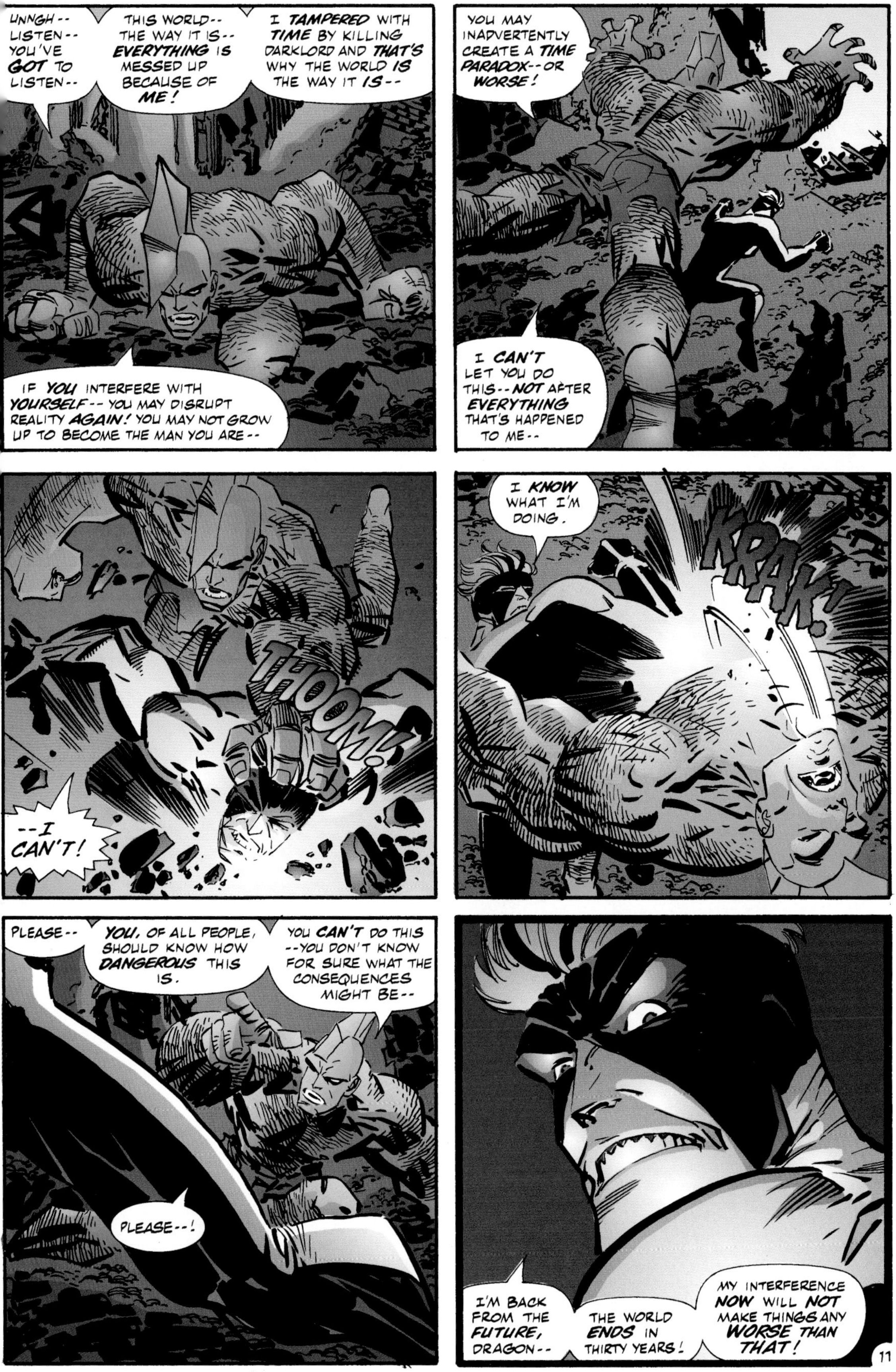
UNNGH -- LISTEN -- YOU'VE GOT TO LISTEN --
THIS WORLD -- THE WAY IT IS -- EVERYTHING IS MESSED UP BECAUSE OF ME!
I TAMPERED WITH TIME BY KILLING DARKLORD AND THAT'S WHY THE WORLD IS THE WAY IT IS --
IF YOU INTERFERE WITH YOURSELF -- YOU MAY DISRUPT REALITY AGAIN! YOU MAY NOT GROW UP TO BECOME THE MAN YOU ARE --
YOU MAY INADVERTENTLY CREATE A TIME PARADOX -- OR WORSE!
I CAN'T LET YOU DO THIS -- NOT AFTER EVERYTHING THAT'S HAPPENED TO ME --
THOOM!
-- I CAN'T!
I KNOW WHAT I'M DOING.
KRAK!
PLEASE --
YOU, OF ALL PEOPLE, SHOULD KNOW HOW DANGEROUS THIS IS.
YOU CAN'T DO THIS -- YOU DON'T KNOW FOR SURE WHAT THE CONSEQUENCES MIGHT BE --
PLEASE -- !
I'M BACK FROM THE FUTURE, DRAGON --
THE WORLD ENDS IN THIRTY YEARS!
MY INTERFERENCE NOW WILL NOT MAKE THINGS ANY WORSE THAN THAT!

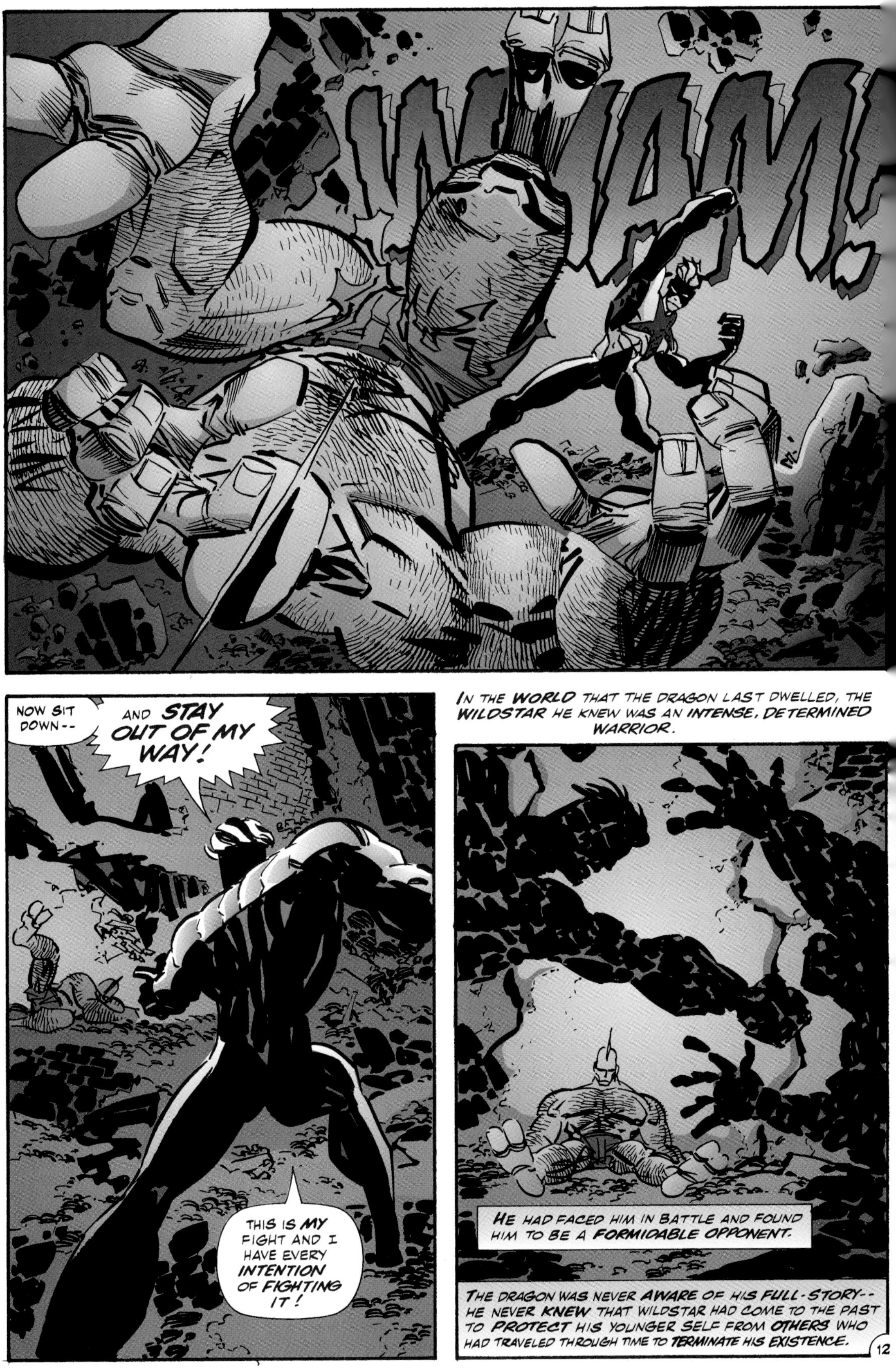
WHAM!
NOW SIT DOWN--
AND STAY OUT OF MY WAY!
THIS IS MY FIGHT AND I HAVE EVERY INTENTION OF FIGHTING IT!
IN THE WORLD THAT THE DRAGON LAST DWELLED, THE WILDSTAR HE KNEW WAS AN INTENSE, DETERMINED WARRIOR.
HE HAD FACED HIM IN BATTLE AND FOUND HIM TO BE A FORMIDABLE OPPONENT.
THE DRAGON WAS NEVER AWARE OF HIS FULL-STORY--HE NEVER KNEW THAT WILDSTAR HAD COME TO THE PAST TO PROTECT HIS YOUNGER SELF FROM OTHERS WHO HAD TRAVELED THROUGH TIME TO TERMINATE HIS EXISTENCE.

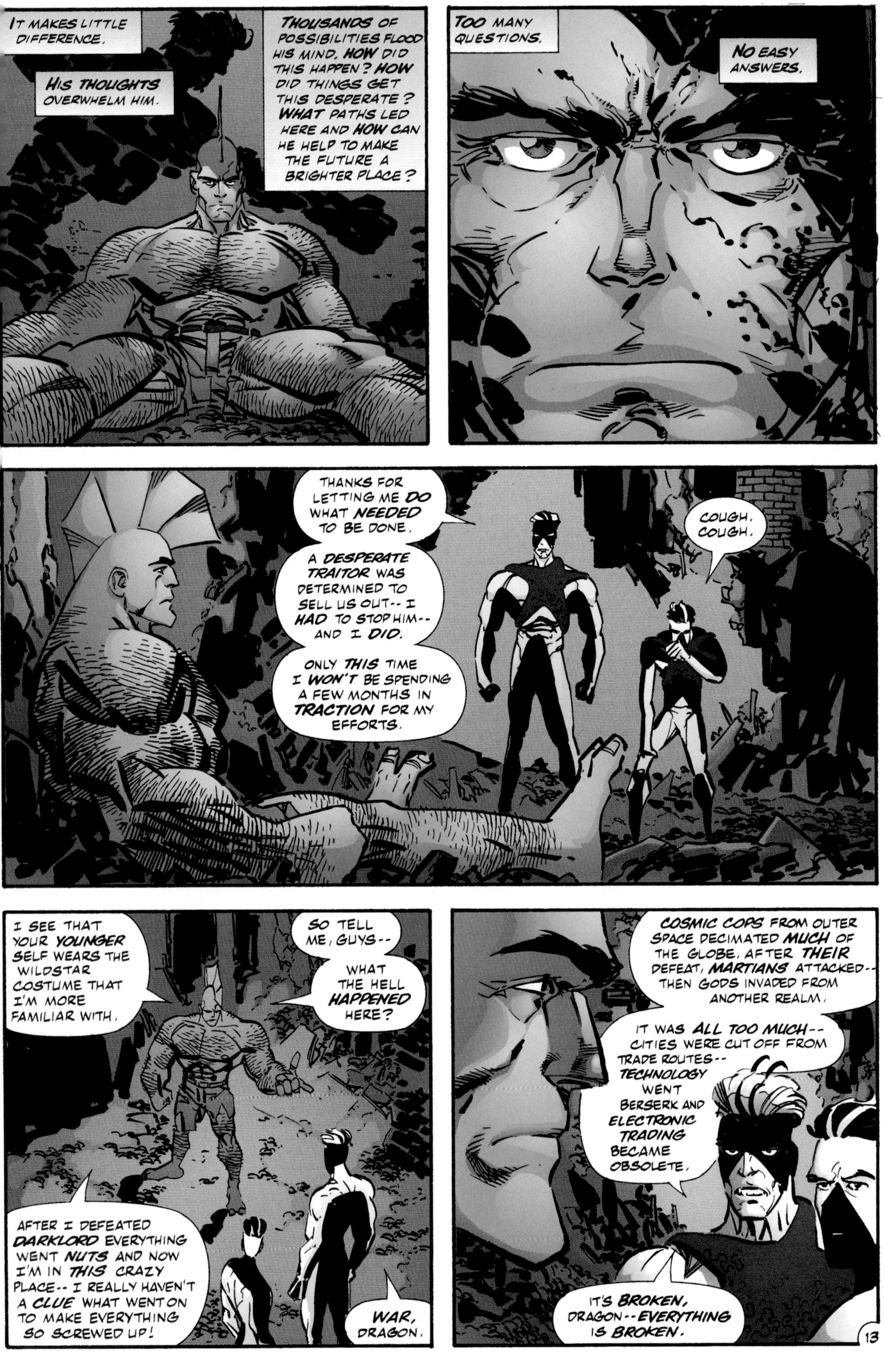
IT MAKES LITTLE DIFFERENCE.
HIS THOUGHTS OVERWHELM HIM.
THOUSANDS OF POSSIBILITIES FLOOD HIS MIND. HOW DID THIS HAPPEN? HOW DID THINGS GET THIS DESPERATE? WHAT PATHS LED HERE AND HOW CAN HE HELP TO MAKE THE FUTURE A BRIGHTER PLACE?
TOO MANY QUESTIONS.
NO EASY ANSWERS.
THANKS FOR LETTING ME DO WHAT NEEDED TO BE DONE.
A DESPERATE TRAITOR WAS DETERMINED TO SELL US OUT-- I HAD TO STOP HIM-- AND I DID.
ONLY THIS TIME I WON'T BE SPENDING A FEW MONTHS IN TRACTION FOR MY EFFORTS.
COUGH. COUGH.
I SEE THAT YOUR YOUNGER SELF WEARS THE WILDSTAR COSTUME THAT I'M MORE FAMILIAR WITH.
SO TELL ME, GUYS--
WHAT THE HELL HAPPENED HERE?
AFTER I DEFEATED DARKLORD EVERYTHING WENT NUTS AND NOW I'M IN THIS CRAZY PLACE-- I REALLY HAVEN'T A CLUE WHAT WENT ON TO MAKE EVERYTHING SO SCREWED UP!
WAR, DRAGON.
COSMIC COPS FROM OUTER SPACE DECIMATED MUCH OF THE GLOBE. AFTER THEIR DEFEAT, MARTIANS ATTACKED-- THEN GODS INVADED FROM ANOTHER REALM.
IT WAS ALL TOO MUCH-- CITIES WERE CUT OFF FROM TRADE ROUTES-- TECHNOLOGY WENT BERSERK AND ELECTRONIC TRADING BECAME OBSOLETE.
IT'S BROKEN, DRAGON-- EVERYTHING IS BROKEN.

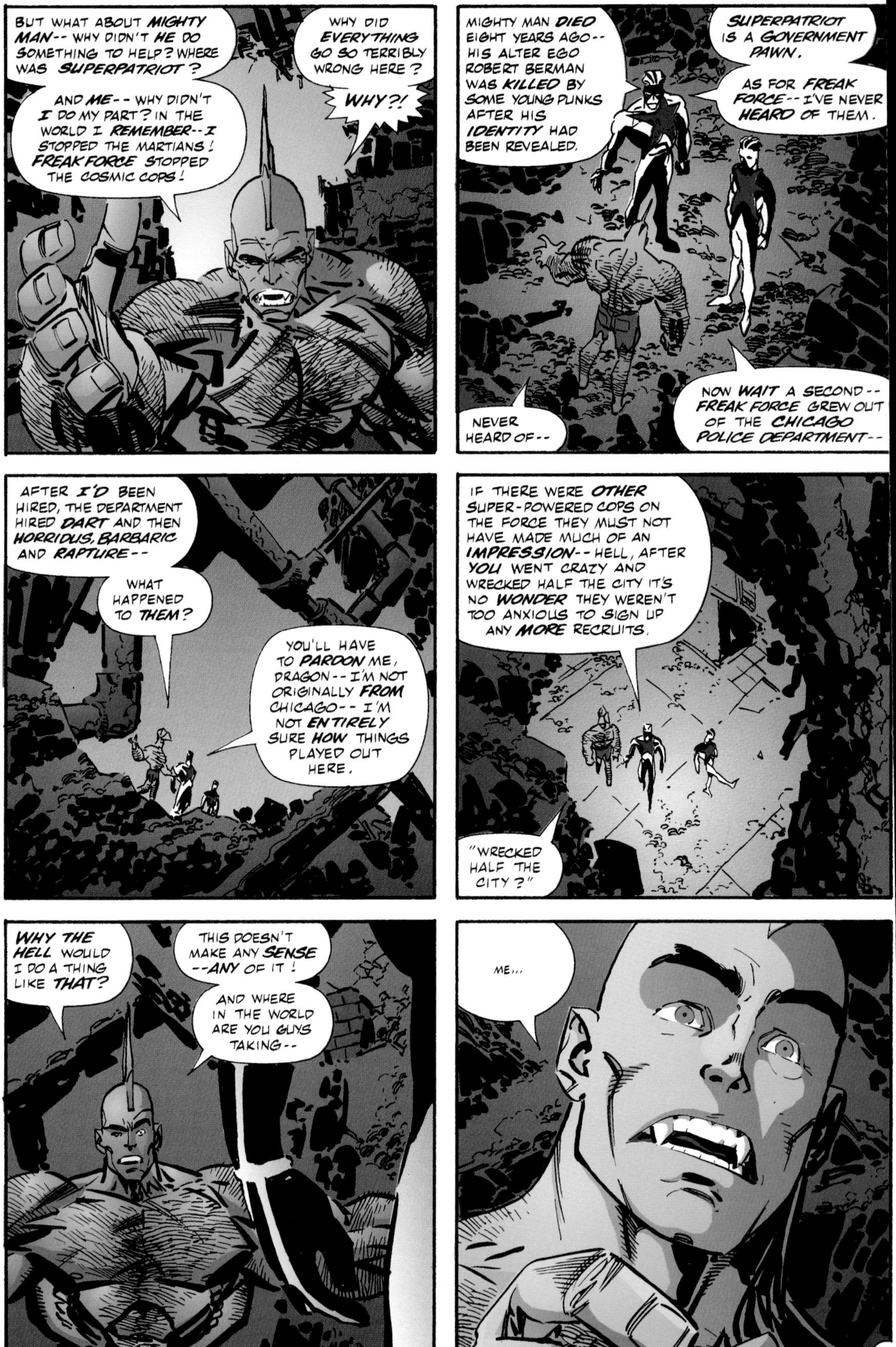
BUT WHAT ABOUT MIGHTY MAN-- WHY DIDN'T HE DO SOMETHING TO HELP? WHERE WAS SUPERPATRIOT?
AND ME-- WHY DIDN'T I DO MY PART? IN THE WORLD I REMEMBER-- I STOPPED THE MARTIANS! FREAK FORCE STOPPED THE COSMIC COPS!
WHY DID EVERYTHING GO SO TERRIBLY WRONG HERE?
WHY?!
MIGHTY MAN DIED EIGHT YEARS AGO-- HIS ALTER EGO ROBERT BERMAN WAS KILLED BY SOME YOUNG PUNKS AFTER HIS IDENTITY HAD BEEN REVEALED.
SUPERPATRIOT IS A GOVERNMENT PAWN.
AS FOR FREAK FORCE-- I'VE NEVER HEARD OF THEM.
NEVER HEARD OF--
NOW WAIT A SECOND-- FREAK FORCE GREW OUT OF THE CHICAGO POLICE DEPARTMENT--
AFTER I'D BEEN HIRED, THE DEPARTMENT HIRED DART AND THEN HORRIDUS, BARBARIC AND RAPTURE--
WHAT HAPPENED TO THEM?
YOU'LL HAVE TO PARDON ME, DRAGON-- I'M NOT ORIGINALLY FROM CHICAGO-- I'M NOT ENTIRELY SURE HOW THINGS PLAYED OUT HERE.
IF THERE WERE OTHER SUPER-POWERED COPS ON THE FORCE THEY MUST NOT HAVE MADE MUCH OF AN IMPRESSION-- HELL, AFTER YOU WENT CRAZY AND WRECKED HALF THE CITY IT'S NO WONDER THEY WEREN'T TOO ANXIOUS TO SIGN UP ANY MORE RECRUITS.
"WRECKED HALF THE CITY?"
WHY THE HELL WOULD I DO A THING LIKE THAT?
THIS DOESN'T MAKE ANY SENSE --ANY OF IT!
AND WHERE IN THE WORLD ARE YOU GUYS TAKING--
ME...

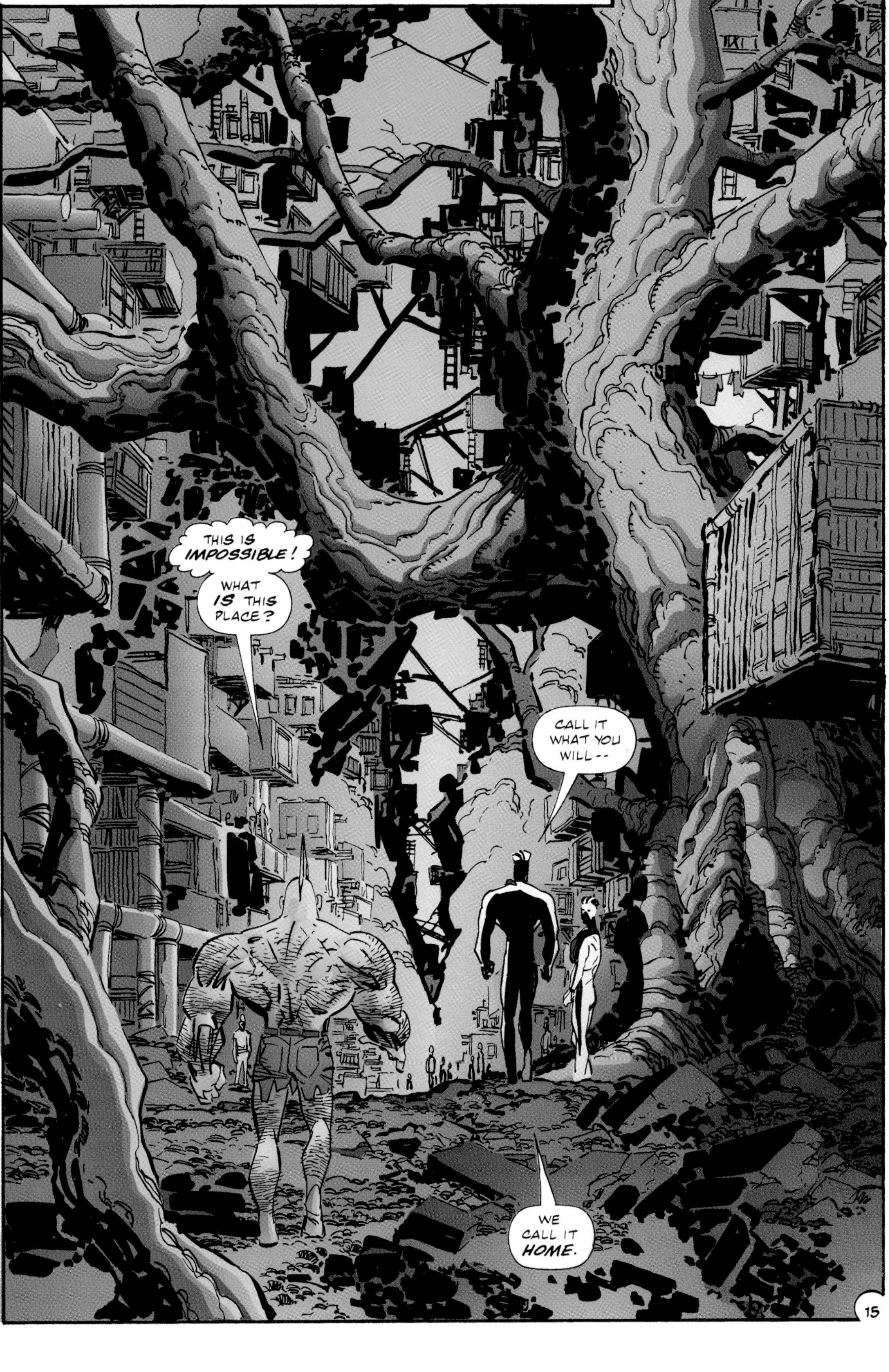
THE DRAGON IS STUNNED TO FIND A MASSIVE MAKESHIFT CITY AMIDST GIGANTIC TREES WHERE NONE HAD STOOD BEFORE. THE DRAGON IS FILLED WITH AN OVERWHELMING FEELING OF AWE.
THIS IS IMPOSSIBLE!
WHAT IS THIS PLACE?
CALL IT WHAT YOU WILL --
WE CALL IT HOME.

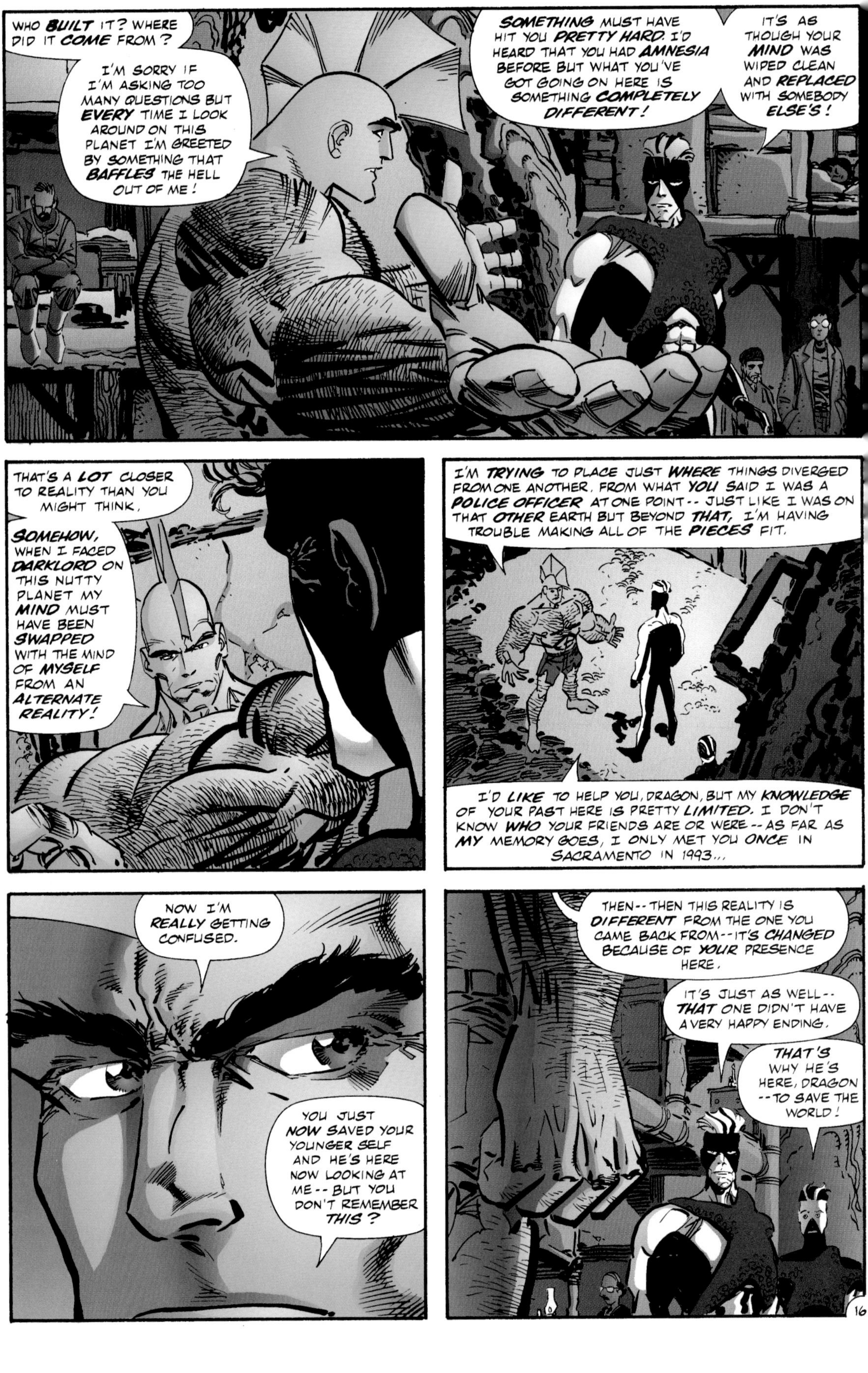
WHO BUILT IT? WHERE DID IT COME FROM?
I'M SORRY IF I'M ASKING TOO MANY QUESTIONS BUT EVERY TIME I LOOK AROUND ON THIS PLANET I'M GREETED BY SOMETHING THAT BAFFLES THE HELL OUT OF ME!
SOMETHING MUST HAVE HIT YOU PRETTY HARD. I'D HEARD THAT YOU HAD AMNESIA BEFORE BUT WHAT YOU'VE GOT GOING ON HERE IS SOMETHING COMPLETELY DIFFERENT!
IT'S AS THOUGH YOUR MIND WAS WIPED CLEAN AND REPLACED WITH SOMEBODY ELSE'S!
THAT'S A LOT CLOSER TO REALITY THAN YOU MIGHT THINK.
SOMEHOW, WHEN I FACED DARKLORD ON THIS NUTTY PLANET MY MIND MUST HAVE BEEN SWAPPED WITH THE MIND OF MYSELF FROM AN ALTERNATE REALITY!
I'M TRYING TO PLACE JUST WHERE THINGS DIVERGED FROM ONE ANOTHER. FROM WHAT YOU SAID I WAS A POLICE OFFICER AT ONE POINT -- JUST LIKE I WAS ON THAT OTHER EARTH BUT BEYOND THAT, I'M HAVING TROUBLE MAKING ALL OF THE PIECES FIT.
I'D LIKE TO HELP YOU, DRAGON, BUT MY KNOWLEDGE OF YOUR PAST HERE IS PRETTY LIMITED. I DON'T KNOW WHO YOUR FRIENDS ARE OR WERE -- AS FAR AS MY MEMORY GOES, I ONLY MET YOU ONCE IN SACRAMENTO IN 1993...
NOW I'M REALLY GETTING CONFUSED.
YOU JUST NOW SAVED YOUR YOUNGER SELF AND HE'S HERE NOW LOOKING AT ME -- BUT YOU DON'T REMEMBER THIS?
THEN -- THEN THIS REALITY IS DIFFERENT FROM THE ONE YOU CAME BACK FROM -- IT'S CHANGED BECAUSE OF YOUR PRESENCE HERE.
IT'S JUST AS WELL -- THAT ONE DIDN'T HAVE A VERY HAPPY ENDING.
THAT'S WHY HE'S HERE, DRAGON -- TO SAVE THE WORLD!

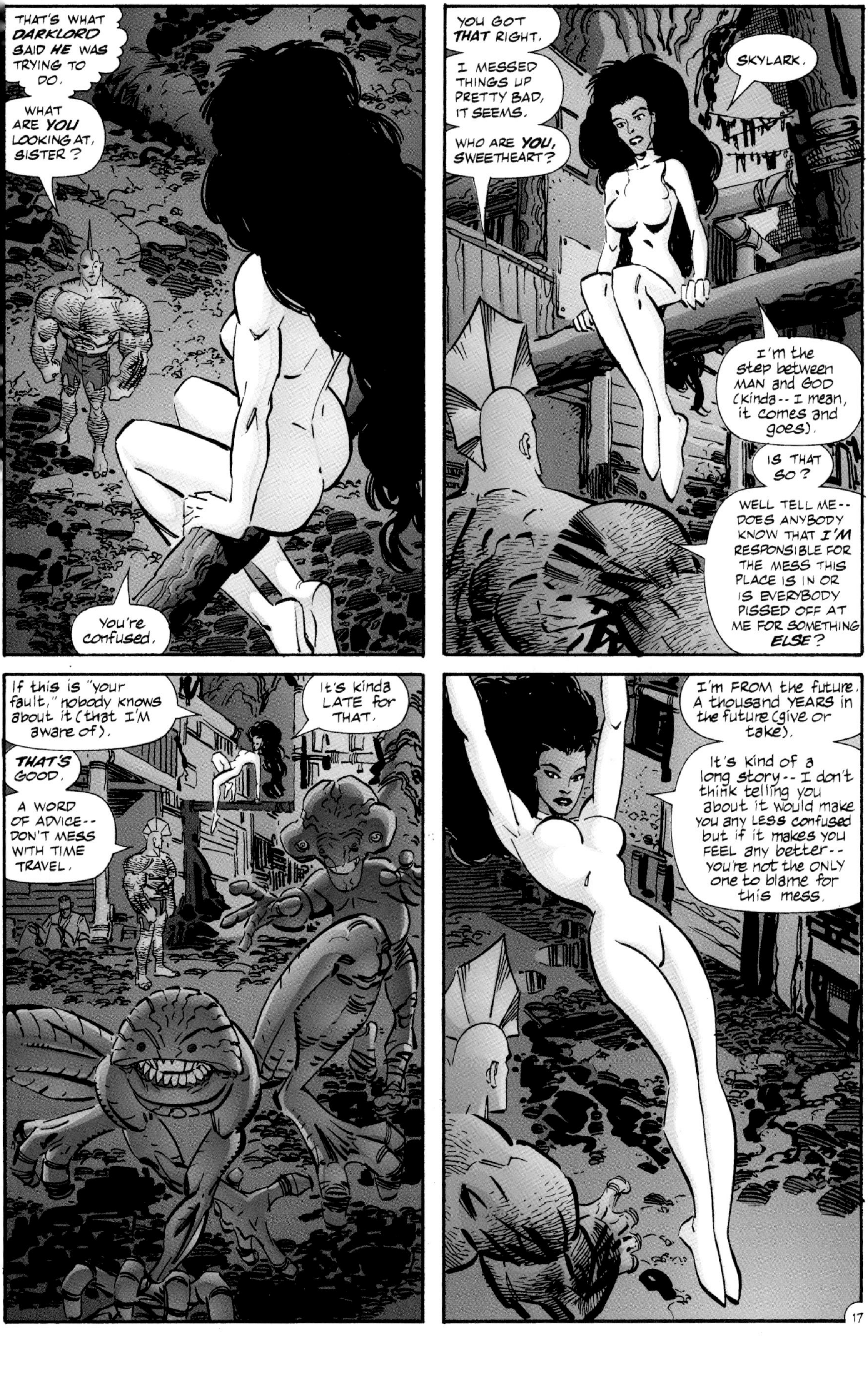
THAT'S WHAT DARKLORD SAID HE WAS TRYING TO DO.
WHAT ARE YOU LOOKING AT, SISTER?
You're confused.
YOU GOT THAT RIGHT.
I MESSED THINGS UP PRETTY BAD, IT SEEMS.
WHO ARE YOU, SWEETHEART?
SKYLARK.
I'm the step between MAN and GOD (kinda -- I mean, it comes and goes).
IS THAT SO?
WELL TELL ME -- DOES ANYBODY KNOW THAT I'M RESPONSIBLE FOR THE MESS THIS PLACE IS IN OR IS EVERYBODY PISSED OFF AT ME FOR SOMETHING ELSE?
If this is "your fault," nobody knows about it (that I'm aware of).
THAT'S GOOD.
A WORD OF ADVICE -- DON'T MESS WITH TIME TRAVEL.
It's kinda LATE for THAT.
I'm FROM the future. A thousand YEARS in the future (give or take).
It's kind of a long story -- I don't think telling you about it would make you any LESS confused but if it makes you FEEL any better -- you're not the ONLY one to blame for this mess.

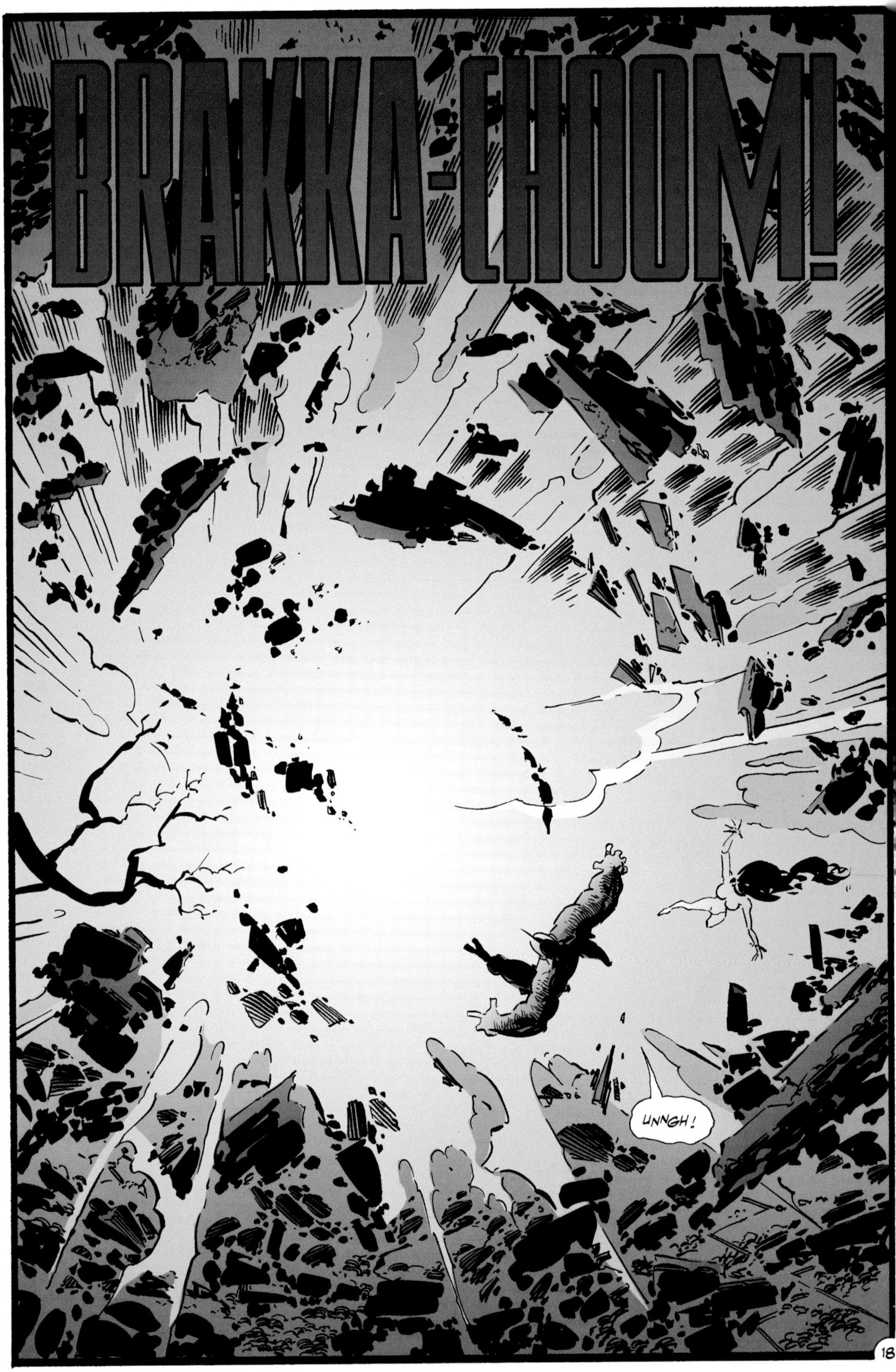
BRAKKA-CHOOM!
UNNGH!

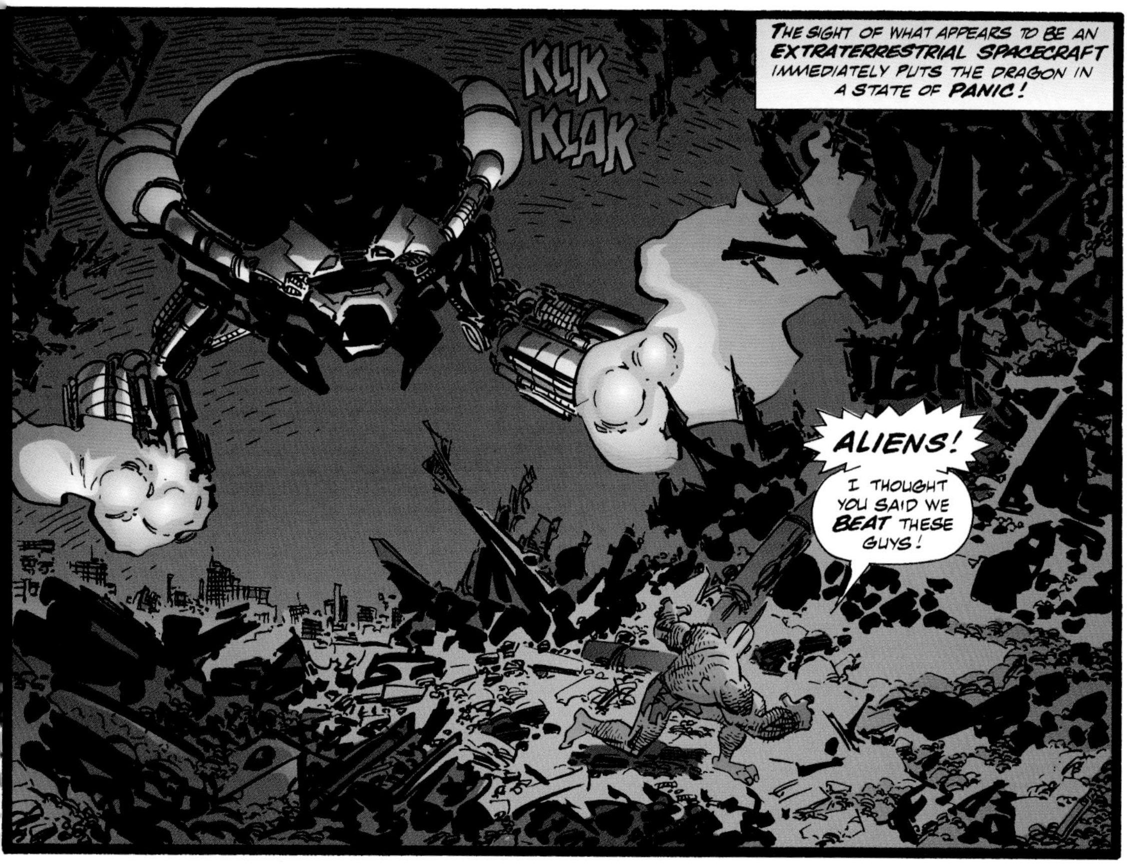
THE SIGHT OF WHAT APPEARS TO BE AN EXTRATERRESTRIAL SPACECRAFT IMMEDIATELY PUTS THE DRAGON IN A STATE OF PANIC!
KLIK KLAK
ALIENS!
I THOUGHT YOU SAID WE BEAT THESE GUYS!

IN A HEARTBEAT HUNDREDS OF MECHANICAL MEN POUR OUT OF THE HOVERING CRAFT WITH A SINGLE UNIFIED PURPOSE--

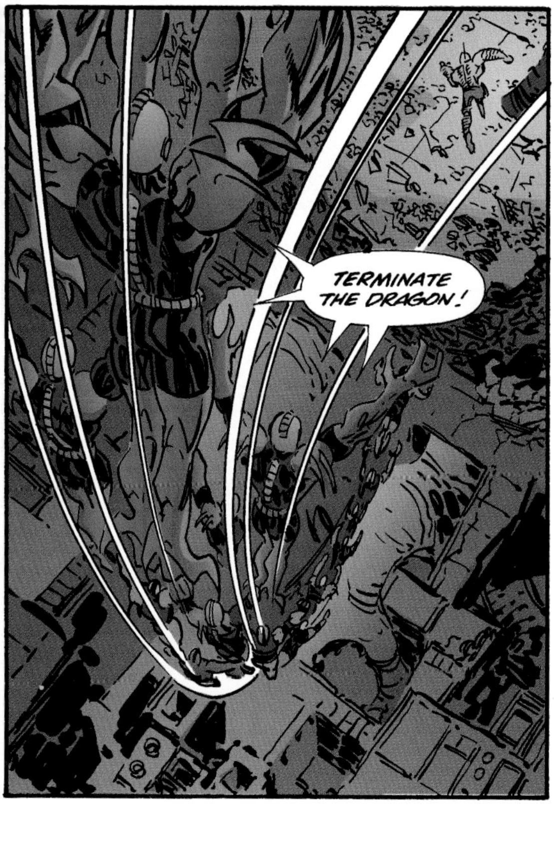
TERMINATE THE DRAGON!

THE DRAGON INSTINCTIVELY RUNS BUT HE'S INSTANTLY OVERCOME AND BROUGHT DOWN BY THE SHEER WEIGHT OF THEIR VAST NUMBERS.

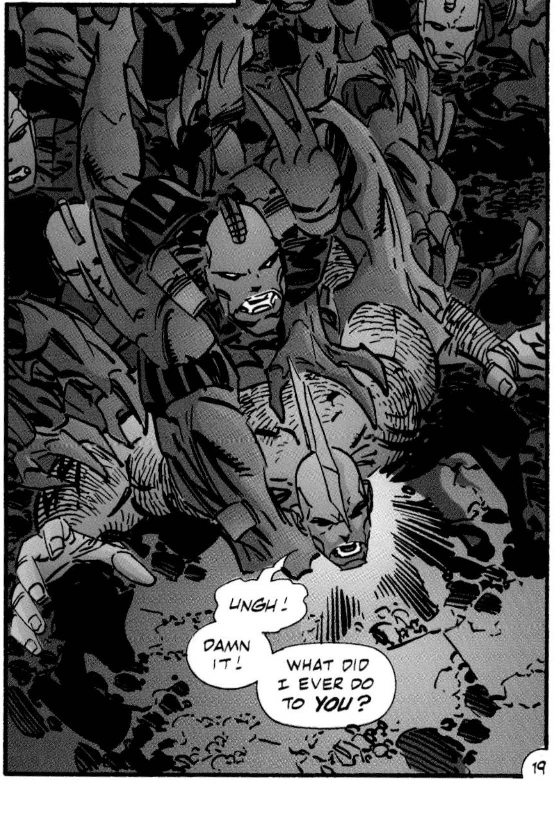
UNGH!
DAMN IT!
WHAT DID I EVER DO TO YOU?

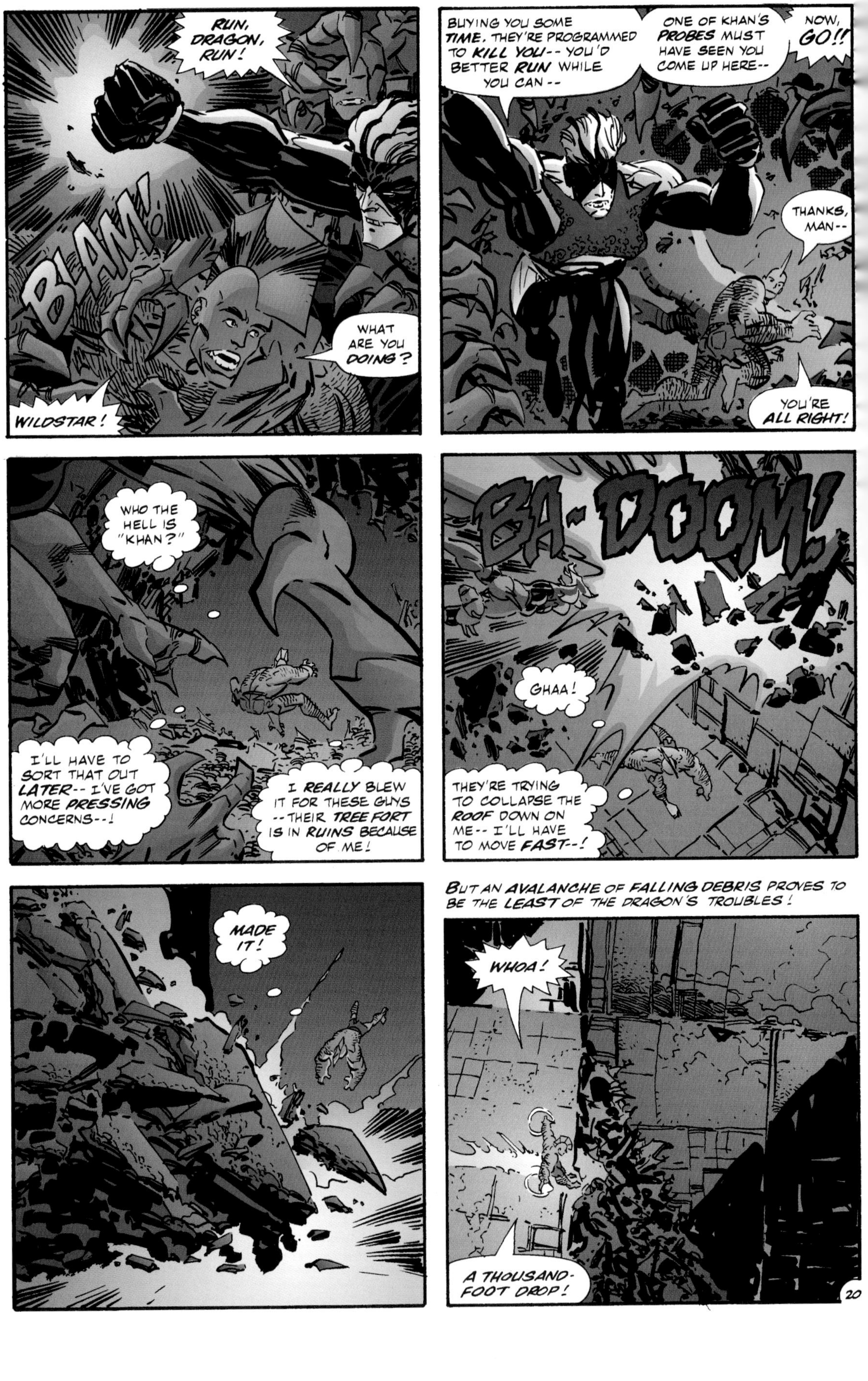
RUN, DRAGON, RUN!
BLAM!
WHAT ARE YOU DOING?
WILDSTAR!
BUYING YOU SOME TIME. THEY'RE PROGRAMMED TO KILL YOU-- YOU'D BETTER RUN WHILE YOU CAN --
ONE OF KHAN'S PROBES MUST HAVE SEEN YOU COME UP HERE--
NOW, GO!!
THANKS, MAN--
YOU'RE ALL RIGHT!
WHO THE HELL IS "KHAN?"
I'LL HAVE TO SORT THAT OUT LATER-- I'VE GOT MORE PRESSING CONCERNS--!
I REALLY BLEW IT FOR THESE GUYS --THEIR TREE FORT IS IN RUINS BECAUSE OF ME!
BA-DOOM!
GHAA!
THEY'RE TRYING TO COLLAPSE THE ROOF DOWN ON ME-- I'LL HAVE TO MOVE FAST--!
MADE IT!
BUT AN AVALANCHE OF FALLING DEBRIS PROVES TO BE THE LEAST OF THE DRAGON'S TROUBLES!
WHOA!
A THOUSAND-FOOT DROP!

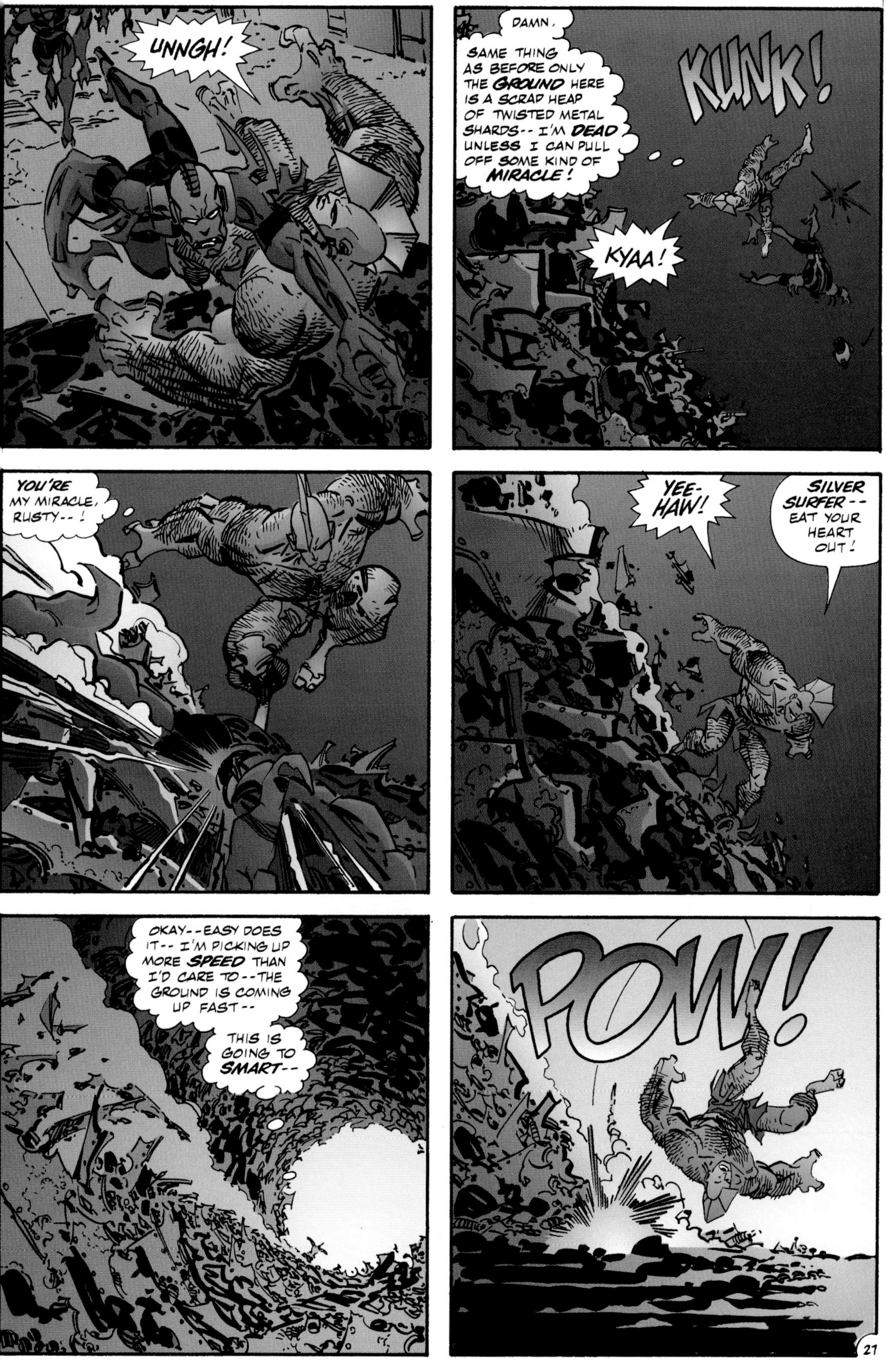
UNNGH!
DAMN,
SAME THING AS BEFORE ONLY THE GROUND HERE IS A SCRAP HEAP OF TWISTED METAL SHARDS-- I'M DEAD UNLESS I CAN PULL OFF SOME KIND OF MIRACLE!
KUNK!
KYAA!
YOU'RE MY MIRACLE, RUSTY--!
YEE-HAW!
SILVER SURFER-- EAT YOUR HEART OUT!
OKAY--EASY DOES IT-- I'M PICKING UP MORE SPEED THAN I'D CARE TO--THE GROUND IS COMING UP FAST--
THIS IS GOING TO SMART--
POW!
27

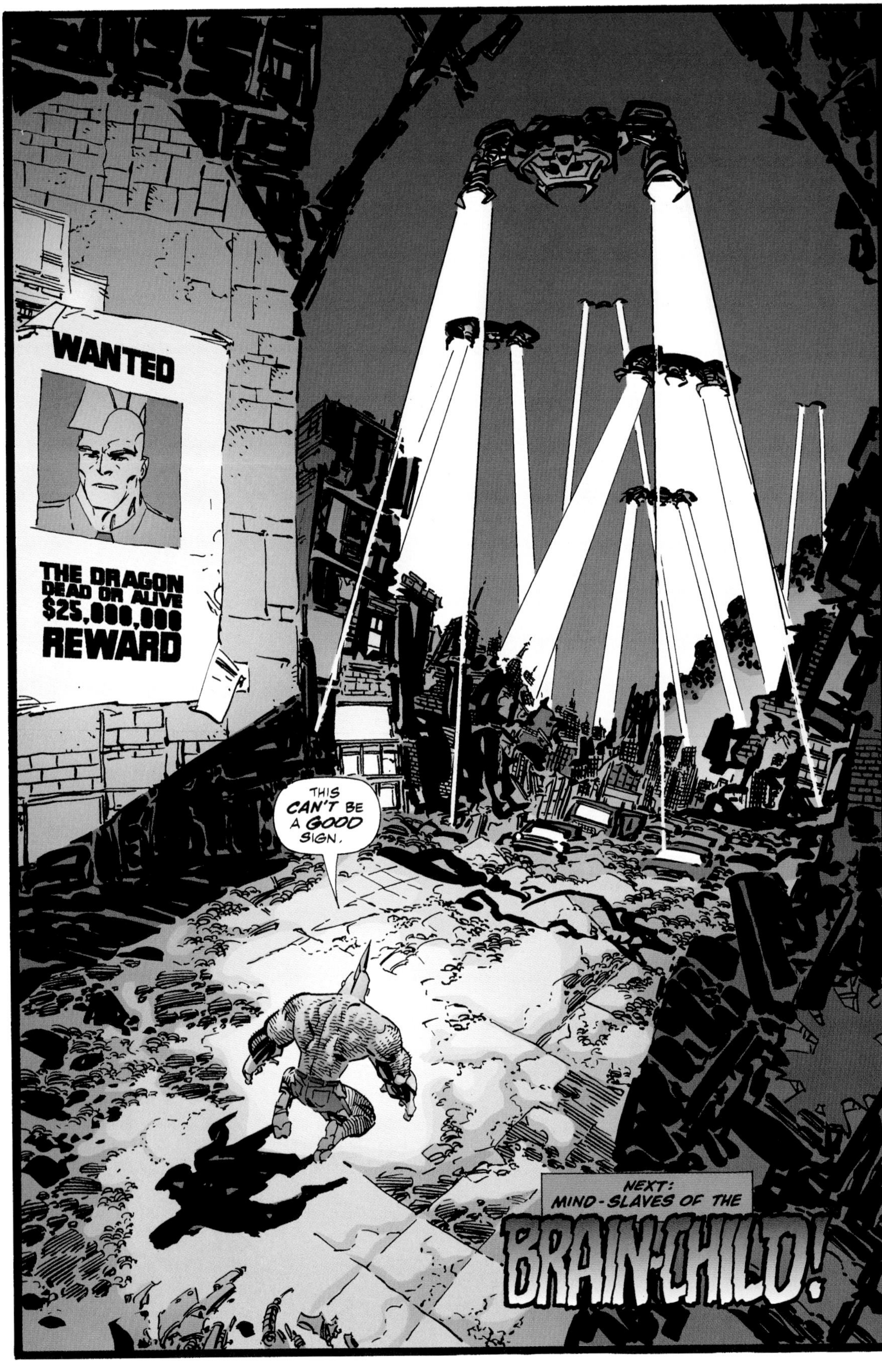
WANTED
THE DRAGON
DEAD OR ALIVE
$25,000,000
REWARD
THIS CAN'T BE A GOOD SIGN.
NEXT: MIND-SLAVES OF THE
BRAIN-CHILD!

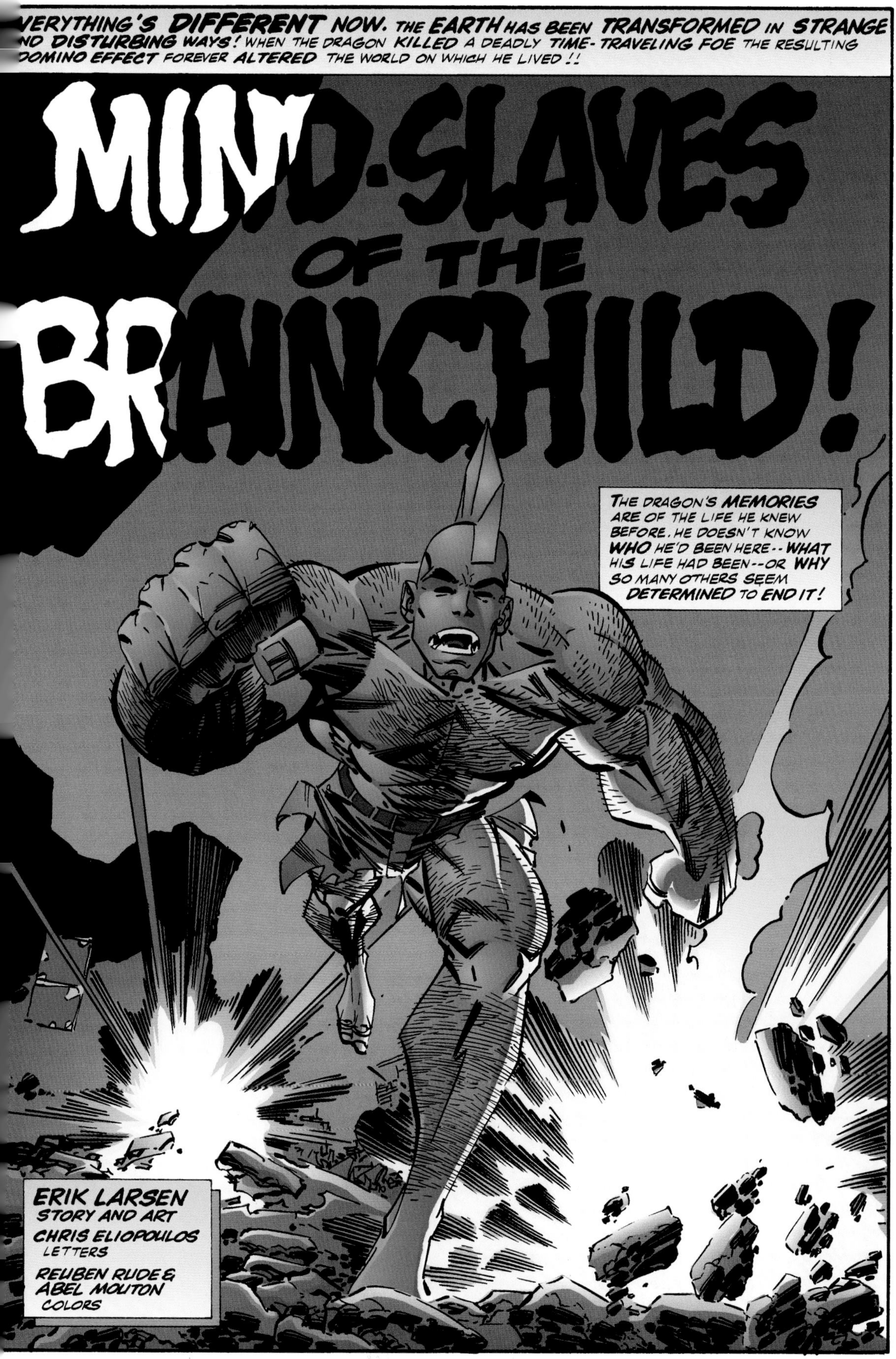
VERYTHING'S DIFFERENT NOW. THE EARTH HAS BEEN TRANSFORMED IN STRANGE
ND DISTURBING WAYS! WHEN THE DRAGON KILLED A DEADLY TIME-TRAVELING FOE THE RESULTING
DOMINO EFFECT FOREVER ALTERED THE WORLD ON WHICH HE LIVED!!
MIND-SLAVES OF THE BRAINCHILD!
THE DRAGON'S MEMORIES ARE OF THE LIFE HE KNEW BEFORE. HE DOESN'T KNOW WHO HE'D BEEN HERE--WHAT HIS LIFE HAD BEEN--OR WHY SO MANY OTHERS SEEM DETERMINED TO END IT!
ERIK LARSEN STORY AND ART
CHRIS ELIOPOULOS LETTERS
REUBEN RUDE & ABEL MOUTON COLORS

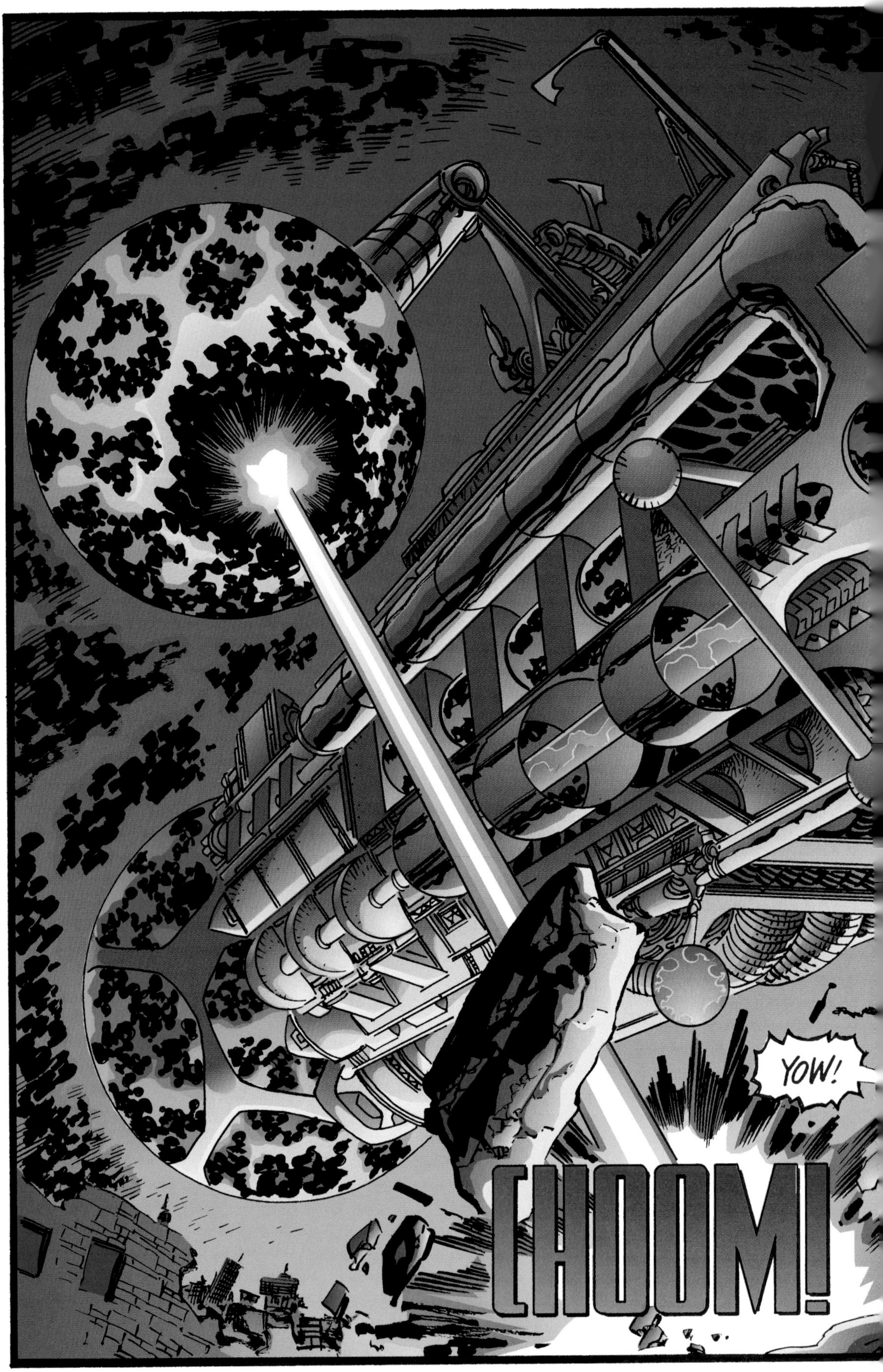
YOW!
CHOOM!

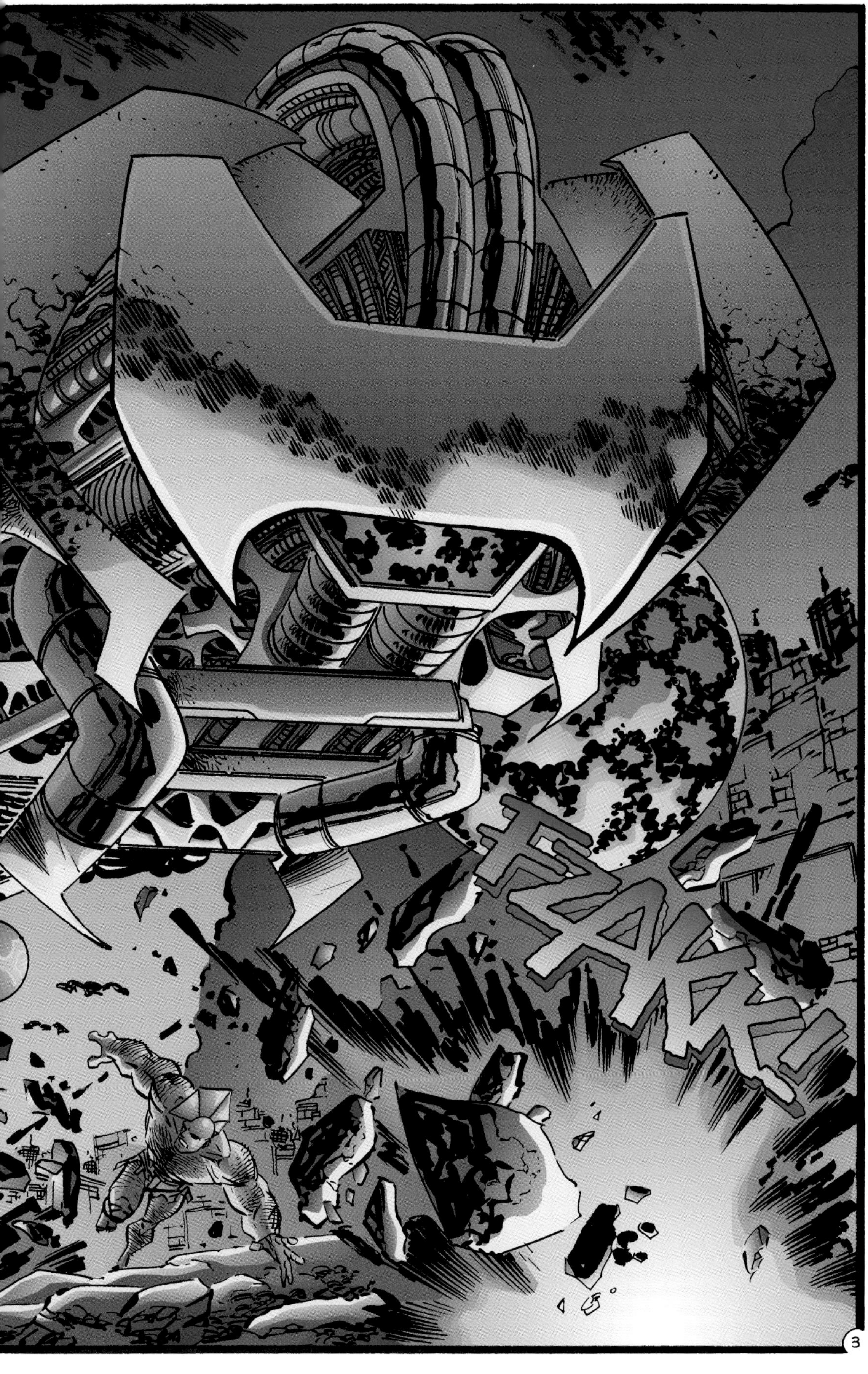

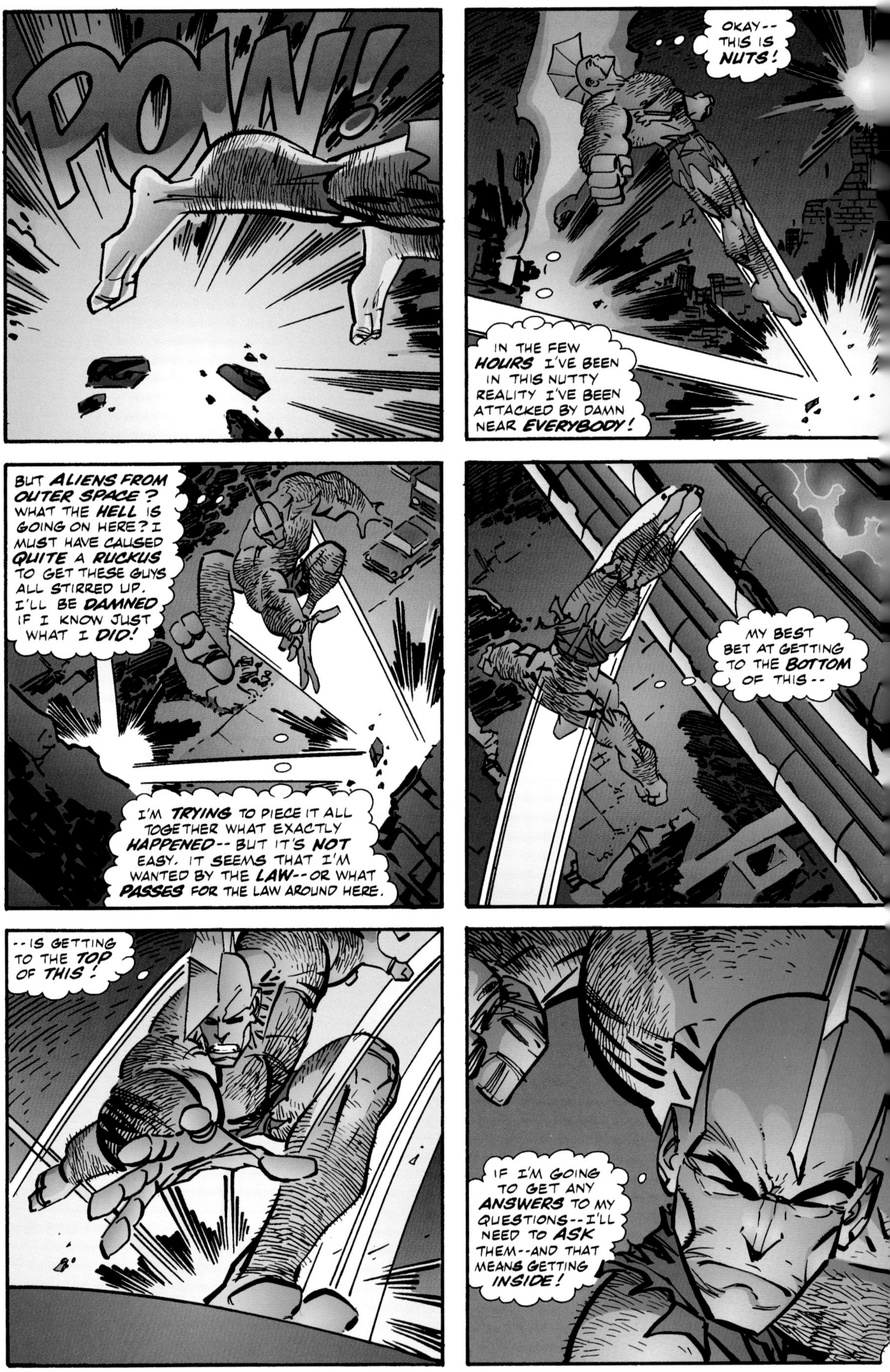
POW!
OKAY-- THIS IS NUTS!
IN THE FEW HOURS I'VE BEEN IN THIS NUTTY REALITY I'VE BEEN ATTACKED BY DAMN NEAR EVERYBODY!
BUT ALIENS FROM OUTER SPACE? WHAT THE HELL IS GOING ON HERE? I MUST HAVE CAUSED QUITE A RUCKUS TO GET THESE GUYS ALL STIRRED UP. I'LL BE DAMNED IF I KNOW JUST WHAT I DID!
I'M TRYING TO PIECE IT ALL TOGETHER WHAT EXACTLY HAPPENED-- BUT IT'S NOT EASY. IT SEEMS THAT I'M WANTED BY THE LAW--OR WHAT PASSES FOR THE LAW AROUND HERE.
MY BEST BET AT GETTING TO THE BOTTOM OF THIS--
--IS GETTING TO THE TOP OF THIS!
IF I'M GOING TO GET ANY ANSWERS TO MY QUESTIONS--I'LL NEED TO ASK THEM--AND THAT MEANS GETTING INSIDE!

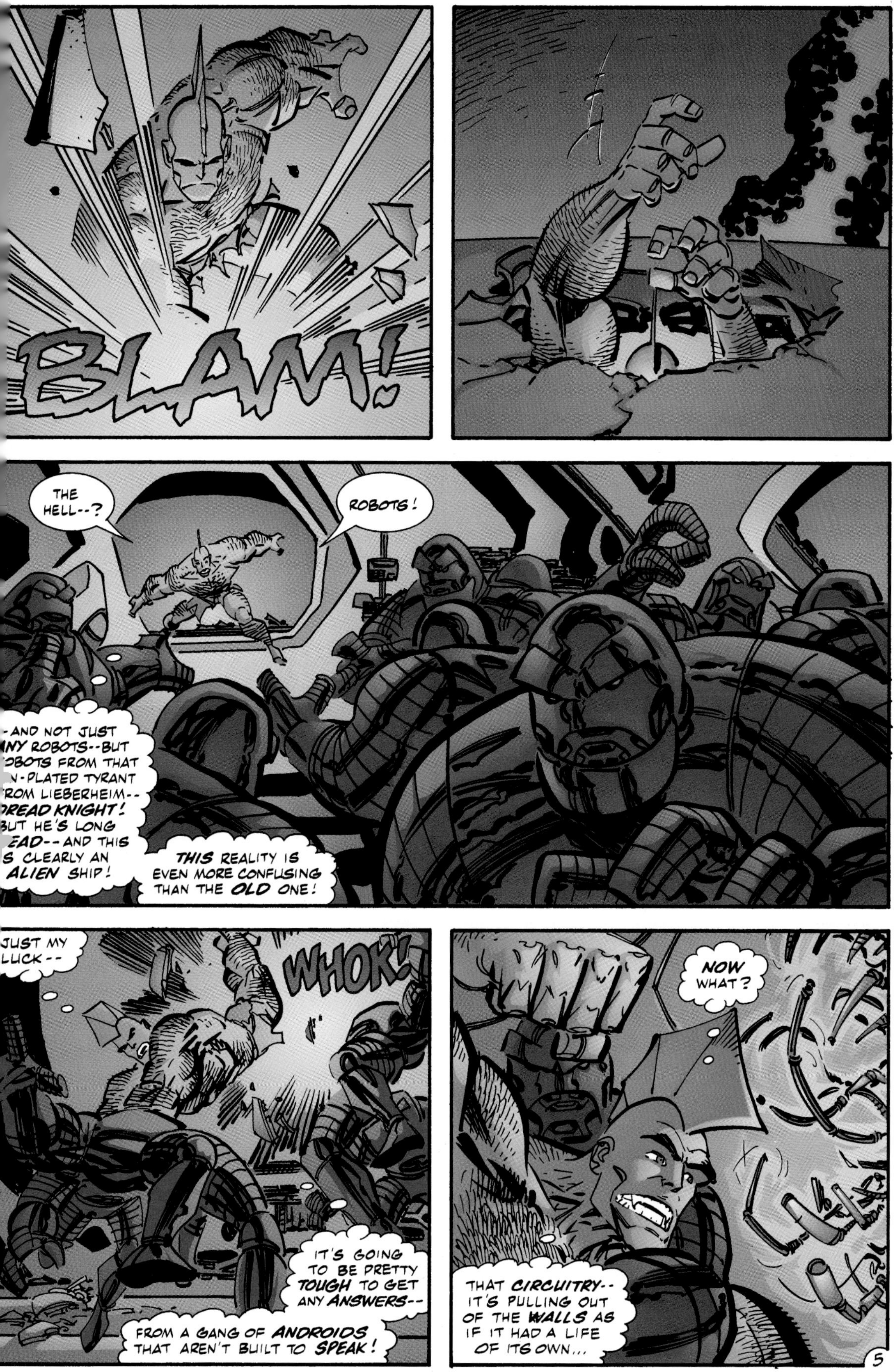
BLAM!
THE HELL--?
ROBOTS!
-AND NOT JUST NY ROBOTS--BUT OBOTS FROM THAT N-PLATED TYRANT ROM LIEBERHEIM-- DREAD KNIGHT! BUT HE'S LONG EAD--AND THIS S CLEARLY AN ALIEN SHIP!
THIS REALITY IS EVEN MORE CONFUSING THAN THE OLD ONE!
JUST MY LUCK--
WHOK!
IT'S GOING TO BE PRETTY TOUGH TO GET ANY ANSWERS--
FROM A GANG OF ANDROIDS THAT AREN'T BUILT TO SPEAK!
NOW WHAT?
THAT CIRCUITRY--IT'S PULLING OUT OF THE WALLS AS IF IT HAD A LIFE OF ITS OWN...

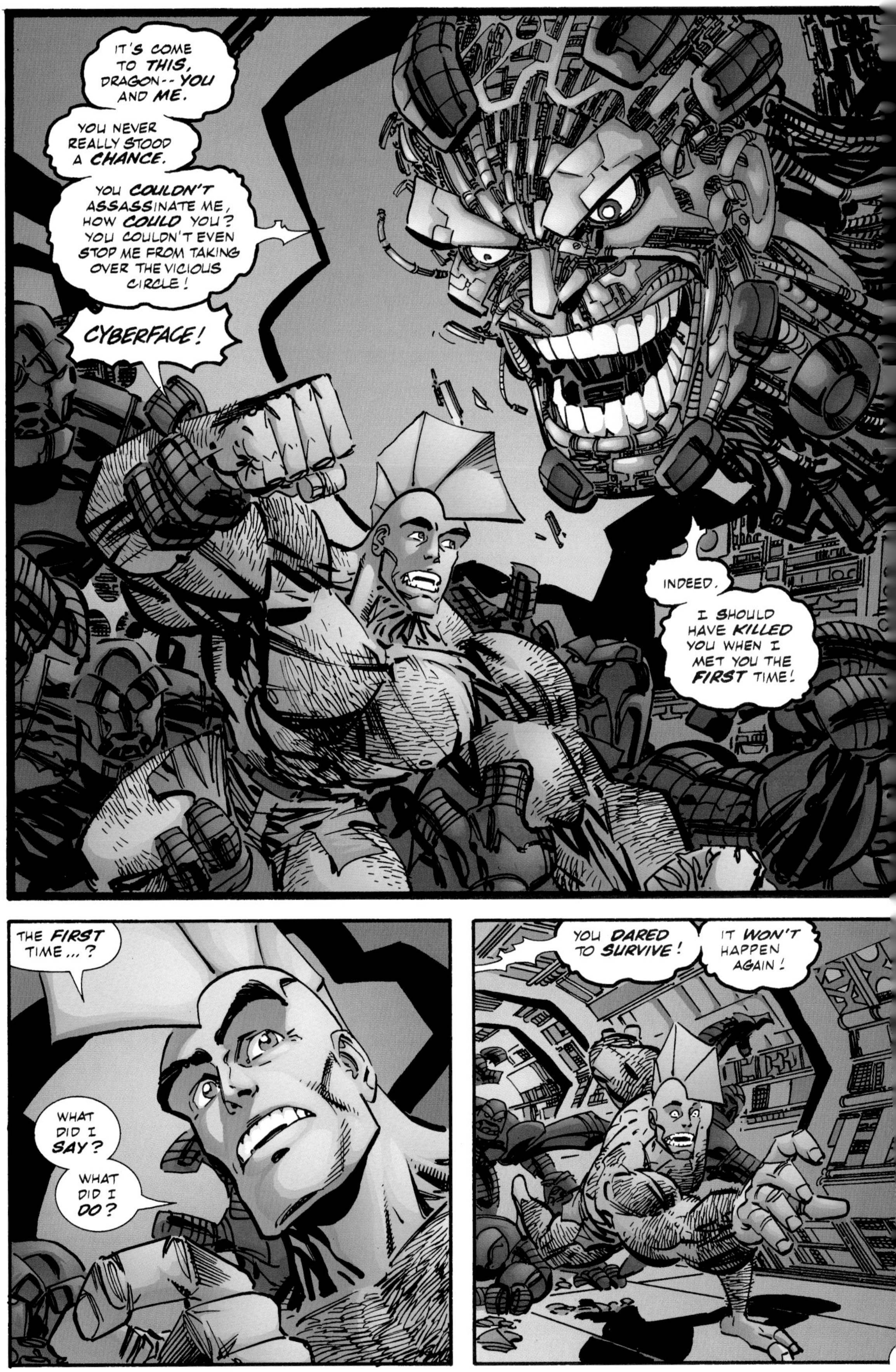
IT'S COME TO THIS, DRAGON-- YOU AND ME.
YOU NEVER REALLY STOOD A CHANCE.
YOU COULDN'T ASSASSINATE ME, HOW COULD YOU? YOU COULDN'T EVEN STOP ME FROM TAKING OVER THE VICIOUS CIRCLE!
CYBERFACE!
INDEED.
I SHOULD HAVE KILLED YOU WHEN I MET YOU THE FIRST TIME!
THE FIRST TIME...?
WHAT DID I SAY?
WHAT DID I DO?
YOU DARED TO SURVIVE!
IT WON'T HAPPEN AGAIN!

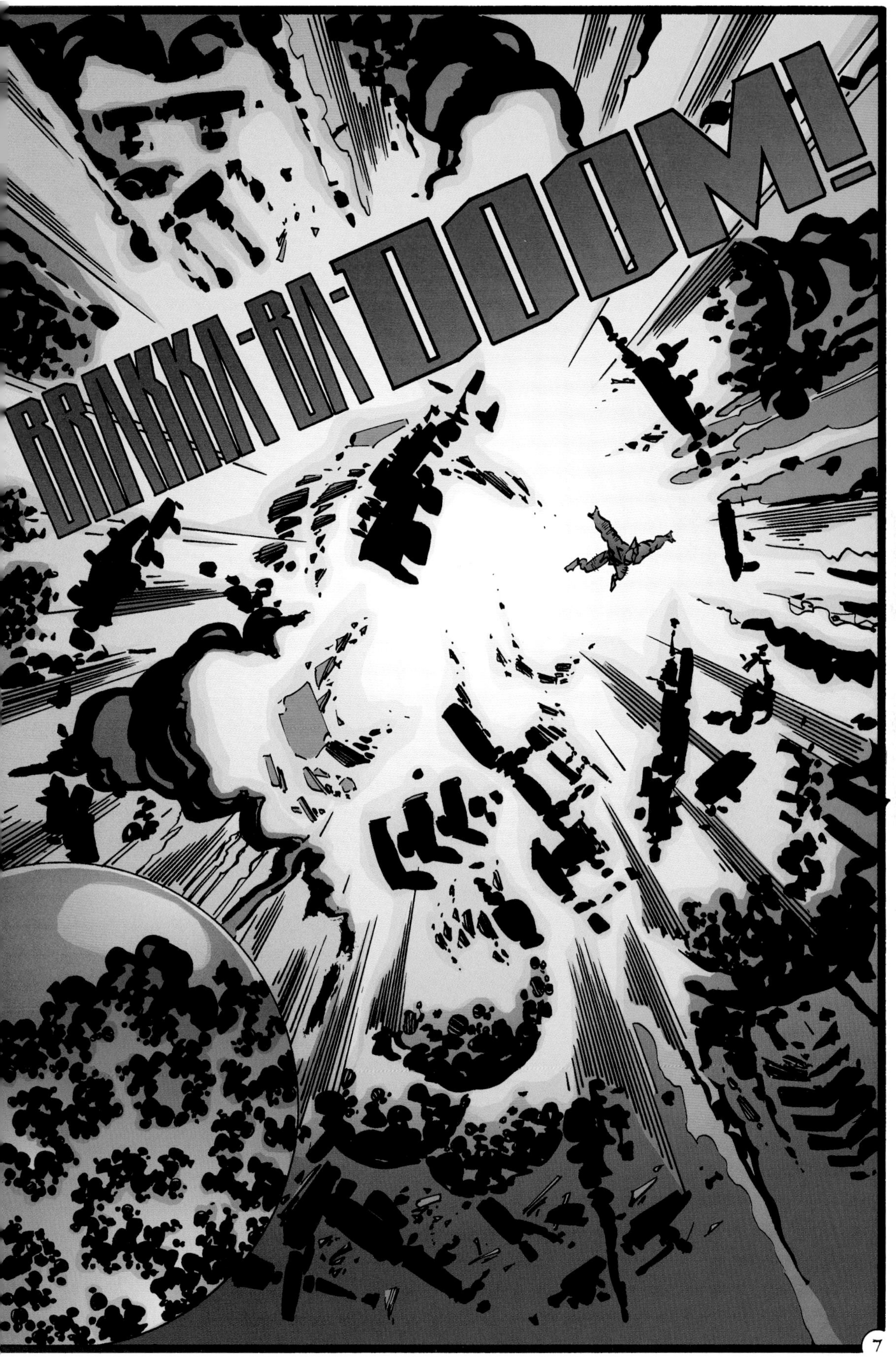
BRAKKA-BA-DOOM!

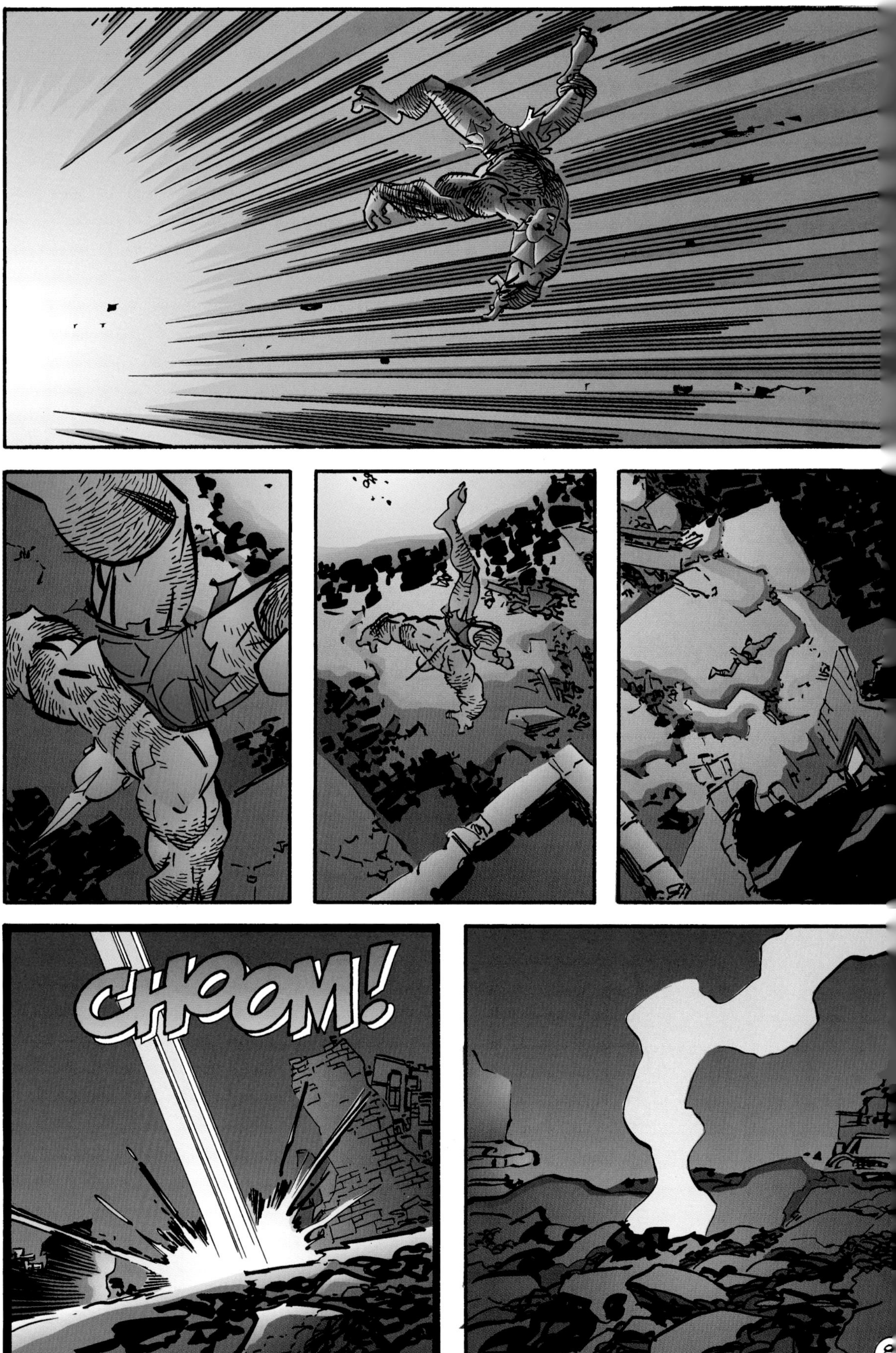
CHOOM!

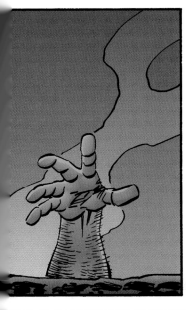

OUCH.

OKAY-- SO FAR, SO GOOD--

I'M ALIVE--

--AND THEY DON'T SEE ME.

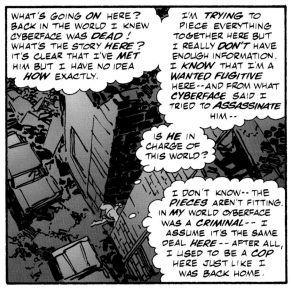

WHAT'S GOING ON HERE? BACK IN THE WORLD I KNEW CYBERFACE WAS DEAD! WHAT'S THE STORY HERE? IT'S CLEAR THAT I'VE MET HIM BUT I HAVE NO IDEA HOW EXACTLY.

I'M TRYING TO PIECE EVERYTHING TOGETHER HERE BUT I REALLY DON'T HAVE ENOUGH INFORMATION. I KNOW THAT I'M A WANTED FUGITIVE HERE--AND FROM WHAT CYBERFACE SAID I TRIED TO ASSASSINATE HIM --

IS HE IN CHARGE OF THIS WORLD?

I DON'T KNOW-- THE PIECES AREN'T FITTING. IN MY WORLD CYBERFACE WAS A CRIMINAL-- I ASSUME IT'S THE SAME DEAL HERE -- AFTER ALL, I USED TO BE A COP HERE JUST LIKE I WAS BACK HOME.

DAMN.

SO NOW WHAT?

I HAVE NO FRIENDS, NO FAMILY, NO HOME AND GUYS ARE TRYING TO KILL ME LEFT AND RIGHT! I TRIED FINDING MY OLD HOUSE BUT IT'S A SMOKING CRATER--EVERYTHING ELSE ISN'T IN MUCH BETTER SHAPE--

IT'S GETTING LATE. I'M GETTING TIRED --HUNGRY.

IF THE BAD GUYS ARE IN CHARGE I'M NOT ABOUT TO TURN MYSELF IN-- BUT WHAT DO I DO NOW? STEAL CLOTHES? STEAL FOOD? HAS MY LIFE COME TO THAT?

9

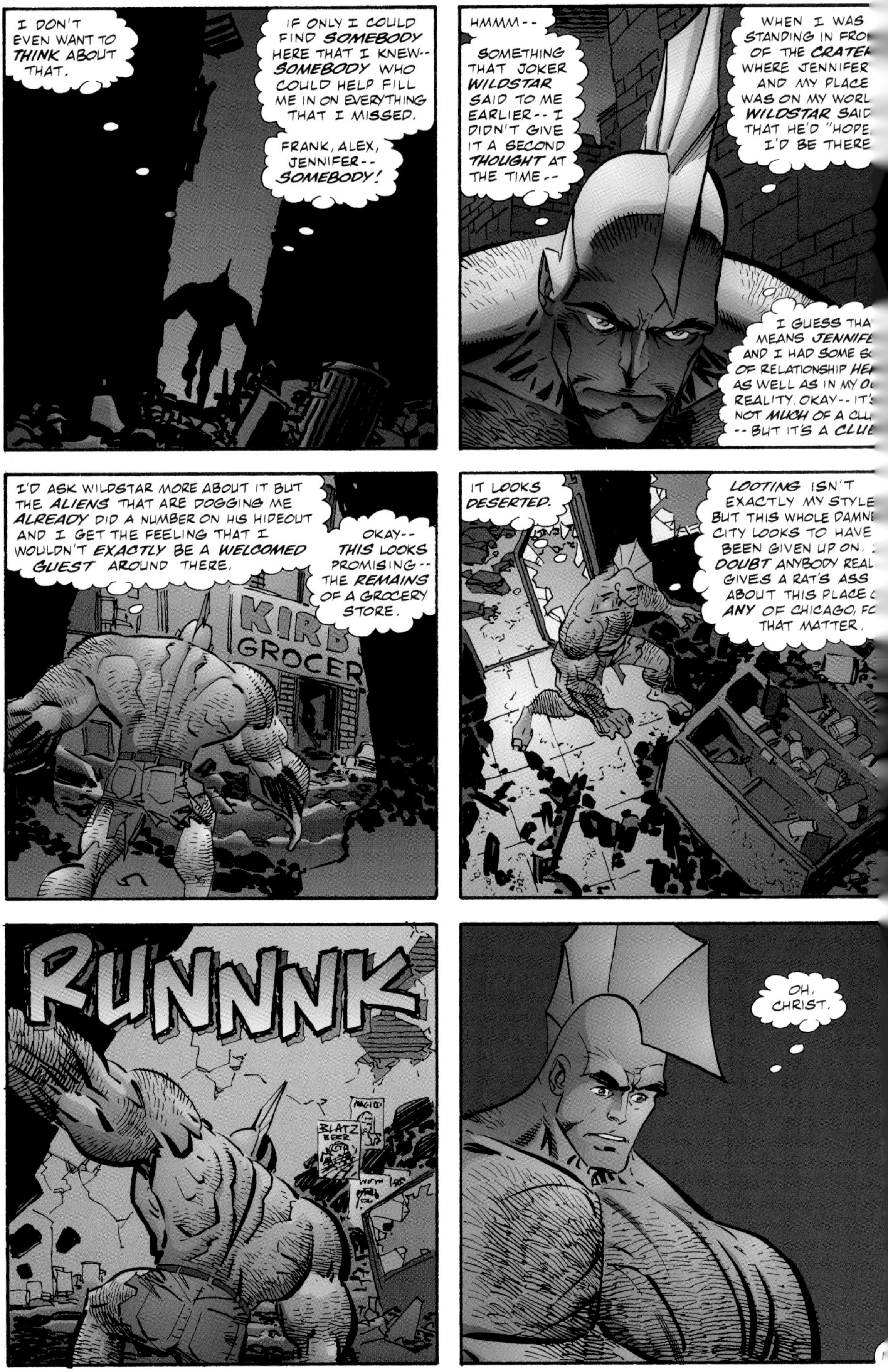
I DON'T EVEN WANT TO THINK ABOUT THAT.
IF ONLY I COULD FIND SOMEBODY HERE THAT I KNEW-- SOMEBODY WHO COULD HELP FILL ME IN ON EVERYTHING THAT I MISSED.
FRANK, ALEX, JENNIFER-- SOMEBODY!
HMMM--
SOMETHING THAT JOKER WILDSTAR SAID TO ME EARLIER-- I DIDN'T GIVE IT A SECOND THOUGHT AT THE TIME--
WHEN I WAS STANDING IN FRO OF THE CRATE WHERE JENNIFER AND MY PLACE WAS ON MY WORL WILDSTAR SAI THAT HE'D "HOPE I'D BE THERE
I GUESS THA MEANS JENNIF AND I HAD SOME S OF RELATIONSHIP HE AS WELL AS IN MY O REALITY. OKAY-- IT' NOT MUCH OF A CL -- BUT IT'S A CLU
I'D ASK WILDSTAR MORE ABOUT IT BUT THE ALIENS THAT ARE DOGGING ME ALREADY DID A NUMBER ON HIS HIDEOUT AND I GET THE FEELING THAT I WOULDN'T EXACTLY BE A WELCOMED GUEST AROUND THERE.
OKAY-- THIS LOOKS PROMISING-- THE REMAINS OF A GROCERY STORE.
KIRB GROCER
IT LOOKS DESERTED.
LOOTING ISN'T EXACTLY MY STYLE BUT THIS WHOLE DAMN CITY LOOKS TO HAVE BEEN GIVEN UP ON. DOUBT ANYBODY REAL GIVES A RAT'S ASS ABOUT THIS PLACE ANY OF CHICAGO, F THAT MATTER.
RUNNNK
BLATZ BEER
OH, CHRIST.

A ...ODY.

FROM THE LOOK OF IT-- I'D SAY HE'S BEEN HERE A WHILE.

THOSE SHOES ARE STILL IN PRETTY DECENT SHAPE.

MAN-- THAT'S JUST WRONG.

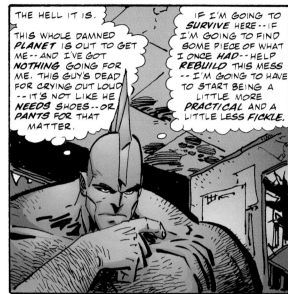

THE HELL IT IS.

THIS WHOLE DAMNED PLANET IS OUT TO GET ME-- AND I'VE GOT NOTHING GOING FOR ME. THIS GUY'S DEAD FOR CRYING OUT LOUD -- IT'S NOT LIKE HE NEEDS SHOES--OR PANTS FOR THAT MATTER.

IF I'M GOING TO SURVIVE HERE--IF I'M GOING TO FIND SOME PIECE OF WHAT I ONCE HAD--HELP REBUILD THIS MESS -- I'M GOING TO HAVE TO START BEING A LITTLE MORE PRACTICAL AND A LITTLE LESS FICKLE.

NOT A ...BAD FIT.

AND IT SURE BEATS THAT PAIR OF DAISY DUKE'S THAT I'VE BEEN WEARING.

LET'S SEE WHO-- TERRY FITZGERALD. NEVER HEARD OF HIM.

I DUNNO IF PAPER MONEY IS STILL ALL THE RAGE HERE BUT HAVING A COUPLE BUCKS IN MY POCKET COULDN'T BE A BAD THING.

FROM THE LOOKS OF IT-- ALL THE FOOD HAS BEEN CARTED OFF-- THE ONLY REASON THIS GUY'S STILL AROUND IS BECAUSE THAT SHELF WEIGHED HALF A TON AND BECAUSE NOBODY KNEW HE WAS HERE.

NO SENSE IN ME HIDING OUT HERE-- THE PLACE IS PRETTY RIPE AND THERE'S NO PRIVACY.

NOT THAT I'M ALL THAT MODEST, BUT IT'D SURE BE NICE TO GET SOME SHELTER AWAY FROM THE SPYING EYES OF THOSE DAMNED ALIEN SPACESHIPS.

I'M BEAT.

HELL.

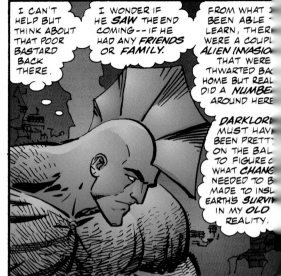

I CAN'T HELP BUT THINK ABOUT THAT POOR BASTARD BACK THERE.

I WONDER IF HE *SAW* THE END COMING--IF HE HAD ANY *FRIENDS* OR *FAMILY.*

FROM WHAT I BEEN ABLE LEARN, THER WERE A COUPL *ALIEN INVASIO* THAT WERE THWARTED BAC HOME BUT REAL DID A *NUMBE* AROUND HERE

DARKLORD MUST HAV BEEN PRETTY ON THE BAL TO FIGURE C WHAT *CHANG* NEEDED TO B MADE TO INSU EARTH'S *SURVI* IN MY *OLD* REALITY.

ONCE I TOOK THAT *MURDERING CREEP* OUT OF THE PICTURE ALL *REALITY* SHIFTED TO WHAT I'VE GOT *HERE.*

I SURE HOPE *SOME* GOOD CAME OUT OF ALL THIS, DARKLORD KILLED A *LOT* OF *GOOD PEOPLE*-- I HOPE *SOME* OF THEM SURVIVED IN THIS SCREWED UP PLACE.

DAMN.

IT'S GETTING *LATE.*

HMMM-- THAT BASEMENT APARTMENT MIGHT *JUST* BE THE TICKET.

LOOKS *RELATIVELY* CLEAN AND I'D WAGER THAT IF SOMEBODY WAS *CURRENTLY* CRASHING HERE THAT THEY'D BE LYING ON THAT WORN OUT MATTRESS BY NOW *SAWING WOOD.*

FACE IT, TIGER -- YOU JUST HIT THE *JACKPOT.*

OKAY -- COAST IS AS *CLEAR* AS IT'S LIKELY TO GET.

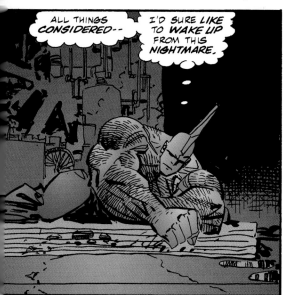

ALL THINGS CONSIDERED-- I'D SURE LIKE TO WAKE UP FROM THIS NIGHTMARE.

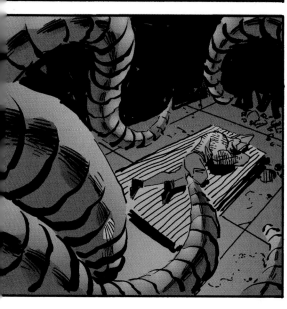

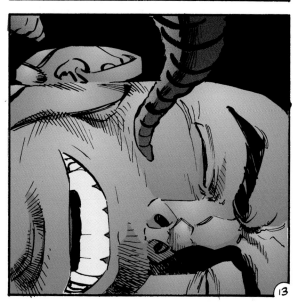

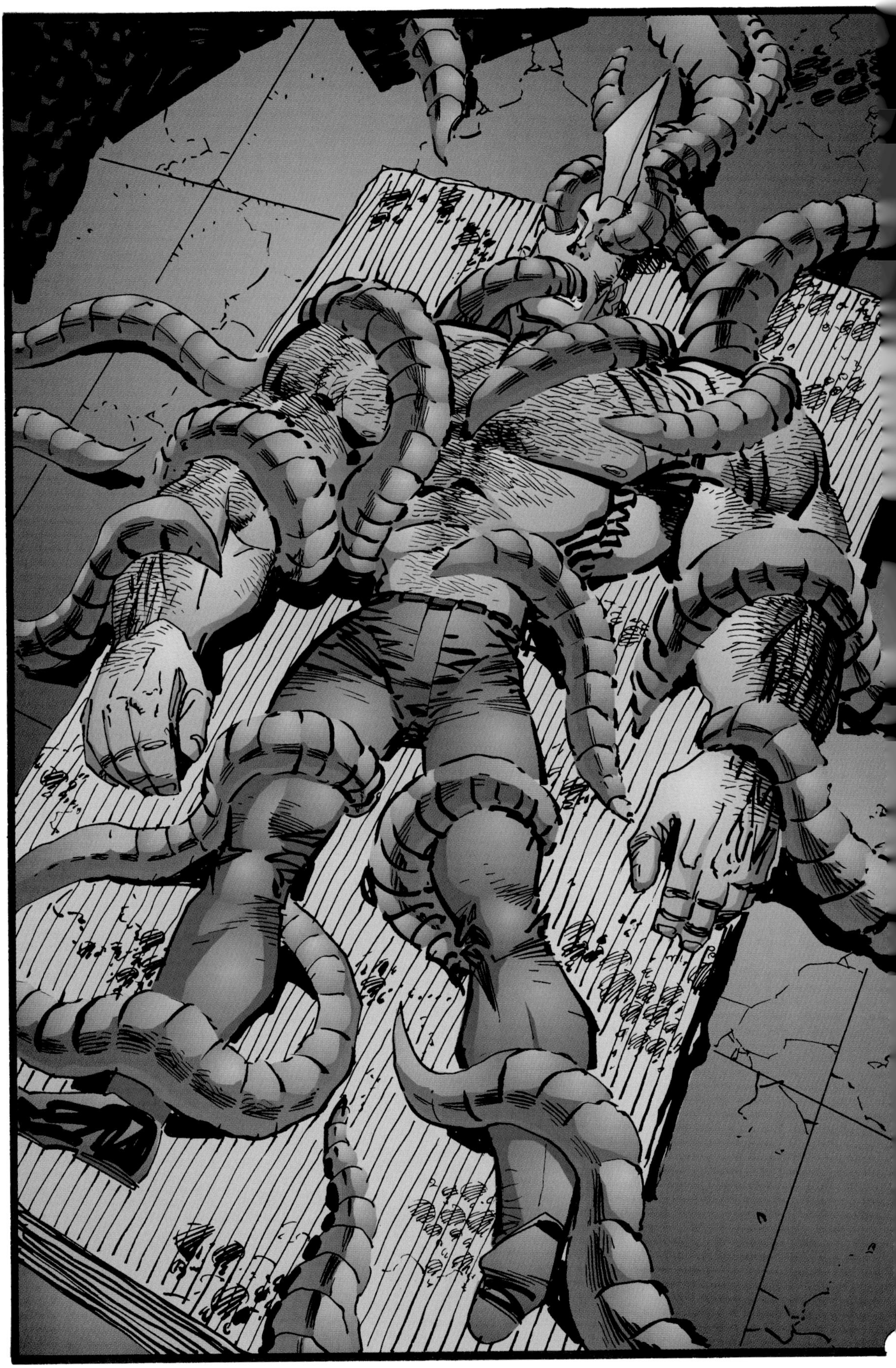

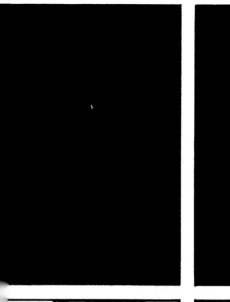

HELLO...?

WHERE IN THE WORLD **AM I** ?

GOD.

JENNIFER,

DRAGON...?

DRAGON-- IS THAT **YOU** ?

YOU'RE **ALIVE**.

I WAS SO **WORRIED**-- I THOUGHT THAT YOU...

I THOUGHT...

15

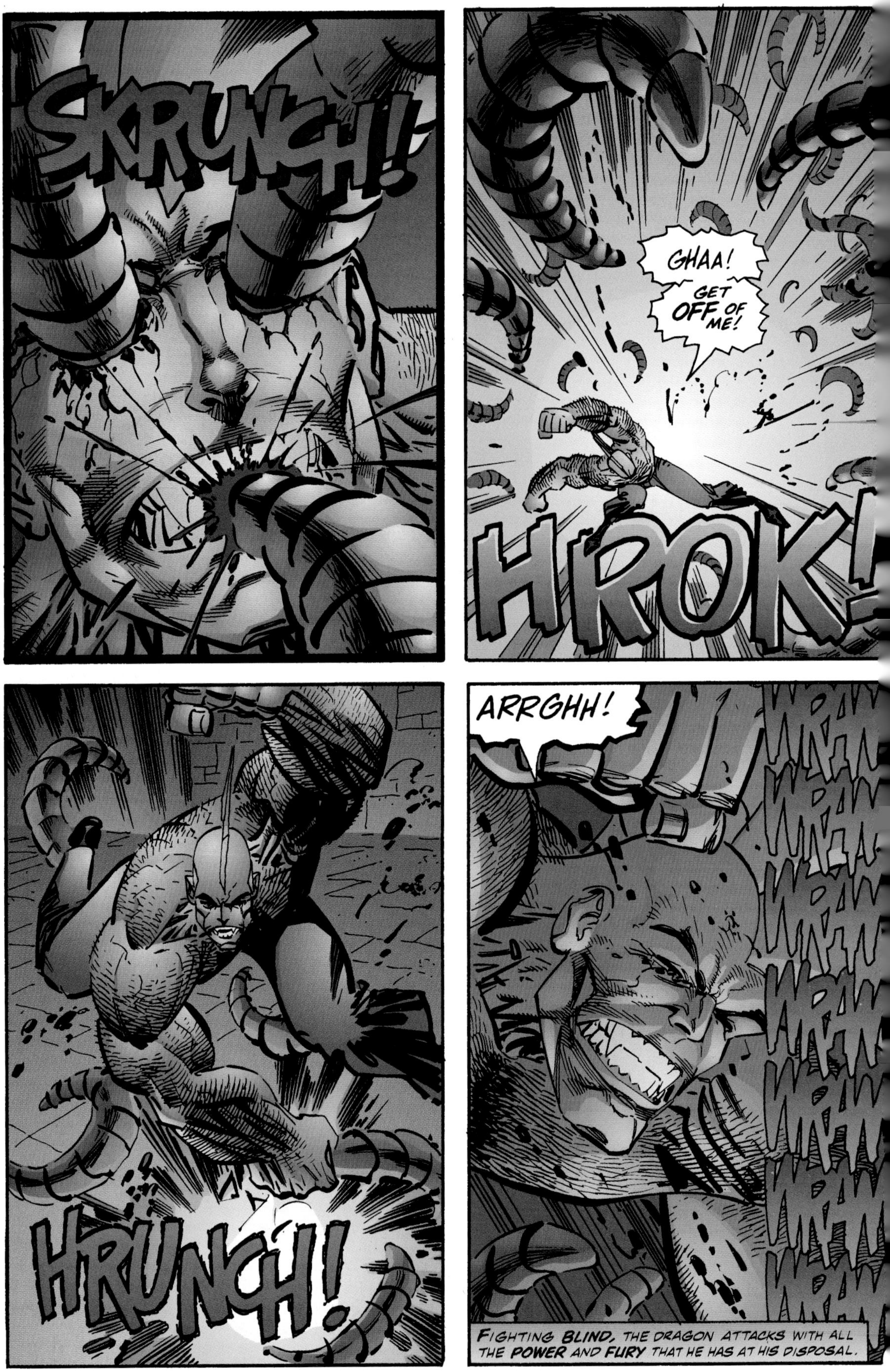
SKRUNCH!
GHAA!
GET OFF OF ME!
HROK!
HRUNCH!
ARRGHH!
WRAW WRAW WRAW WRAW WRAW WRAW WRAW WRAW WRAW
FIGHTING BLIND, THE DRAGON ATTACKS WITH ALL THE POWER AND FURY THAT HE HAS AT HIS DISPOSAL.

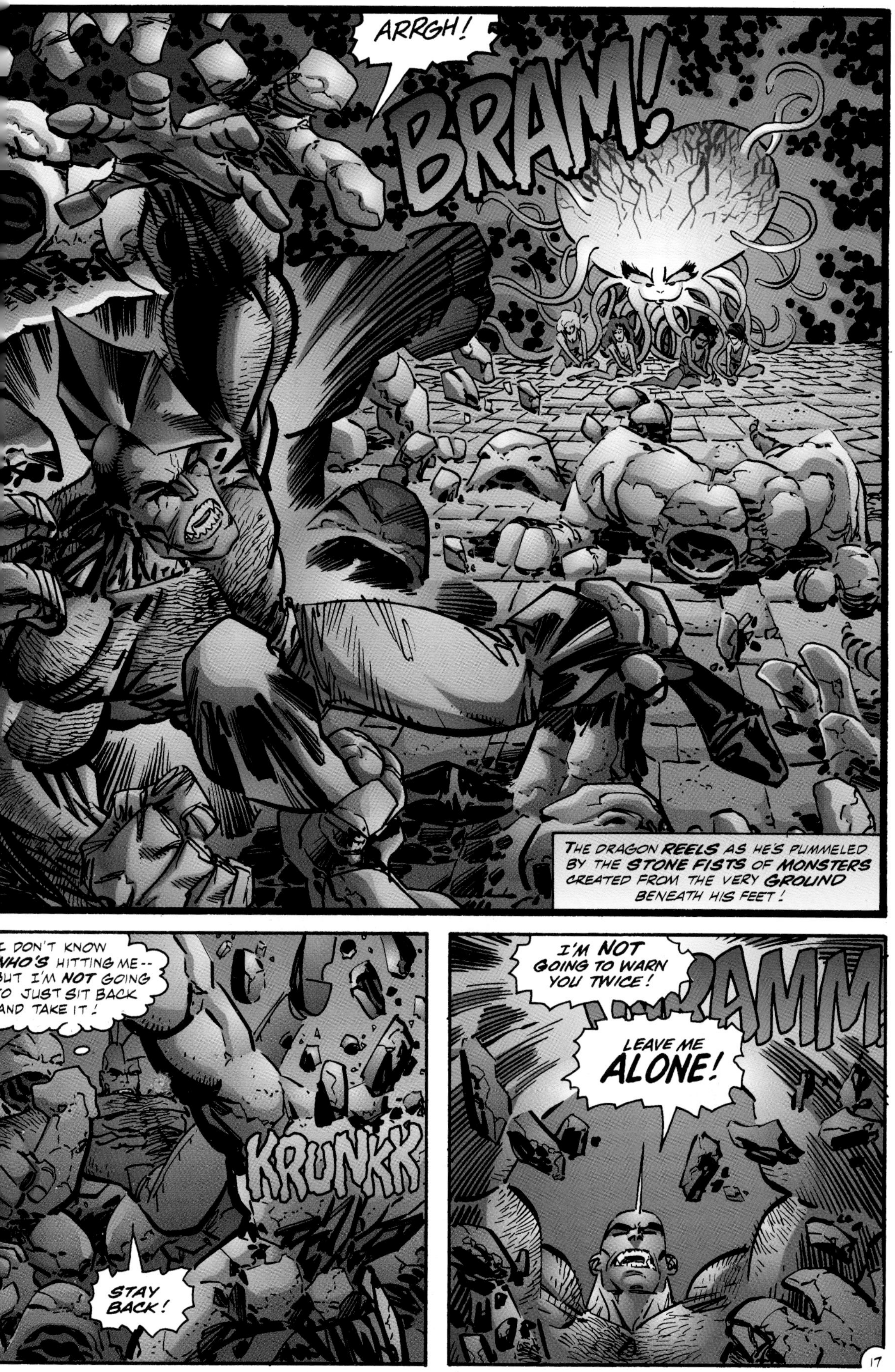
ARRGH!
BRAM!
THE DRAGON REELS AS HE'S PUMMELED BY THE STONE FISTS OF MONSTERS CREATED FROM THE VERY GROUND BENEATH HIS FEET!
I DON'T KNOW WHO'S HITTING ME-- BUT I'M NOT GOING TO JUST SIT BACK AND TAKE IT!
KRUNKK
STAY BACK!
I'M NOT GOING TO WARN YOU TWICE!
AMM
LEAVE ME ALONE!

BUT THE DRAGON'S WORDS FALL ON DEAF EARS.

THE STONE CREATURES CONTINUE TO ASSAULT THEIR QUARRY.

THEY OVERWHELM HIM, THEIR NUMBERS INCREASING WITH EACH PASSING MOMENT. AN ARMY OF BEHEMOTH INTENT ON CRUSHING THEIR GREEN-SKINNED ADVERSAR TO THE GROUND!

ENOUGH!

FWOOM!

THE MUTATED INFANT STARES IN WILD WONDER AS HIS MIND-SLAVES ARE DESTROYED IN A MATTER OF SECONDS.

SPAK!

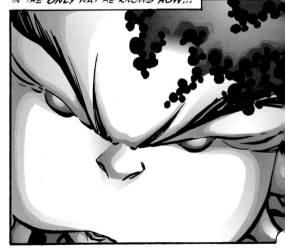

THE BRAIN-CHILD IS NOT USED TO DEFEAT. FRUSTRATIC IS A NEW FEELING FOR THE YOUTH. HATRED GROWS AND HE PREPARES TO DEAL WITH THE SOURCE OF HIS ANGE IN THE ONLY WAY HE KNOWS HOW...

'HOA!

MY *EYES* HAVE *HEALED* THEMSELVES-- AND *JUST* IN TIME.

NOW IF I CAN MANAGE TO STAY OUT OF THIS BIG *GORILLA'S WAY* I *JUST* MIGHT STAY IN *BUSINESS!*

HEAD'S UP, SPARKY--!

THOOM!

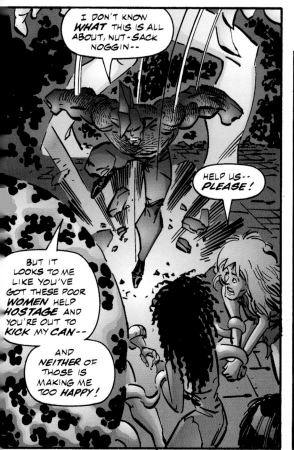

I DON'T KNOW *WHAT* THIS IS ALL ABOUT, NUT-SACK NOGGIN--

HELP US-- *PLEASE!*

BUT IT LOOKS TO ME LIKE YOU'VE GOT THESE POOR *WOMEN* HELP *HOSTAGE* AND YOU'RE OUT TO *KICK MY CAN--*

AND *NEITHER* OF THOSE IS MAKING ME TOO *HAPPY!*

THE *BRAIN-CHILD* SPEAKS NOT A WORD. SUDDENLY HIS *CAPTIVES* ATTACK THE *DRAGON!* WITH A *MENTAL PUSH* HE TURNS THEM AGAINST HIM AND THEY *STRIKE* WITH A *FEROCITY* THAT *BELIES* THEIR *STATURE!*

STOP HIM!

YOU *MUST FREE US!*

NO *SWEAT,* SWEETHEART!

ONCE I *PASTE* THIS *PRECOCIOUS PRESCHOOLER* IN THE *PUSS* YOU'LL BE FREE AS A BIRD.

19

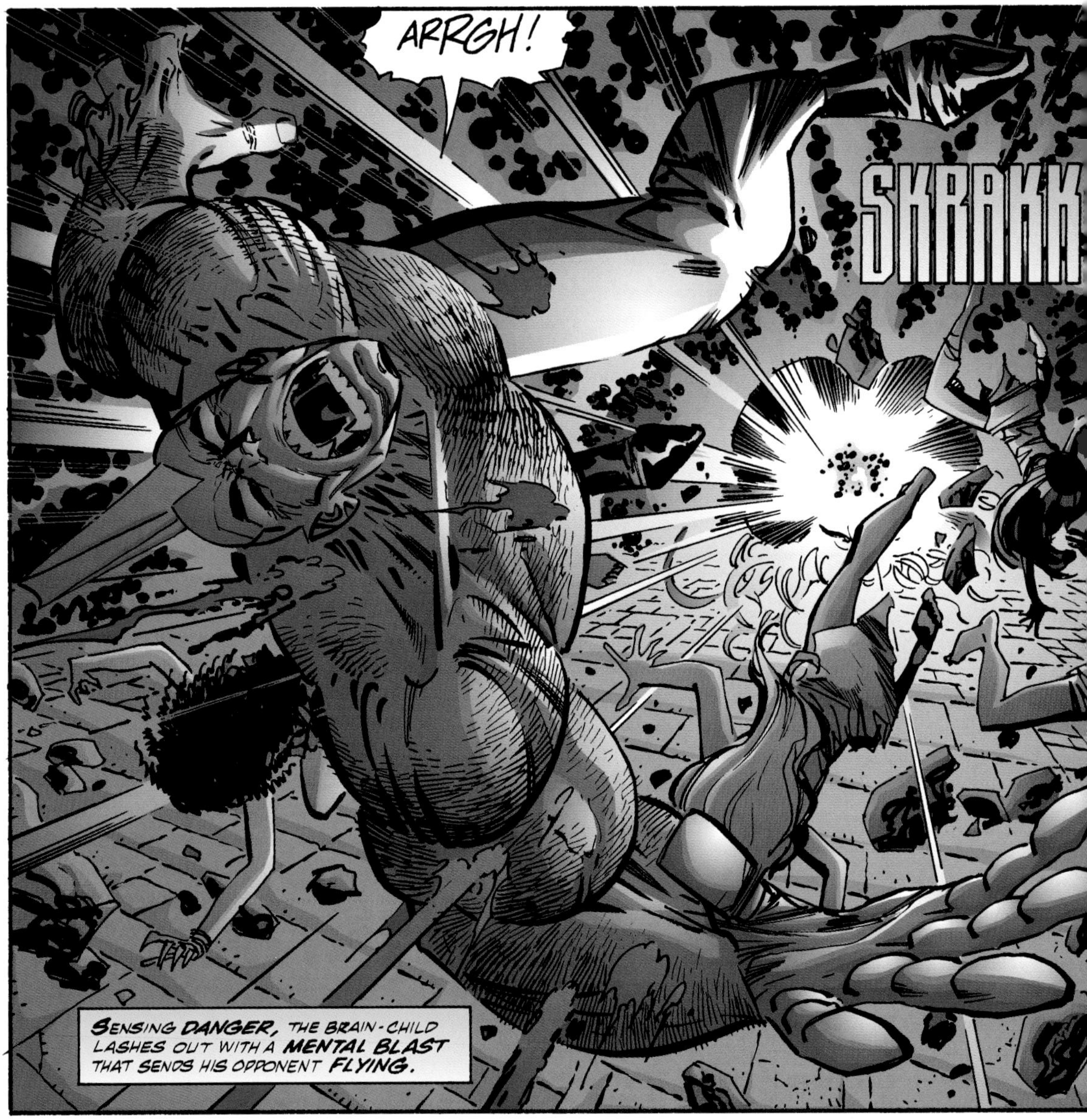

ARRGH!
SKRAKK
SENSING DANGER, THE BRAIN-CHILD LASHES OUT WITH A MENTAL BLAST THAT SENDS HIS OPPONENT FLYING.

THE BRAIN-CHILD IS AWARE OF HIS ADVERSARY'S POWER! IN AN EFFORT TO STOP HIS FOE HE UNLEASHES WAVE AFTER WAVE OF ENERGY THAT WOULD TURN AN ORDINARY MAN TO POWDER!

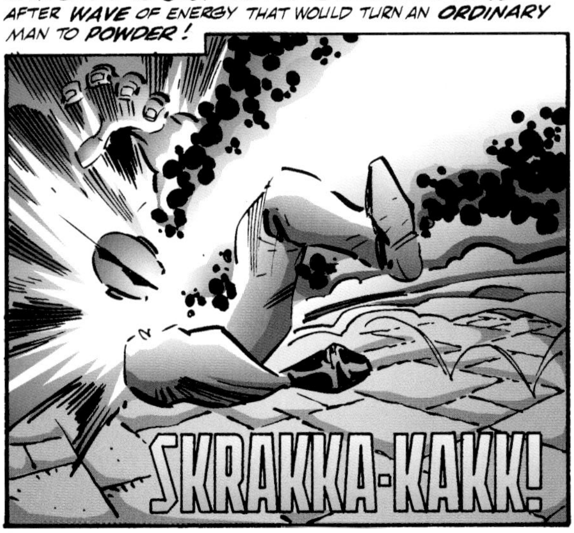

SKRAKKA-KAKK!

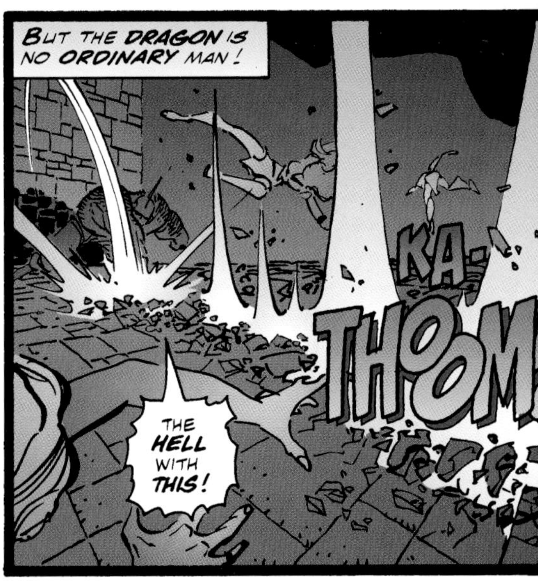

BUT THE DRAGON IS NO ORDINARY MAN!
KA-THOOM!
THE HELL WITH THIS!

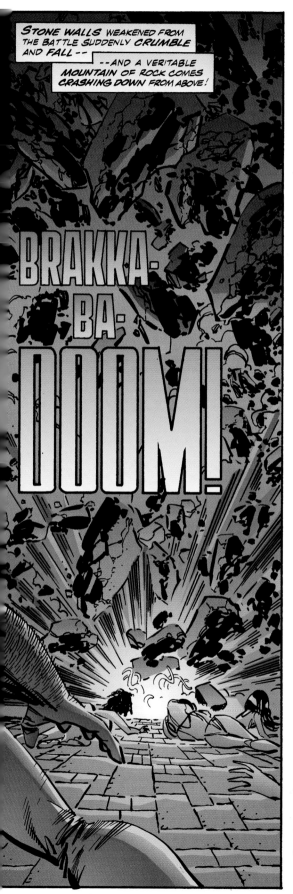

STONE WALLS WEAKENED FROM THE BATTLE SUDDENLY *CRUMBLE* AND *FALL*--

--AND A VERITABLE *MOUNTAIN* OF ROCK COMES *CRASHING* DOWN FROM ABOVE!

BRAKKA-
BA-
DOOM!

HANG IN THERE, SISTER --HELP IS ON ITS WAY!

THOOM!

AAA!!

THE WHOLE *PLACE* IS COMING *DOWN* AROUND OUR *EARS!*

FOLLOW ME!

OH NO!

NO!

THE BABY!

WHAT ABOUT THE *BABY?!*

THE BRAIN-CHILD IS *PINNED* BENEATH CRUMBLING DEBRIS THAT RAINS DOWN UPON HIM.

AND IN *LESS TIME* THAN IT TAKES TO *SCREAM*--

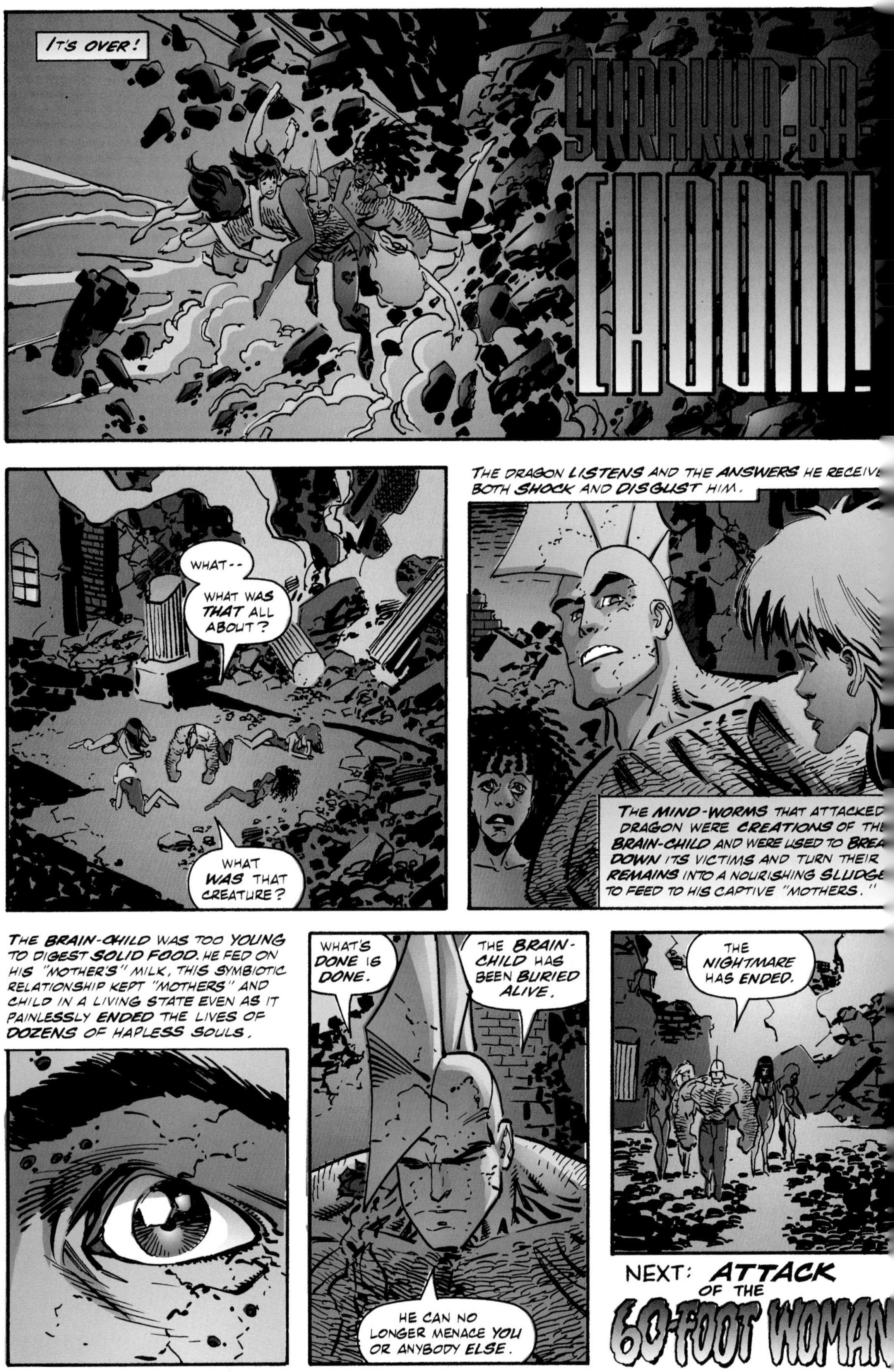
IT'S OVER!
SKRAKKA-BA-CHOOM!
WHAT--
WHAT WAS THAT ALL ABOUT?
WHAT WAS THAT CREATURE?
THE DRAGON LISTENS AND THE ANSWERS HE RECEIVE BOTH SHOCK AND DISGUST HIM.
THE MIND-WORMS THAT ATTACKED DRAGON WERE CREATIONS OF THE BRAIN-CHILD AND WERE USED TO BREA DOWN ITS VICTIMS AND TURN THEIR REMAINS INTO A NOURISHING SLUDGE TO FEED TO HIS CAPTIVE "MOTHERS."
THE BRAIN-CHILD WAS TOO YOUNG TO DIGEST SOLID FOOD. HE FED ON HIS "MOTHER'S" MILK. THIS SYMBIOTIC RELATIONSHIP KEPT "MOTHERS" AND CHILD IN A LIVING STATE EVEN AS IT PAINLESSLY ENDED THE LIVES OF DOZENS OF HAPLESS SOULS.
WHAT'S DONE IS DONE.
THE BRAIN-CHILD HAS BEEN BURIED ALIVE.
HE CAN NO LONGER MENACE YOU OR ANYBODY ELSE.
THE NIGHTMARE HAS ENDED.
NEXT: ATTACK OF THE 60-FOOT WOMAN

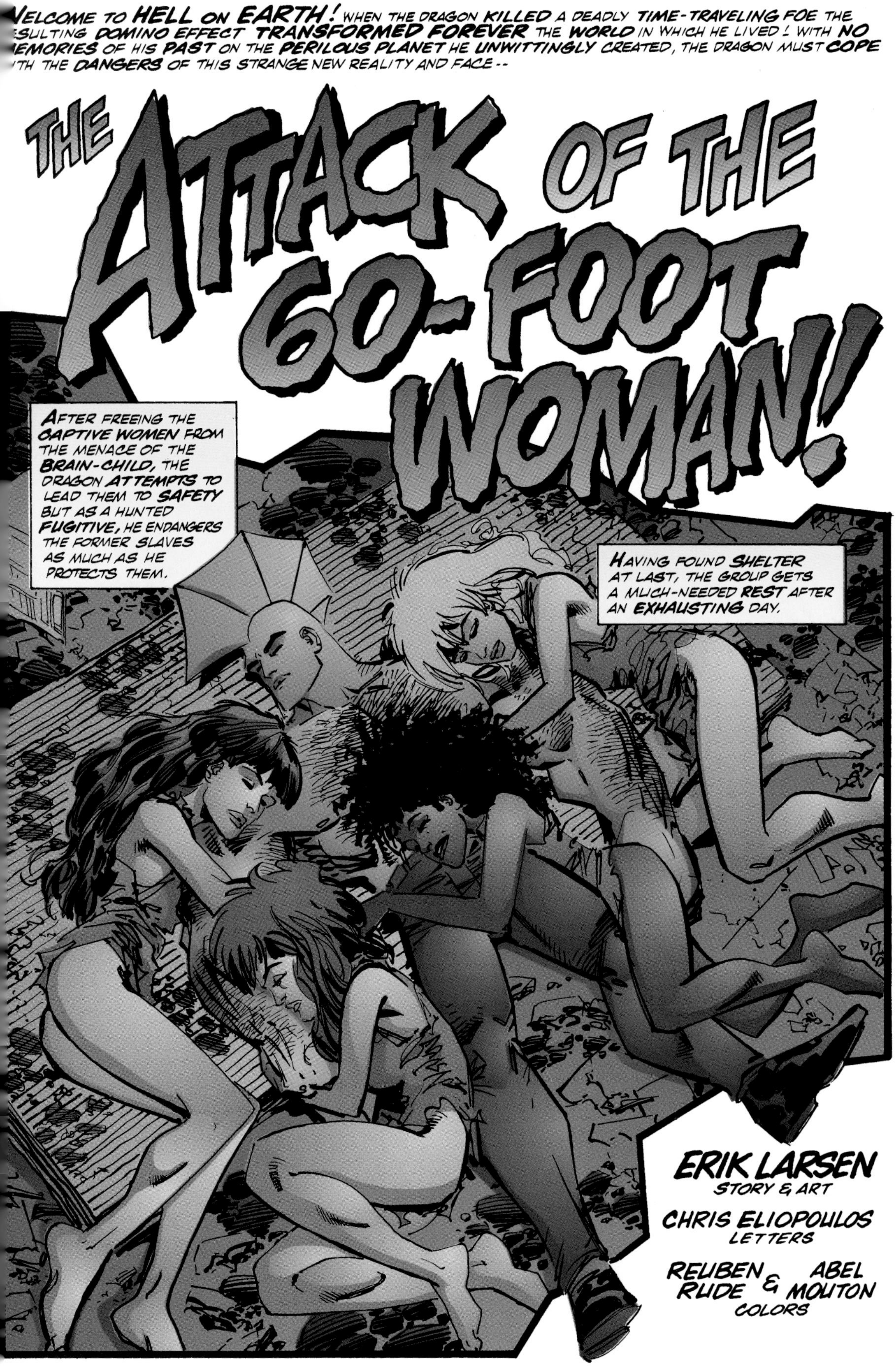
WELCOME TO HELL ON EARTH! WHEN THE DRAGON KILLED A DEADLY TIME-TRAVELING FOE THE ESULTING DOMINO EFFECT TRANSFORMED FOREVER THE WORLD IN WHICH HE LIVED! WITH NO EMORIES OF HIS PAST ON THE PERILOUS PLANET HE UNWITTINGLY CREATED, THE DRAGON MUST COPE ITH THE DANGERS OF THIS STRANGE NEW REALITY AND FACE --
THE ATTACK OF THE 60-FOOT WOMAN!
AFTER FREEING THE CAPTIVE WOMEN FROM THE MENACE OF THE BRAIN-CHILD, THE DRAGON ATTEMPTS TO LEAD THEM TO SAFETY BUT AS A HUNTED FUGITIVE, HE ENDANGERS THE FORMER SLAVES AS MUCH AS HE PROTECTS THEM.
HAVING FOUND SHELTER AT LAST, THE GROUP GETS A MUCH-NEEDED REST AFTER AN EXHAUSTING DAY.
ERIK LARSEN STORY & ART
CHRIS ELIOPOULOS LETTERS
REUBEN RUDE & ABEL MOUTON COLORS

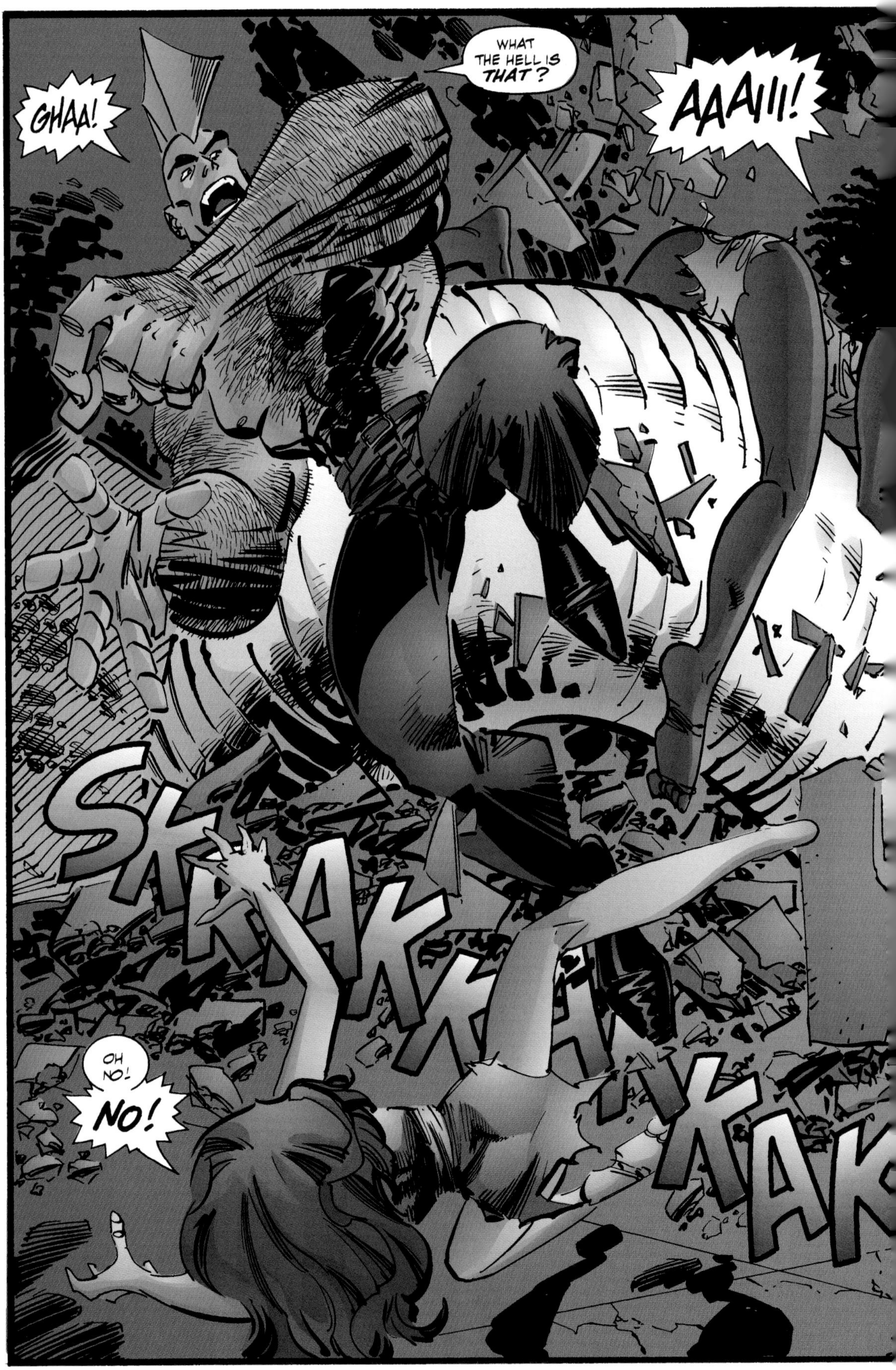
GHAA!
WHAT THE HELL IS THAT?
AAAIII!
SKRAKKAKKAKKAK
OH NO!
NO!

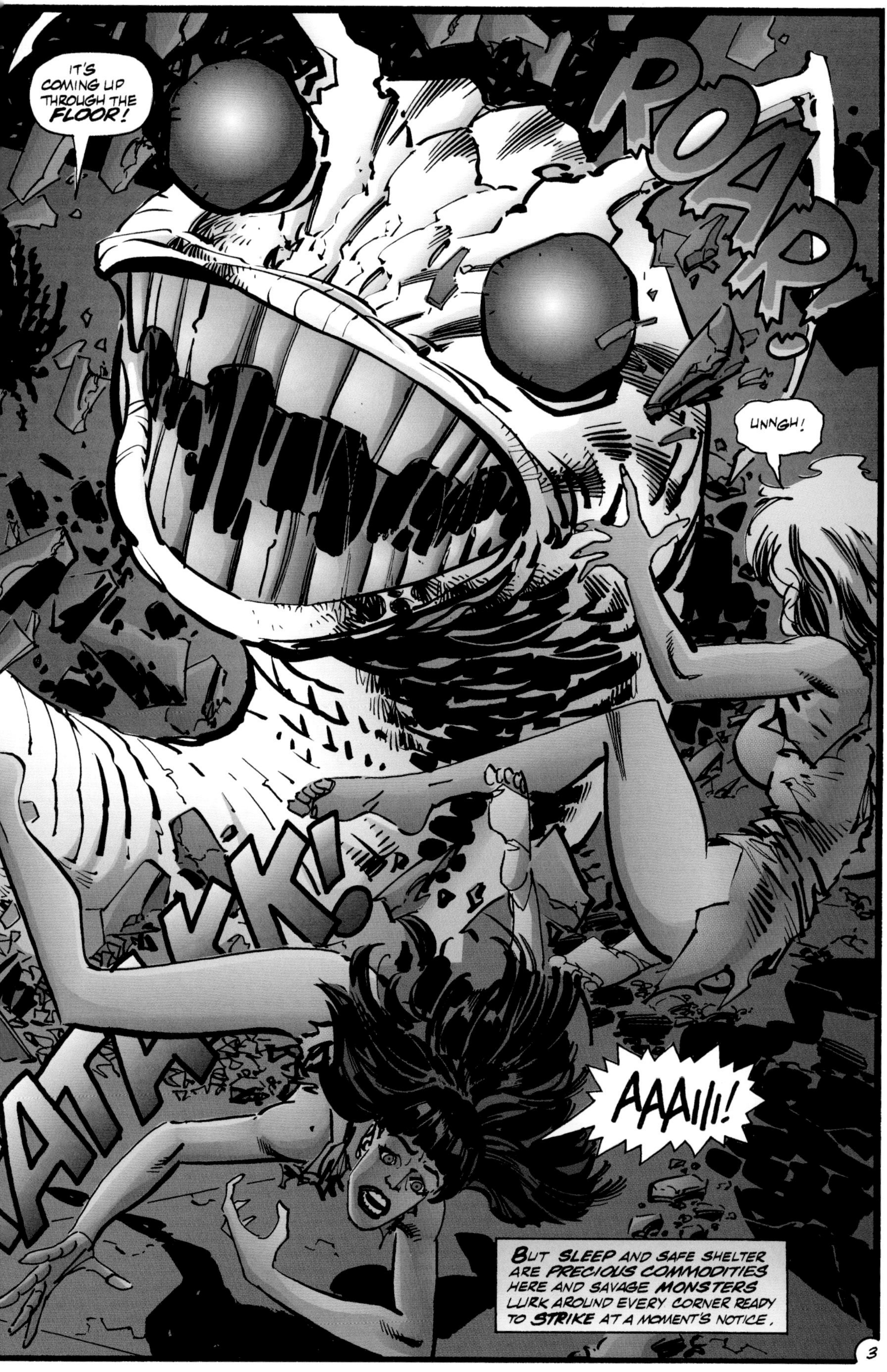
IT'S COMING UP THROUGH THE FLOOR!
ROAR
UNNGH!
ATTAKK!
AAAIII!
BUT SLEEP AND SAFE SHELTER ARE PRECIOUS COMMODITIES HERE AND SAVAGE MONSTERS LURK AROUND EVERY CORNER READY TO STRIKE AT A MOMENT'S NOTICE.

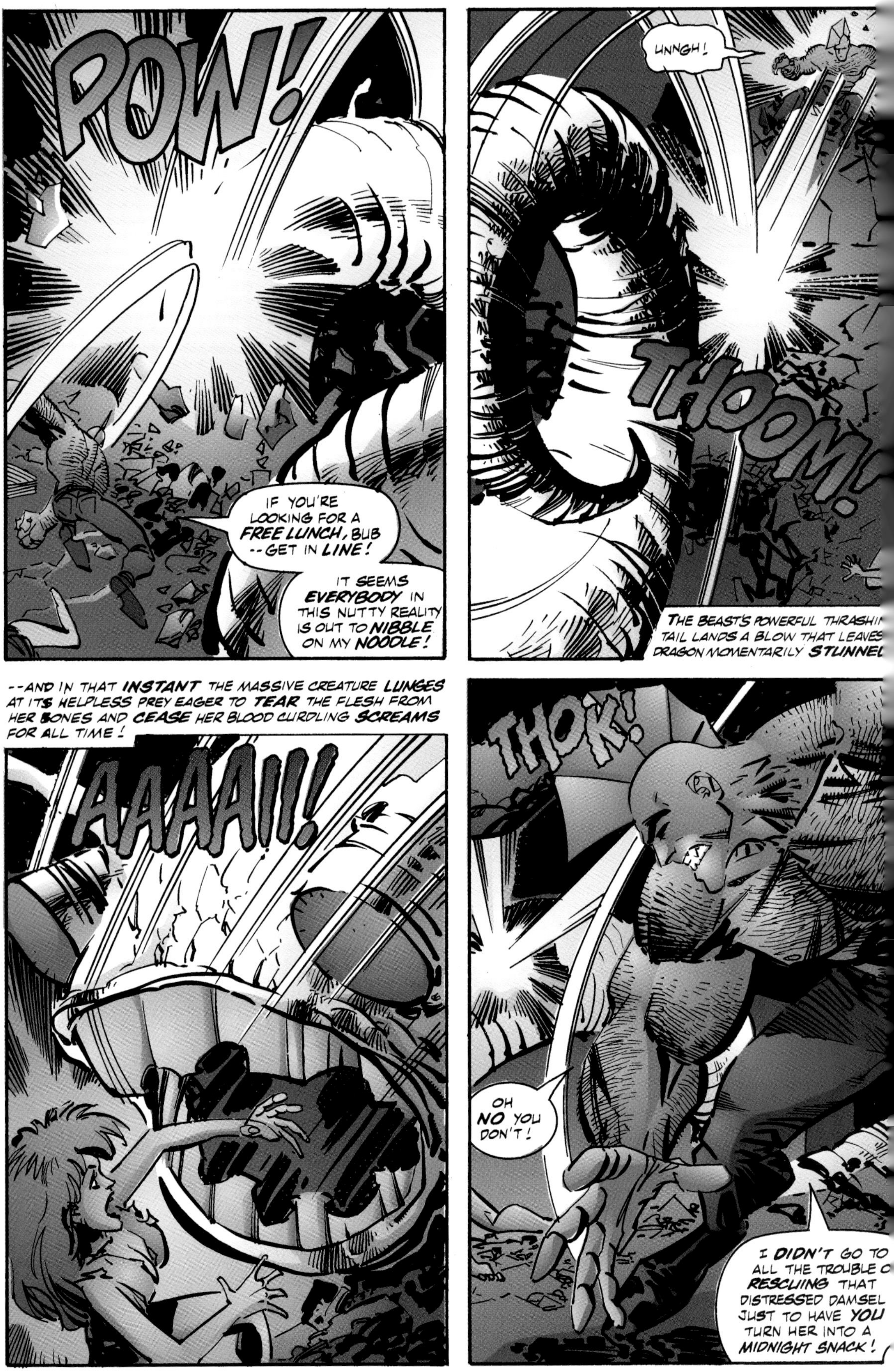
POW!!
IF YOU'RE LOOKING FOR A FREE LUNCH, BUB --GET IN LINE!
IT SEEMS EVERYBODY IN THIS NUTTY REALITY IS OUT TO NIBBLE ON MY NOODLE!
UNNGH!
THOOM!
THE BEAST'S POWERFUL THRASHI TAIL LANDS A BLOW THAT LEAVES DRAGON MOMENTARILY STUNNE
--AND IN THAT INSTANT THE MASSIVE CREATURE LUNGES AT ITS HELPLESS PREY EAGER TO TEAR THE FLESH FROM HER BONES AND CEASE HER BLOOD CURDLING SCREAMS FOR ALL TIME!
AAAAII!
THOK!
OH NO YOU DON'T!
I DIDN'T GO TO ALL THE TROUBLE O RESCUING THAT DISTRESSED DAMSEL JUST TO HAVE YOU TURN HER INTO A MIDNIGHT SNACK!

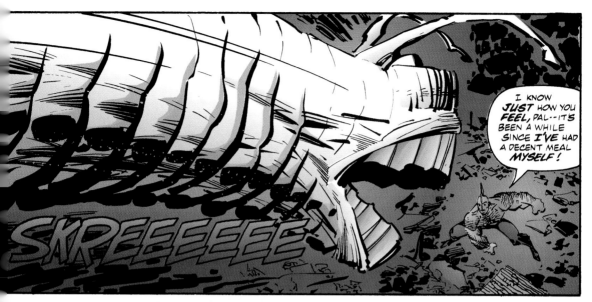

SKREEEEEE

I KNOW *JUST* HOW YOU *FEEL*, PAL--IT'S BEEN A WHILE SINCE *I'VE* HAD A DECENT MEAL *MYSELF!*

THRAKKASH!

=WHEW!=

HE'S *FASTER* THAN HE LOOKS--

SEEMS LIKE THAT'S *ALWAYS* THE CASE!

DAMN!

CHOMP!

OH GOD-- NO.

5

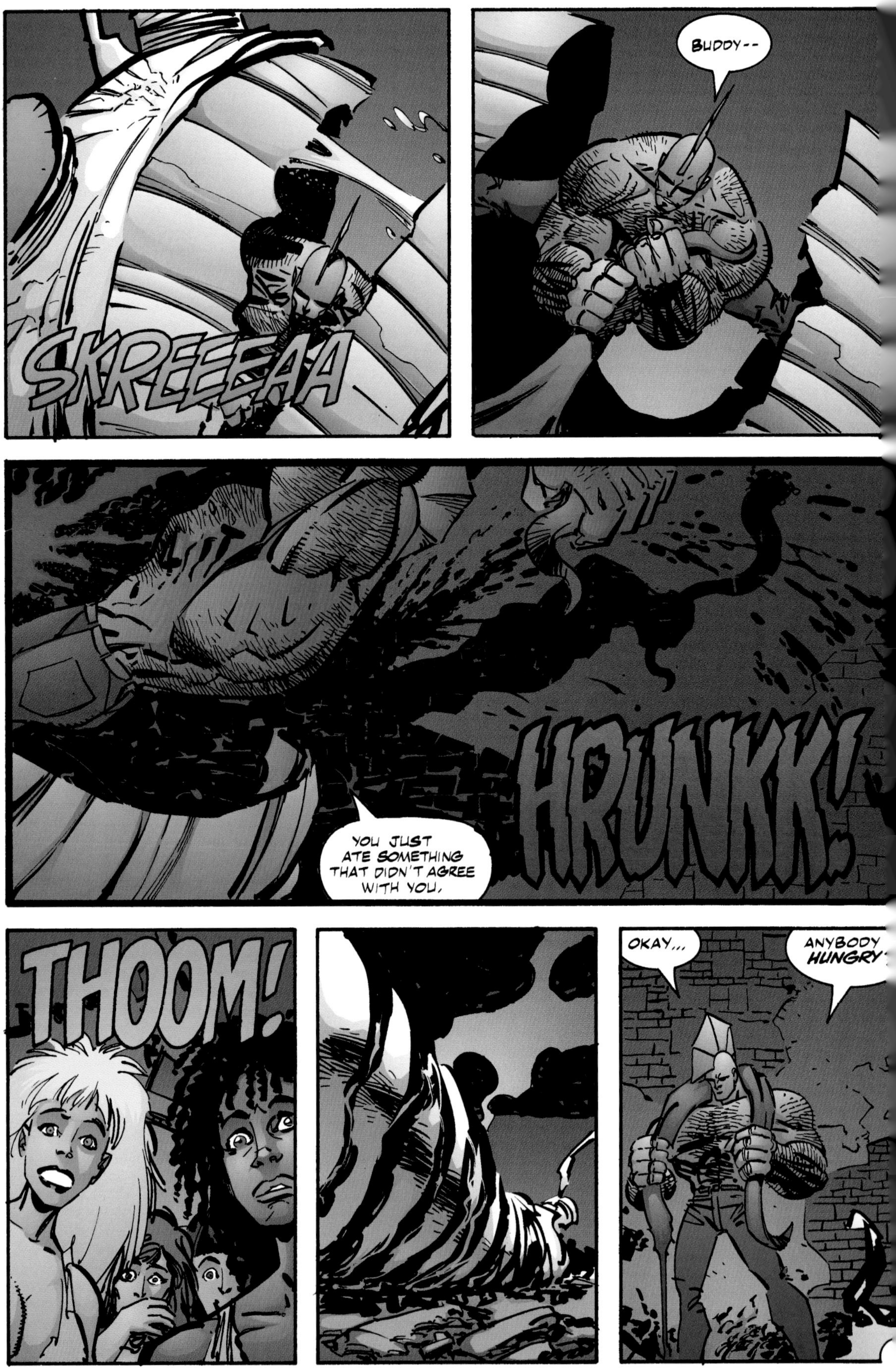
SKREEEAA
BUDDY--
HRUNKK!
YOU JUST ATE SOMETHING THAT DIDN'T AGREE WITH YOU.
THOOM!
OKAY...
ANYBODY HUNGRY

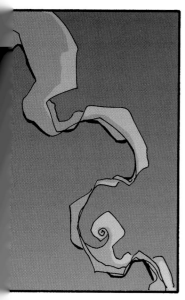

IT SMELLS GOOD.

LET'S JUST HOPE THIS SUCKER'S EDIBLE.

I'M SURE THAT I CAN CHOKE IT DOWN BUT I'D HATE TO HAVE YOU GIRLS GET FOOD POISONING FROM THIS GUY.

7

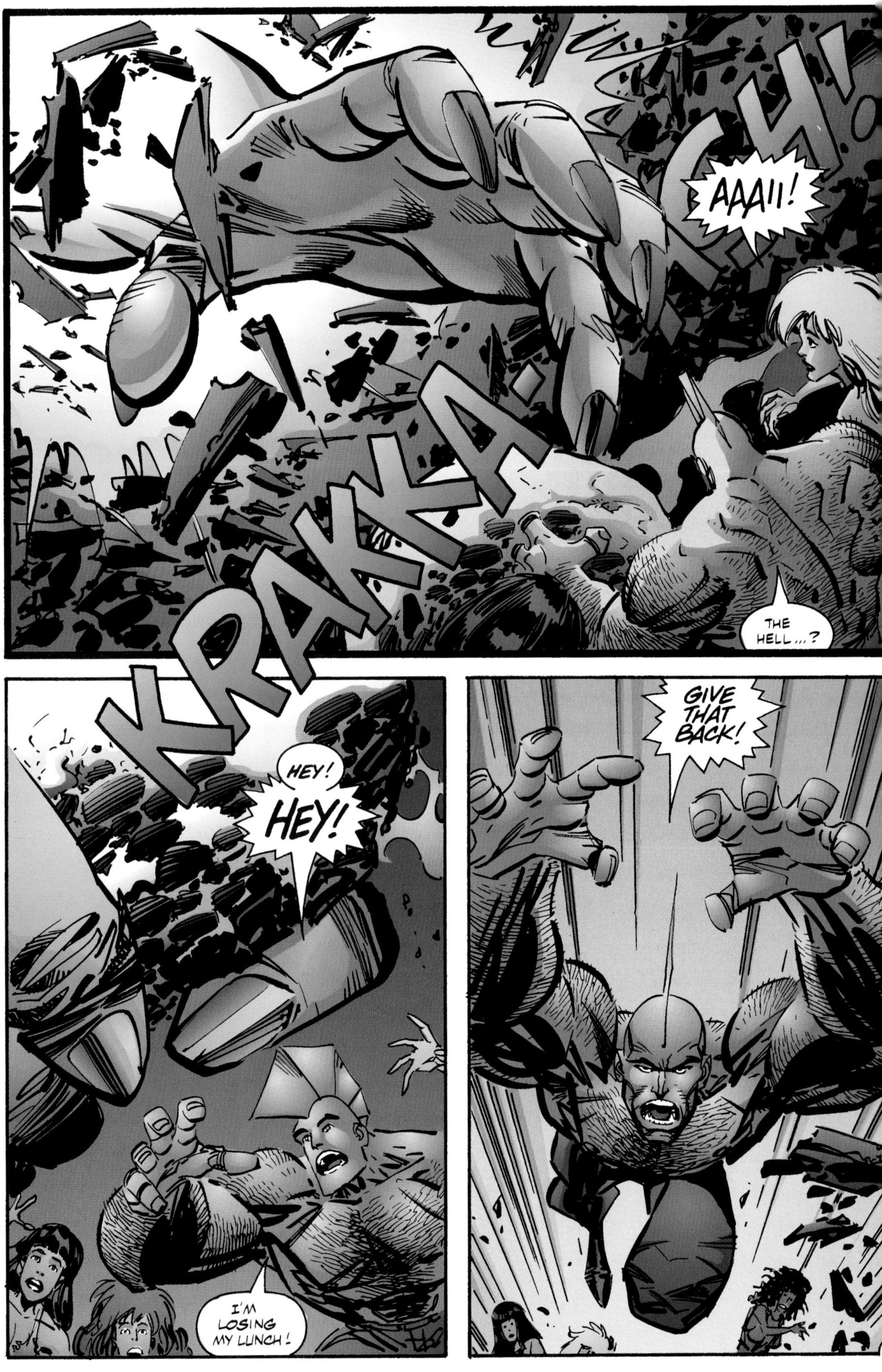
AAAII!
CH!
THE HELL...?
KRAKKA
HEY!
HEY!
I'M LOSING MY LUNCH!
GIVE THAT BACK!

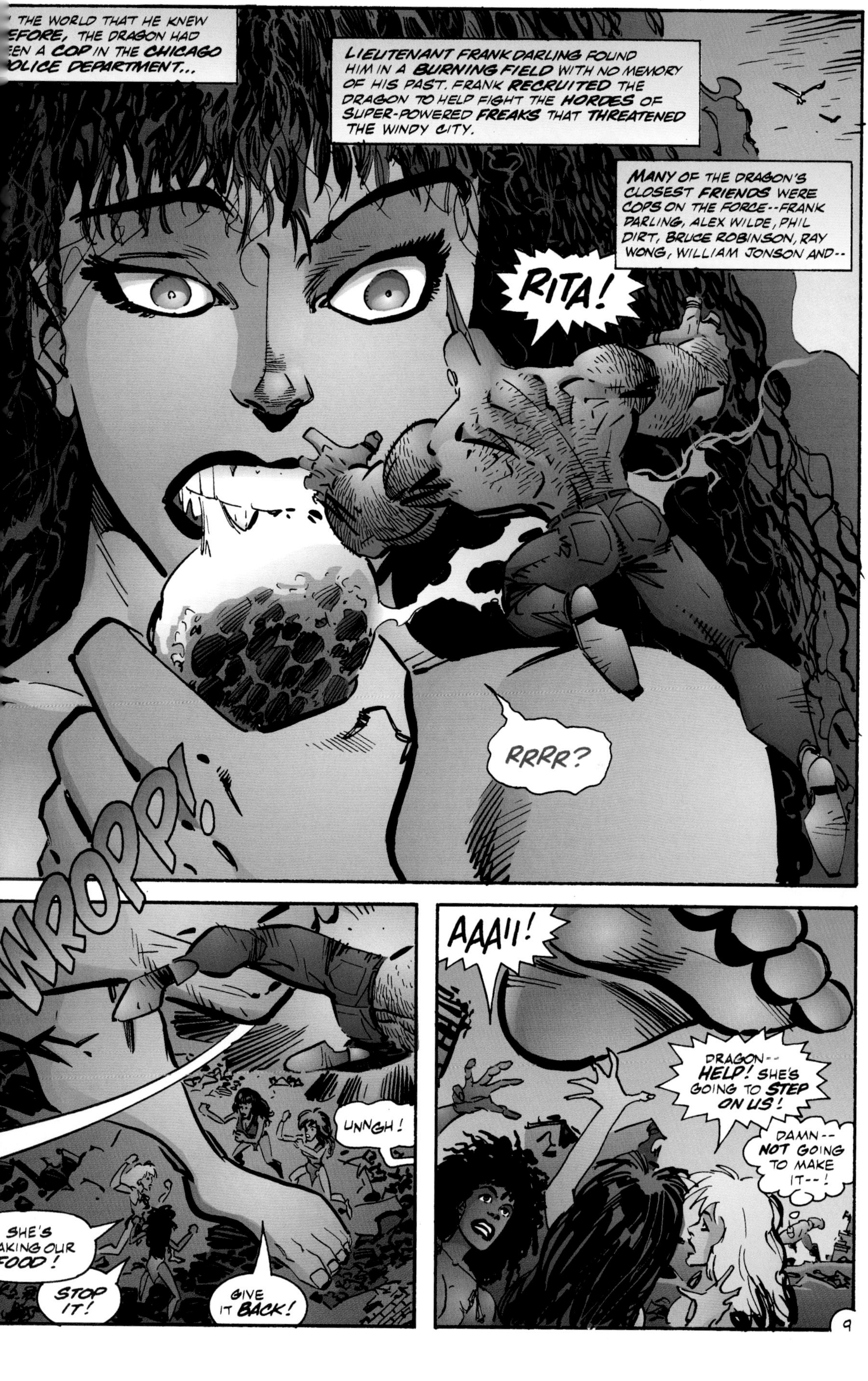
THE WORLD THAT HE KNEW
EFORE, THE DRAGON HAD
EEN A COP IN THE CHICAGO
OLICE DEPARTMENT...
LIEUTENANT FRANK DARLING FOUND HIM IN A BURNING FIELD WITH NO MEMORY OF HIS PAST. FRANK RECRUITED THE DRAGON TO HELP FIGHT THE HORDES OF SUPER-POWERED FREAKS THAT THREATENED THE WINDY CITY.
MANY OF THE DRAGON'S CLOSEST FRIENDS WERE COPS ON THE FORCE--FRANK DARLING, ALEX WILDE, PHIL DIRT, BRUCE ROBINSON, RAY WONG, WILLIAM JONSON AND--
RITA!
RRRR?
WROPP!
UNNGH!
SHE'S TAKING OUR FOOD!
STOP IT!
GIVE IT BACK!
AAA!!!
DRAGON-- HELP! SHE'S GOING TO STEP ON US!
DAMN-- NOT GOING TO MAKE IT--!

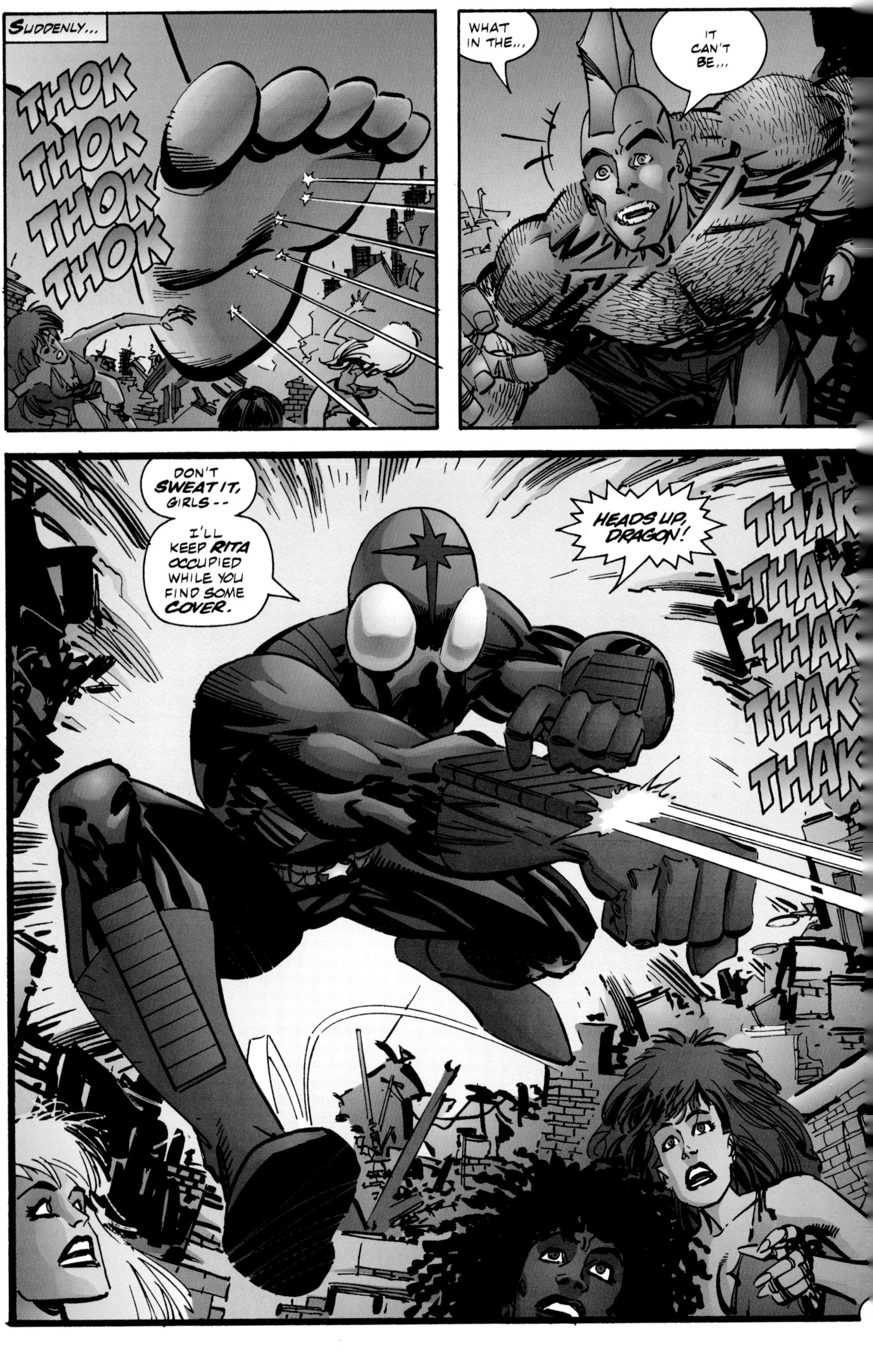
SUDDENLY...
THOK THOK THOK THOK
WHAT IN THE...
IT CAN'T BE...
DON'T SWEAT IT, GIRLS --
I'LL KEEP RITA OCCUPIED WHILE YOU FIND SOME COVER.
HEADS UP, DRAGON!
THAK THAK THAK THAK THAK

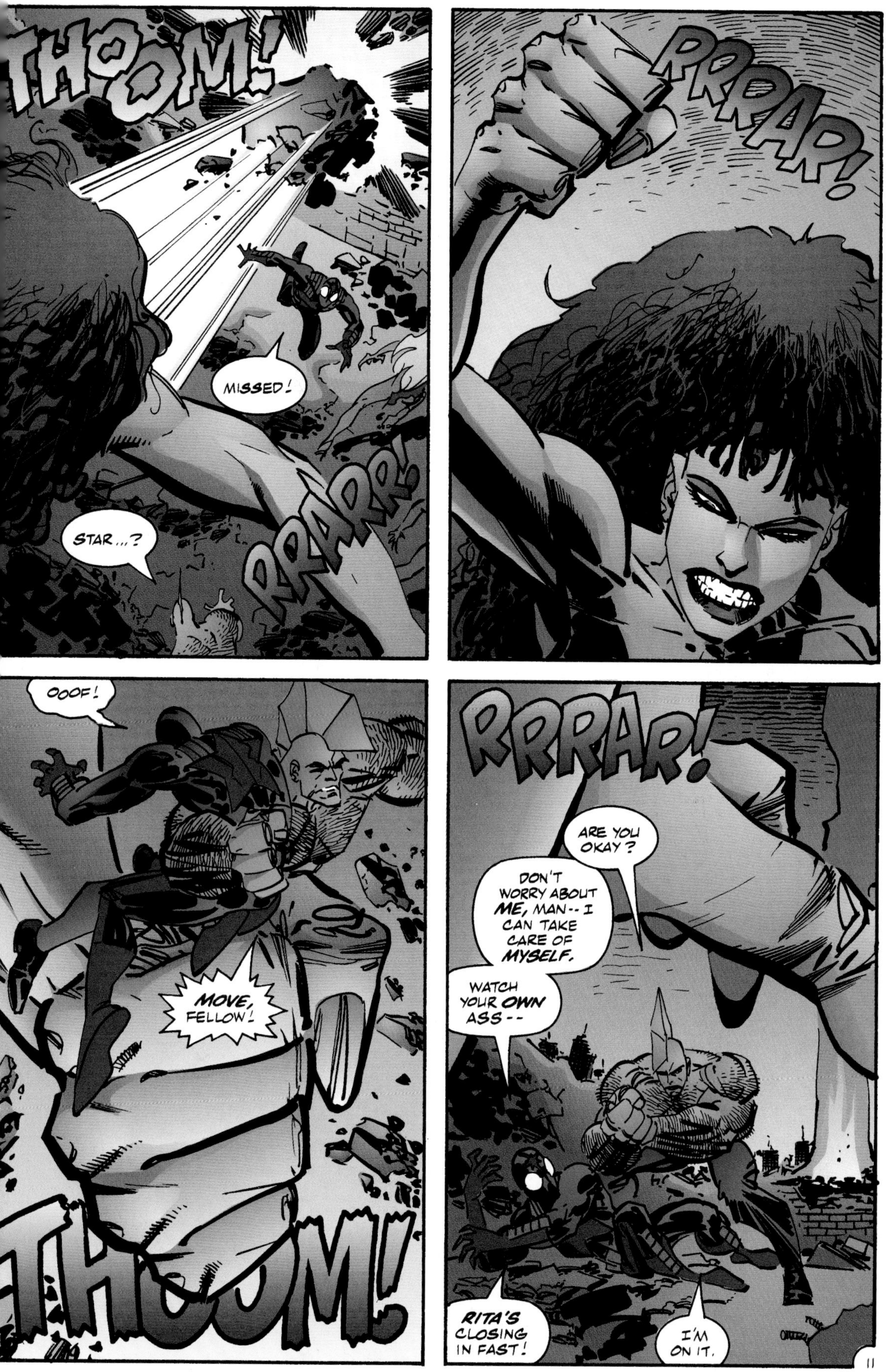
THOOM!
MISSED!
STAR...?
RRARR!
RRRAR!
OOOF!
MOVE, FELLOW!
THOOM!
RRRAR!
ARE YOU OKAY?
DON'T WORRY ABOUT ME, MAN -- I CAN TAKE CARE OF MYSELF.
WATCH YOUR OWN ASS --
RITA'S CLOSING IN FAST!
I'M ON IT.

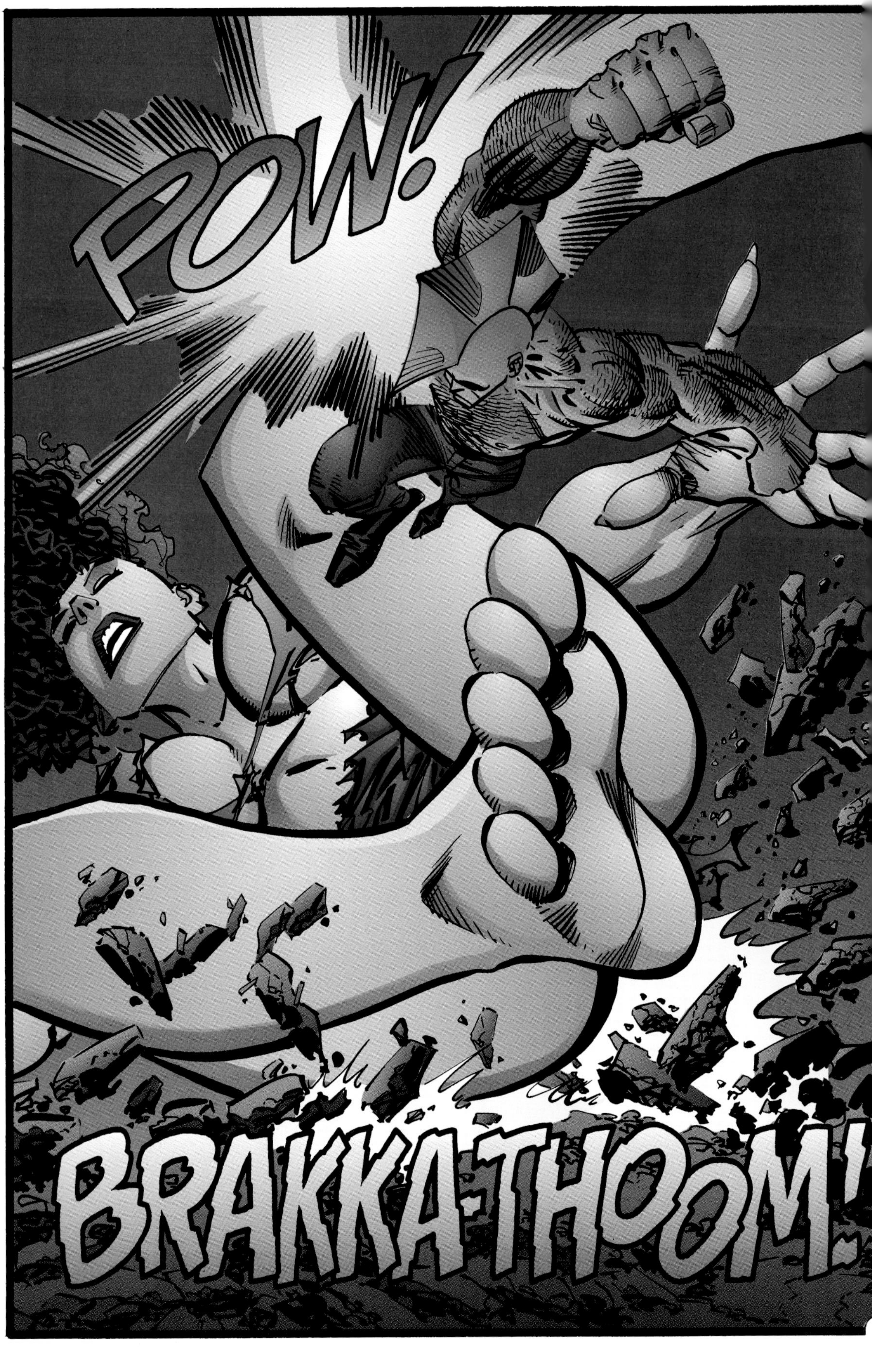
POW!
BRAKKA-THOOM!

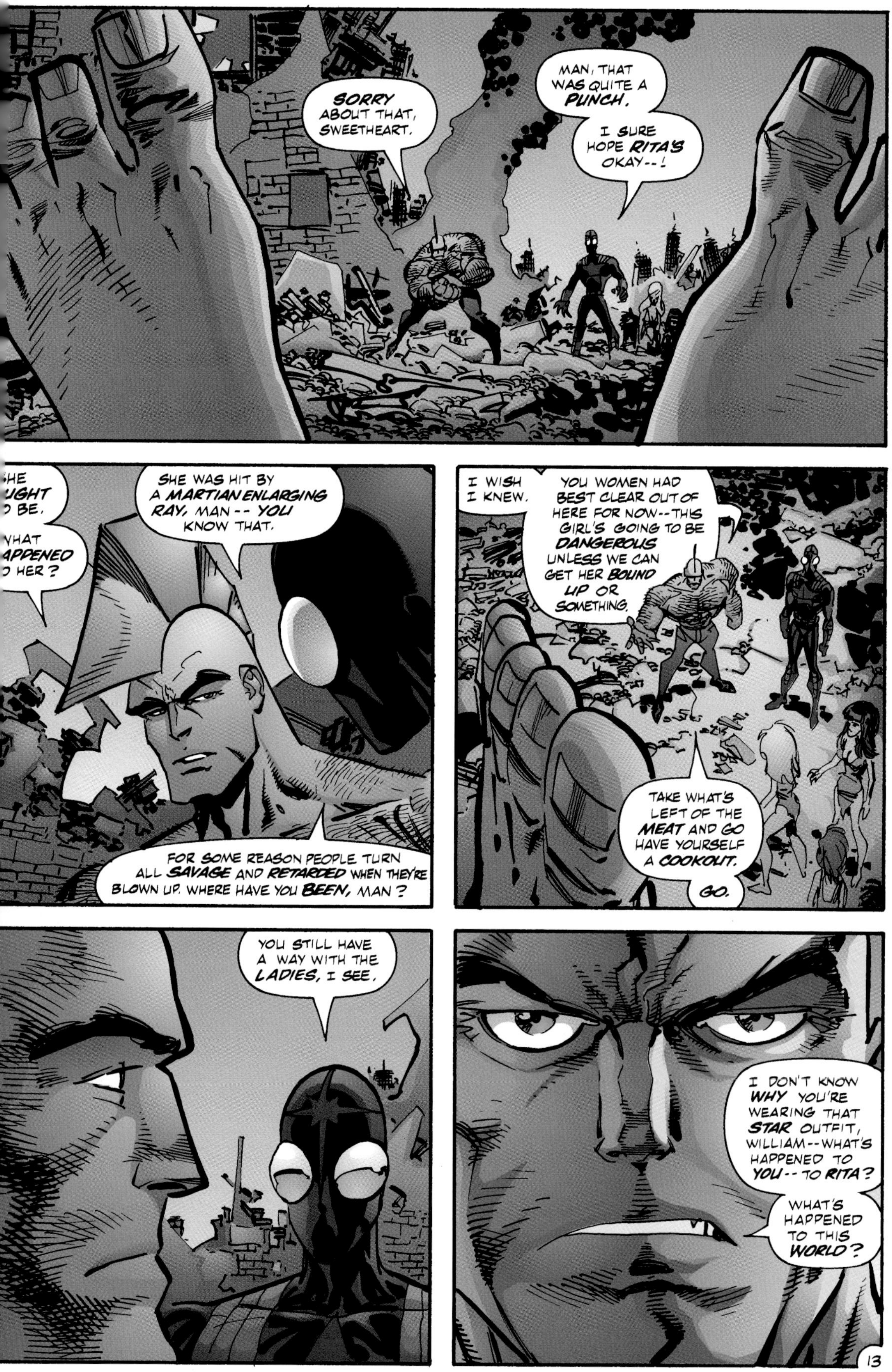

SORRY ABOUT THAT, SWEETHEART.
MAN, THAT WAS QUITE A PUNCH.
I SURE HOPE RITA'S OKAY--!
HE UGHT O BE.
VHAT APPENED O HER?
SHE WAS HIT BY A MARTIAN ENLARGING RAY, MAN -- YOU KNOW THAT.
FOR SOME REASON PEOPLE TURN ALL SAVAGE AND RETARDED WHEN THEY'RE BLOWN UP. WHERE HAVE YOU BEEN, MAN?
I WISH I KNEW.
YOU WOMEN HAD BEST CLEAR OUT OF HERE FOR NOW--THIS GIRL'S GOING TO BE DANGEROUS UNLESS WE CAN GET HER BOUND UP OR SOMETHING.
TAKE WHAT'S LEFT OF THE MEAT AND GO HAVE YOURSELF A COOKOUT.
GO.
YOU STILL HAVE A WAY WITH THE LADIES, I SEE.
I DON'T KNOW WHY YOU'RE WEARING THAT STAR OUTFIT, WILLIAM--WHAT'S HAPPENED TO YOU--TO RITA?
WHAT'S HAPPENED TO THIS WORLD?

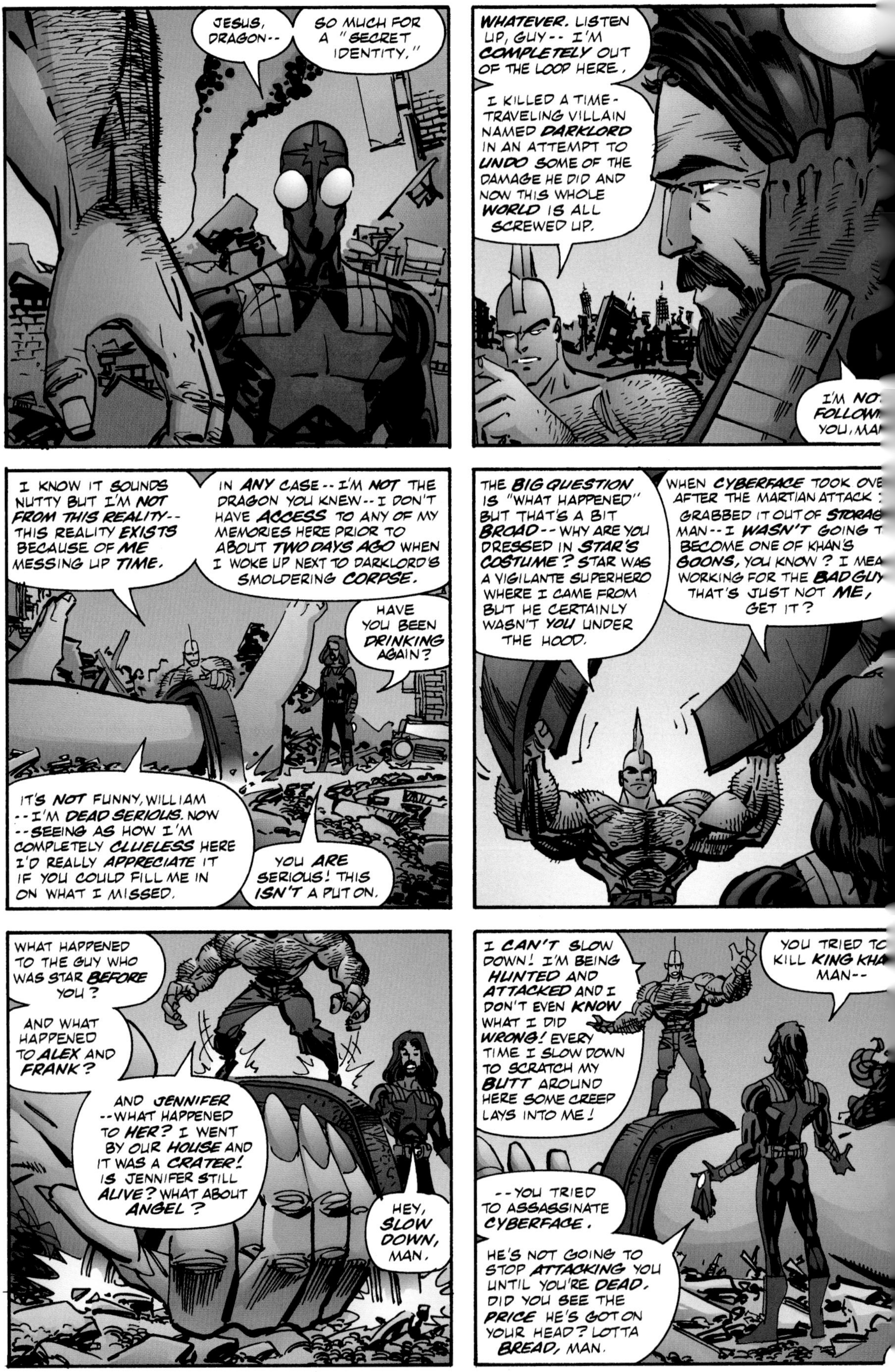
JESUS, DRAGON--
SO MUCH FOR A "SECRET IDENTITY."
WHATEVER. LISTEN UP, GUY-- I'M COMPLETELY OUT OF THE LOOP HERE.
I KILLED A TIME-TRAVELING VILLAIN NAMED DARKLORD IN AN ATTEMPT TO UNDO SOME OF THE DAMAGE HE DID AND NOW THIS WHOLE WORLD IS ALL SCREWED UP.
I'M NO FOLLOWI YOU, MA
I KNOW IT SOUNDS NUTTY BUT I'M NOT FROM THIS REALITY-- THIS REALITY EXISTS BECAUSE OF ME MESSING UP TIME.
IN ANY CASE-- I'M NOT THE DRAGON YOU KNEW-- I DON'T HAVE ACCESS TO ANY OF MY MEMORIES HERE PRIOR TO ABOUT TWO DAYS AGO WHEN I WOKE UP NEXT TO DARKLORD'S SMOLDERING CORPSE.
HAVE YOU BEEN DRINKING AGAIN?
IT'S NOT FUNNY, WILLIAM --I'M DEAD SERIOUS. NOW --SEEING AS HOW I'M COMPLETELY CLUELESS HERE I'D REALLY APPRECIATE IT IF YOU COULD FILL ME IN ON WHAT I MISSED.
YOU ARE SERIOUS! THIS ISN'T A PUT ON.
THE BIG QUESTION IS "WHAT HAPPENED" BUT THAT'S A BIT BROAD-- WHY ARE YOU DRESSED IN STAR'S COSTUME? STAR WAS A VIGILANTE SUPERHERO WHERE I CAME FROM BUT HE CERTAINLY WASN'T YOU UNDER THE HOOD.
WHEN CYBERFACE TOOK OVE AFTER THE MARTIAN ATTACK GRABBED IT OUT OF STORAG MAN-- I WASN'T GOING T BECOME ONE OF KHAN'S GOONS, YOU KNOW? I MEA WORKING FOR THE BAD GUY THAT'S JUST NOT ME, GET IT?
WHAT HAPPENED TO THE GUY WHO WAS STAR BEFORE YOU?
AND WHAT HAPPENED TO ALEX AND FRANK?
AND JENNIFER --WHAT HAPPENED TO HER? I WENT BY OUR HOUSE AND IT WAS A CRATER! IS JENNIFER STILL ALIVE? WHAT ABOUT ANGEL?
HEY, SLOW DOWN, MAN.
I CAN'T SLOW DOWN! I'M BEING HUNTED AND ATTACKED AND I DON'T EVEN KNOW WHAT I DID WRONG! EVERY TIME I SLOW DOWN TO SCRATCH MY BUTT AROUND HERE SOME CREEP LAYS INTO ME!
YOU TRIED TO KILL KING KHA MAN--
--YOU TRIED TO ASSASSINATE CYBERFACE.
HE'S NOT GOING TO STOP ATTACKING YOU UNTIL YOU'RE DEAD. DID YOU SEE THE PRICE HE'S GOT ON YOUR HEAD? LOTTA BREAD, MAN.

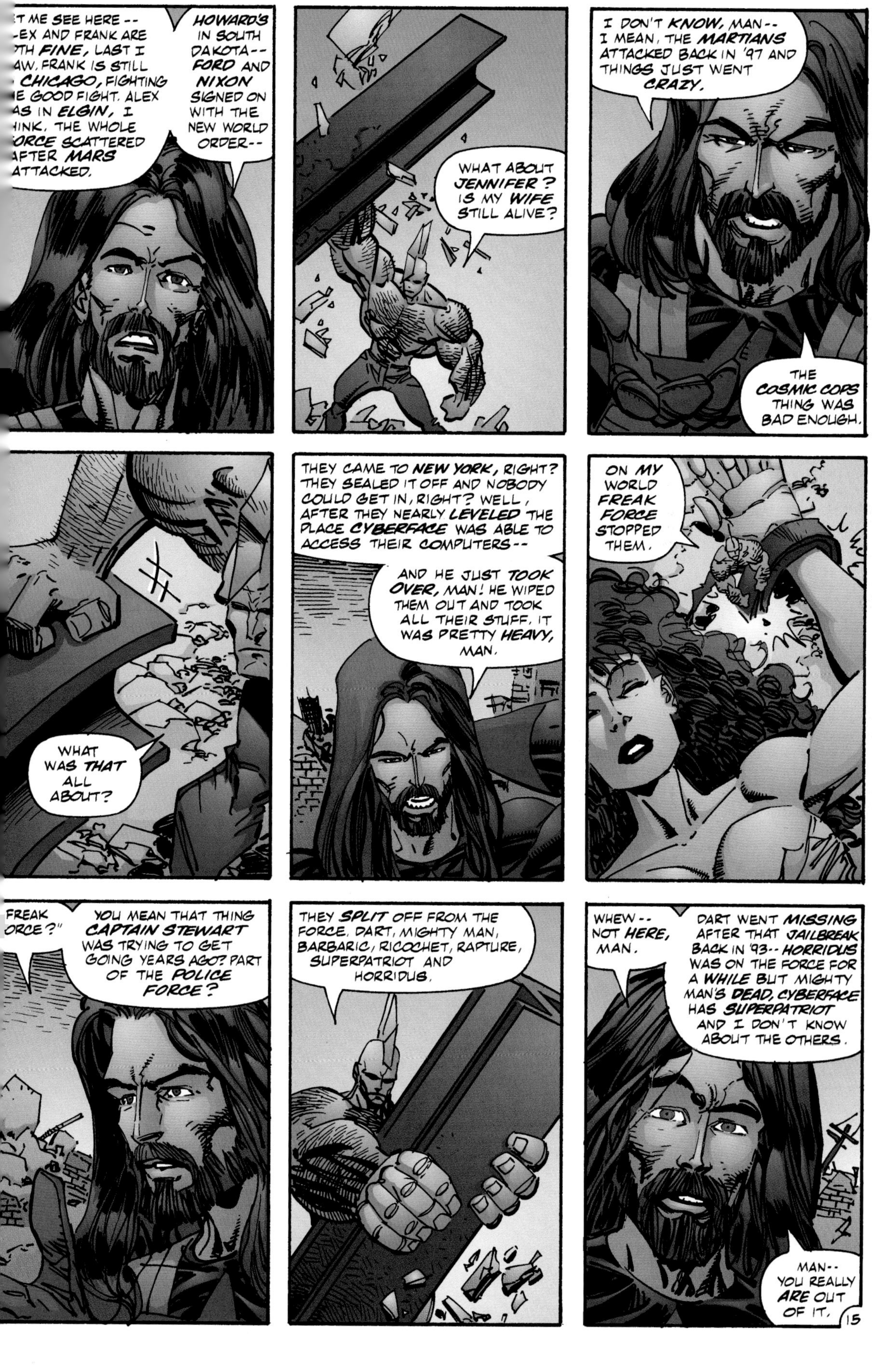

T ME SEE HERE -- -EX AND FRANK ARE OTH FINE, LAST I AW. FRANK IS STILL CHICAGO, FIGHTING E GOOD FIGHT. ALEX AS IN ELGIN, I HINK. THE WHOLE ORCE SCATTERED AFTER MARS ATTACKED.
HOWARD'S IN SOUTH DAKOTA-- FORD AND NIXON SIGNED ON WITH THE NEW WORLD ORDER--
WHAT ABOUT JENNIFER? IS MY WIFE STILL ALIVE?
I DON'T KNOW, MAN-- I MEAN, THE MARTIANS ATTACKED BACK IN '97 AND THINGS JUST WENT CRAZY.
THE COSMIC COPS THING WAS BAD ENOUGH.
WHAT WAS THAT ALL ABOUT?
THEY CAME TO NEW YORK, RIGHT? THEY SEALED IT OFF AND NOBODY COULD GET IN, RIGHT? WELL, AFTER THEY NEARLY LEVELED THE PLACE CYBERFACE WAS ABLE TO ACCESS THEIR COMPUTERS--
AND HE JUST TOOK OVER, MAN! HE WIPED THEM OUT AND TOOK ALL THEIR STUFF. IT WAS PRETTY HEAVY, MAN.
ON MY WORLD FREAK FORCE STOPPED THEM.
FREAK ORCE?"
YOU MEAN THAT THING CAPTAIN STEWART WAS TRYING TO GET GOING YEARS AGO? PART OF THE POLICE FORCE?
THEY SPLIT OFF FROM THE FORCE. DART, MIGHTY MAN, BARBARIC, RICOCHET, RAPTURE, SUPERPATRIOT AND HORRIDUS.
WHEW-- NOT HERE, MAN.
DART WENT MISSING AFTER THAT JAILBREAK BACK IN '93-- HORRIDUS WAS ON THE FORCE FOR A WHILE BUT MIGHTY MAN'S DEAD, CYBERFACE HAS SUPERPATRIOT AND I DON'T KNOW ABOUT THE OTHERS.
MAN-- YOU REALLY ARE OUT OF IT.

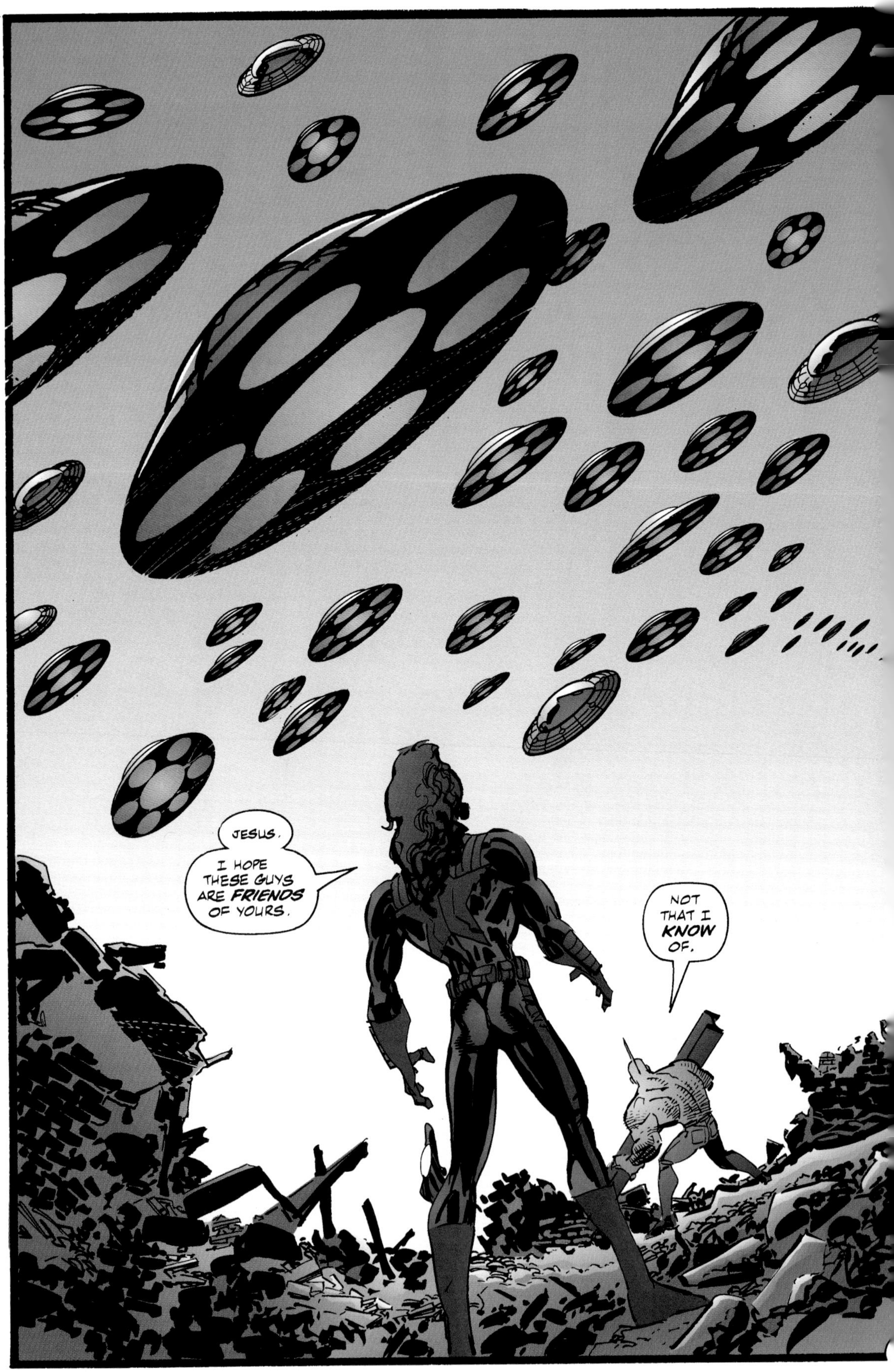
JESUS.
I HOPE THESE GUYS ARE FRIENDS OF YOURS.
NOT THAT I KNOW OF.

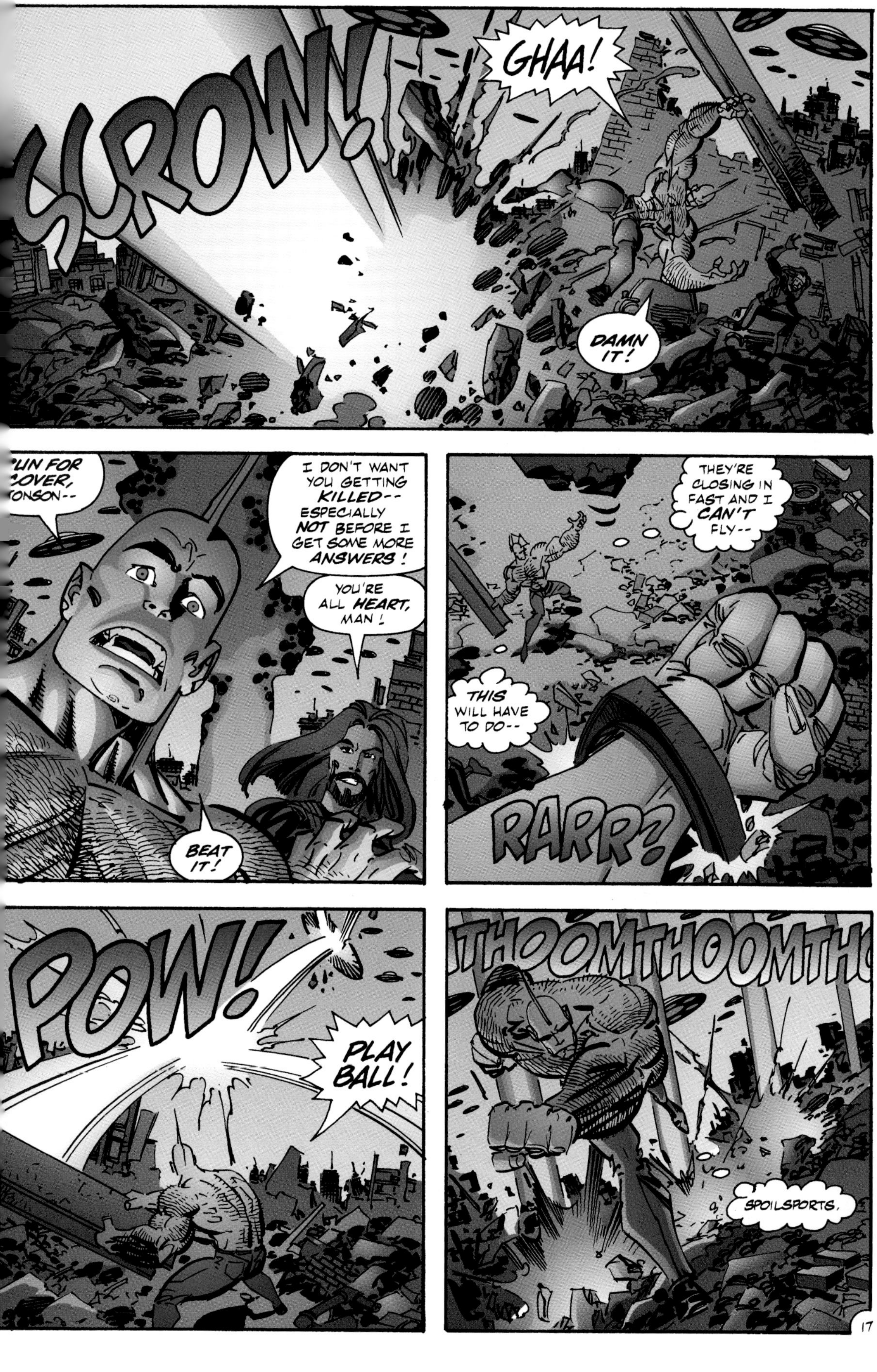
SCROW!!
GHAA!
DAMN IT!
RUN FOR COVER, TONSON--
I DON'T WANT YOU GETTING KILLED-- ESPECIALLY NOT BEFORE I GET SOME MORE ANSWERS!
YOU'RE ALL HEART, MAN!
BEAT IT!
THEY'RE CLOSING IN FAST AND I CAN'T FLY--
THIS WILL HAVE TO DO--
RARR?
POW!
PLAY BALL!
THOOMTHOOMTHOOMTHO
SPOILSPORTS.

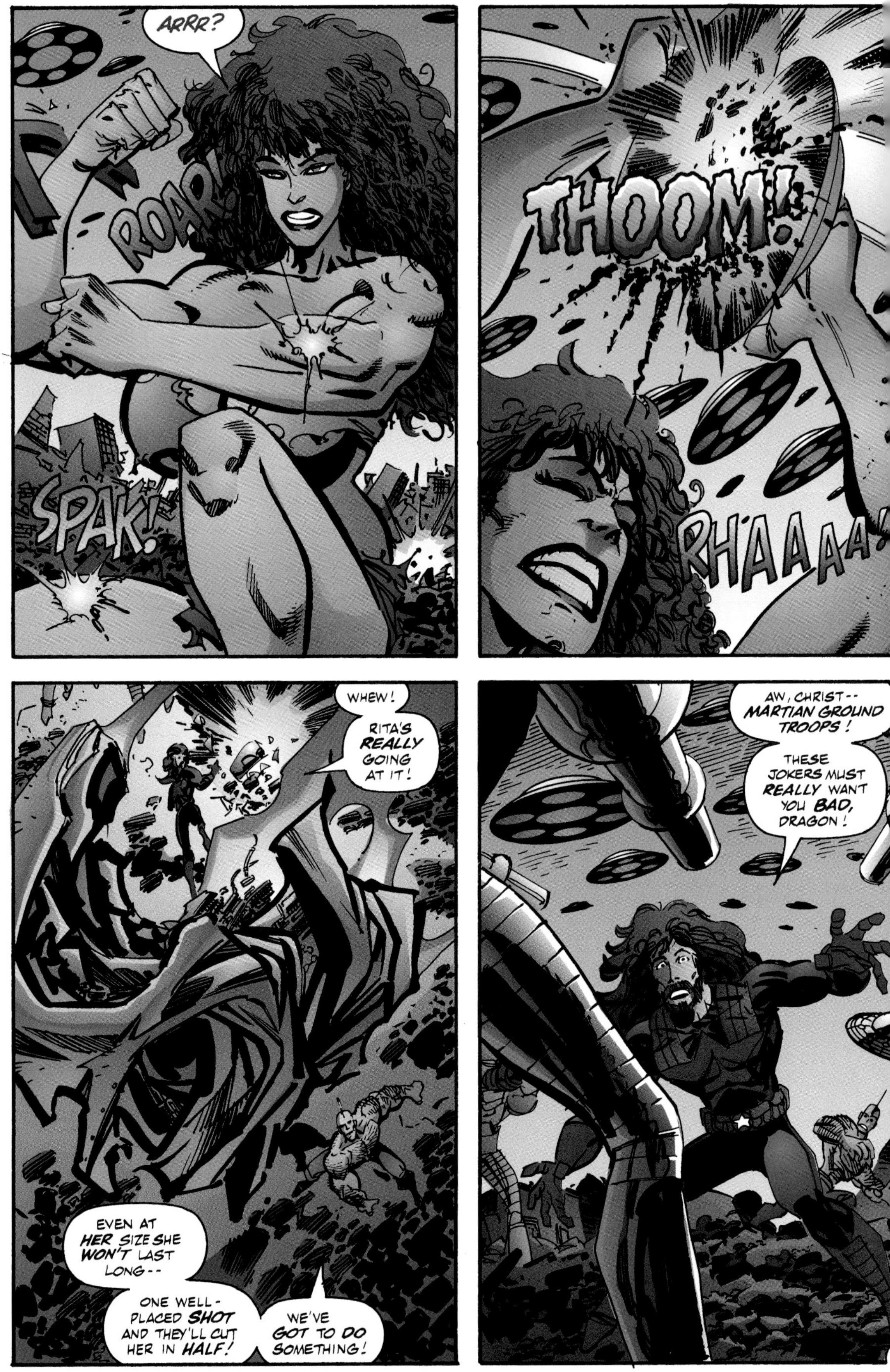
ARRR?
ROAR!
SPAK!
THOOM!
RHAAAAA!
WHEW!
RITA'S REALLY GOING AT IT!
EVEN AT HER SIZE SHE WON'T LAST LONG--
ONE WELL-PLACED SHOT AND THEY'LL CUT HER IN HALF!
WE'VE GOT TO DO SOMETHING!
AW, CHRIST-- MARTIAN GROUND TROOPS!
THESE JOKERS MUST REALLY WANT YOU BAD, DRAGON!

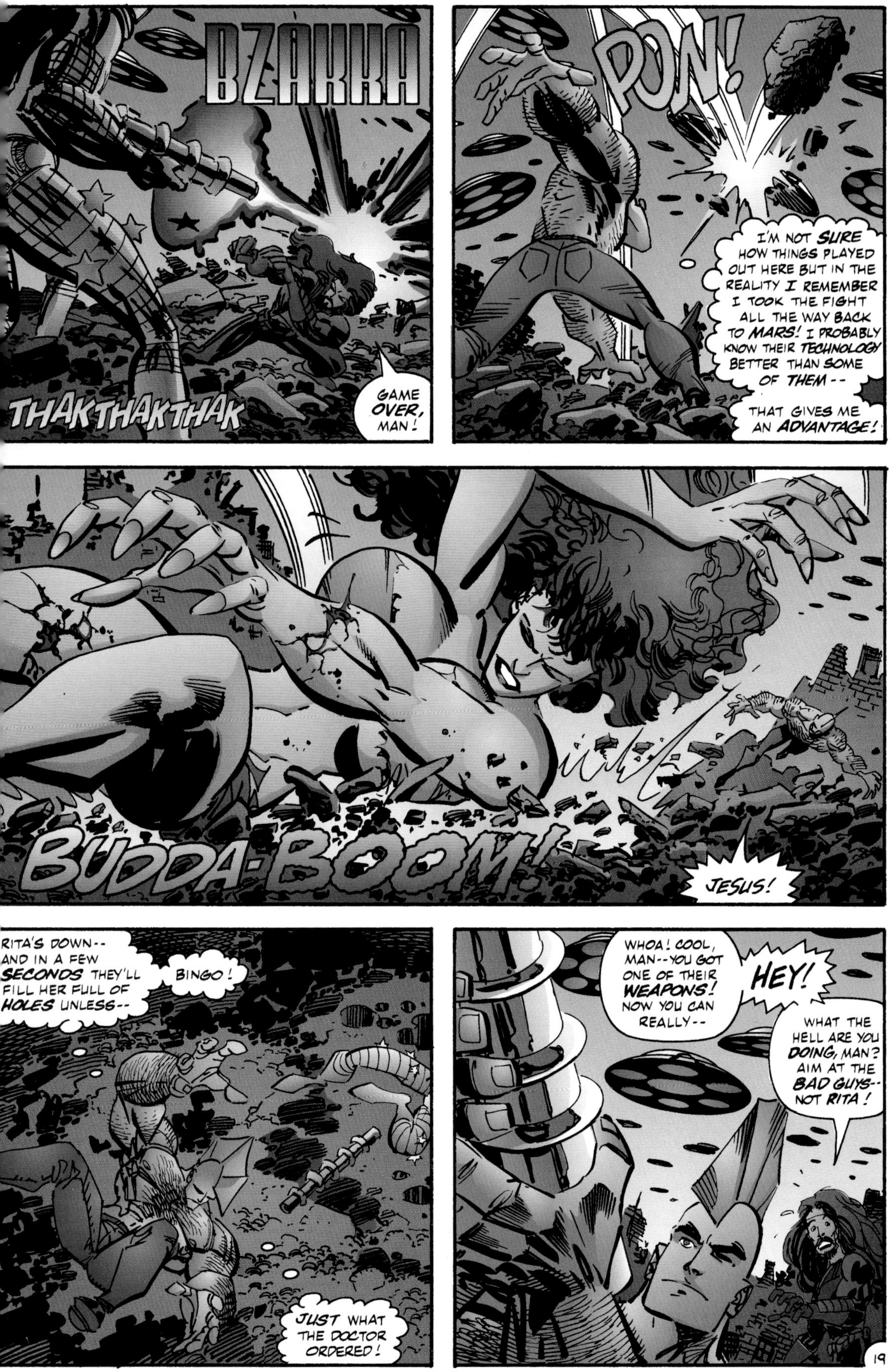
BZAKKA
THAKTHAKTHAK
GAME OVER, MAN!
PON!
I'M NOT SURE HOW THINGS PLAYED OUT HERE BUT IN THE REALITY I REMEMBER I TOOK THE FIGHT ALL THE WAY BACK TO MARS! I PROBABLY KNOW THEIR TECHNOLOGY BETTER THAN SOME OF THEM --
THAT GIVES ME AN ADVANTAGE!
BUDDA-BOOM!
JESUS!
RITA'S DOWN-- AND IN A FEW SECONDS THEY'LL FILL HER FULL OF HOLES UNLESS--
BINGO!
JUST WHAT THE DOCTOR ORDERED!
WHOA! COOL, MAN--YOU GOT ONE OF THEIR WEAPONS! NOW YOU CAN REALLY--
HEY!
WHAT THE HELL ARE YOU DOING, MAN? AIM AT THE BAD GUYS-- NOT RITA!

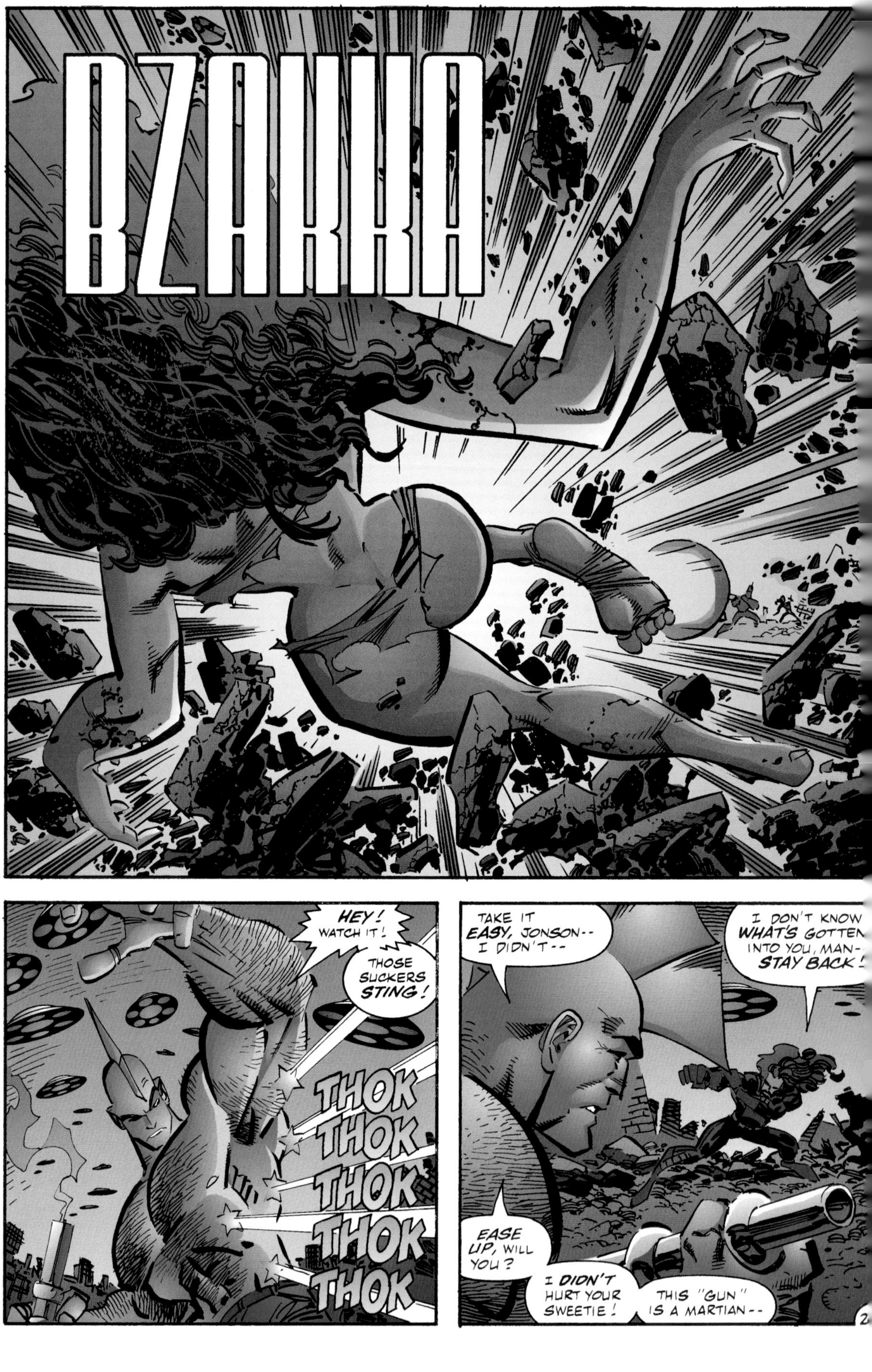
BZAKKA
HEY! WATCH IT!
THOSE SUCKERS STING!
THOK THOK THOK THOK THOK
TAKE IT EASY, JONSON-- I DIDN'T--
I DON'T KNOW WHAT'S GOTTEN INTO YOU, MAN-- STAY BACK!
EASE UP, WILL YOU?
I DIDN'T HURT YOUR SWEETIE!
THIS "GUN" IS A MARTIAN--

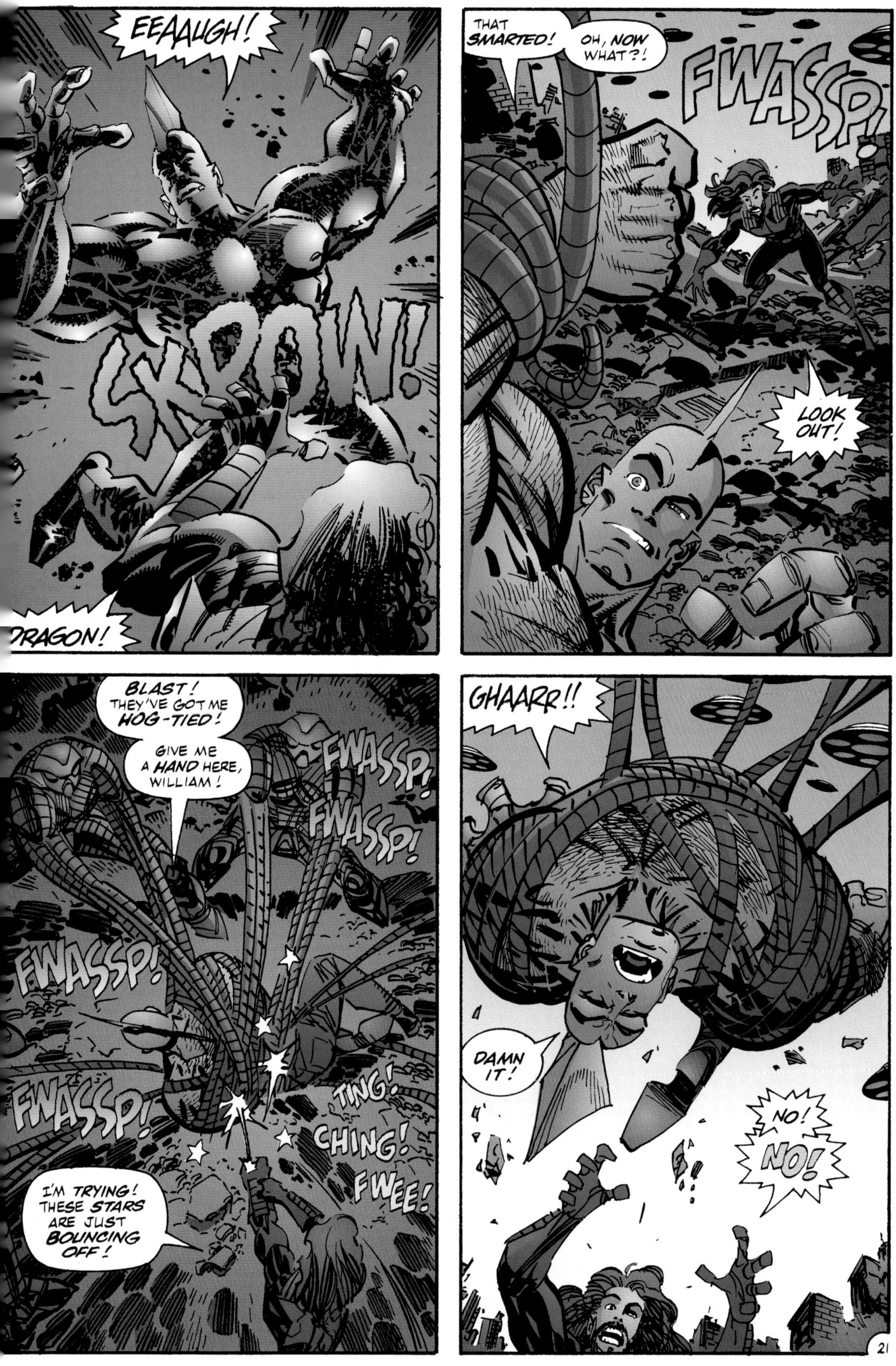
EEAAUGH!
SKOOM!
DRAGON!
THAT SMARTED!
OH, NOW WHAT?!
FWASSP!
LOOK OUT!
BLAST! THEY'VE GOT ME HOG-TIED!
GIVE ME A HAND HERE, WILLIAM!
FWASSP!
FWASSP!
FWASSP!
FWASSP!
TING!
CHING!
FWEE!
I'M TRYING! THESE STARS ARE JUST BOUNCING OFF!
GHAARR!!
DAMN IT!
NO!
NO!

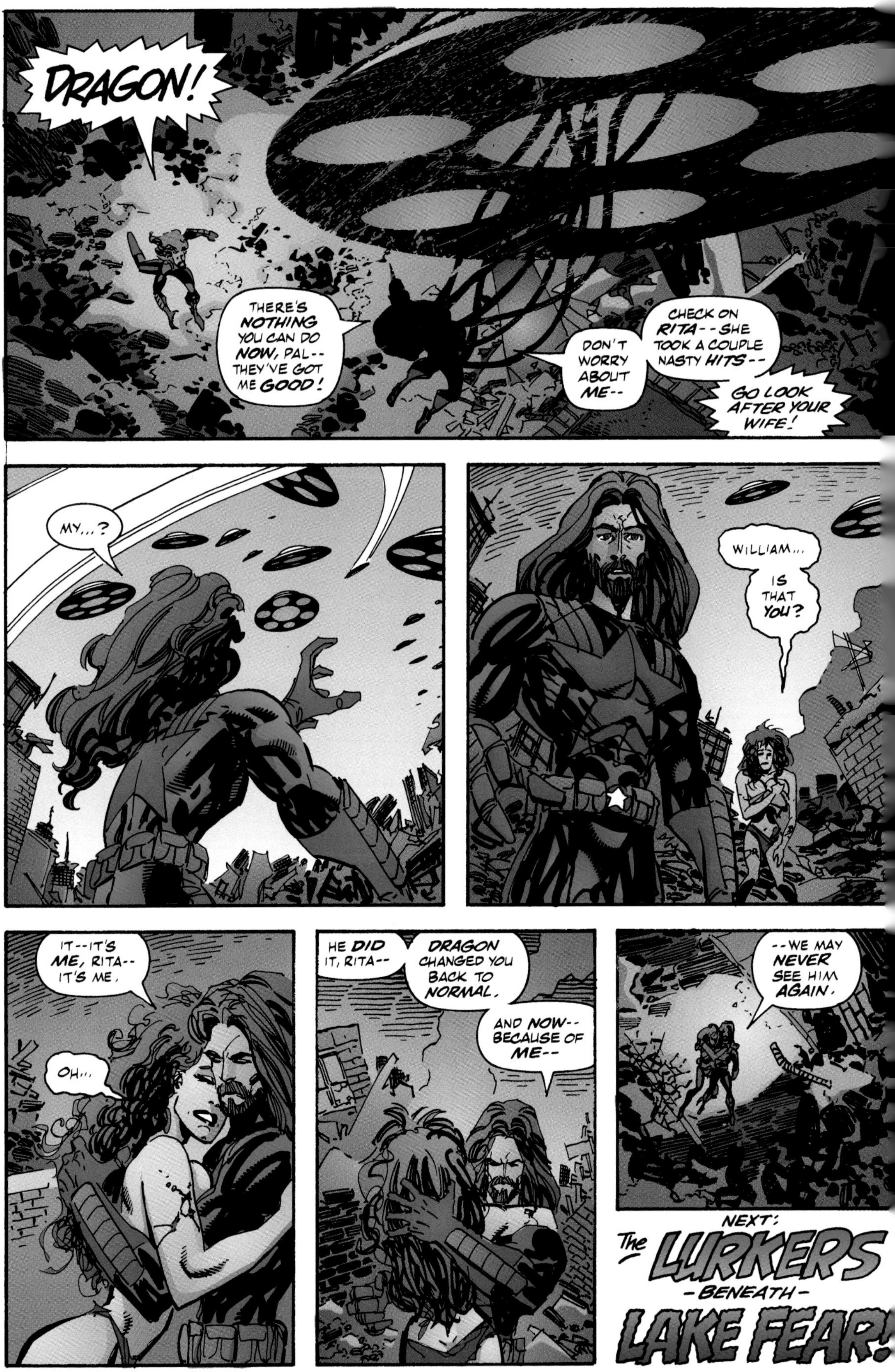
DRAGON!
THERE'S NOTHING YOU CAN DO NOW, PAL-- THEY'VE GOT ME GOOD!
DON'T WORRY ABOUT ME--
CHECK ON RITA--SHE TOOK A COUPLE NASTY HITS--
GO LOOK AFTER YOUR WIFE!
MY...?
WILLIAM...
IS THAT YOU?
IT--IT'S ME, RITA-- IT'S ME.
OH...
HE DID IT, RITA--
DRAGON CHANGED YOU BACK TO NORMAL.
AND NOW-- BECAUSE OF ME--
--WE MAY NEVER SEE HIM AGAIN.
NEXT:
The LURKERS -BENEATH- LAKE FEAR!

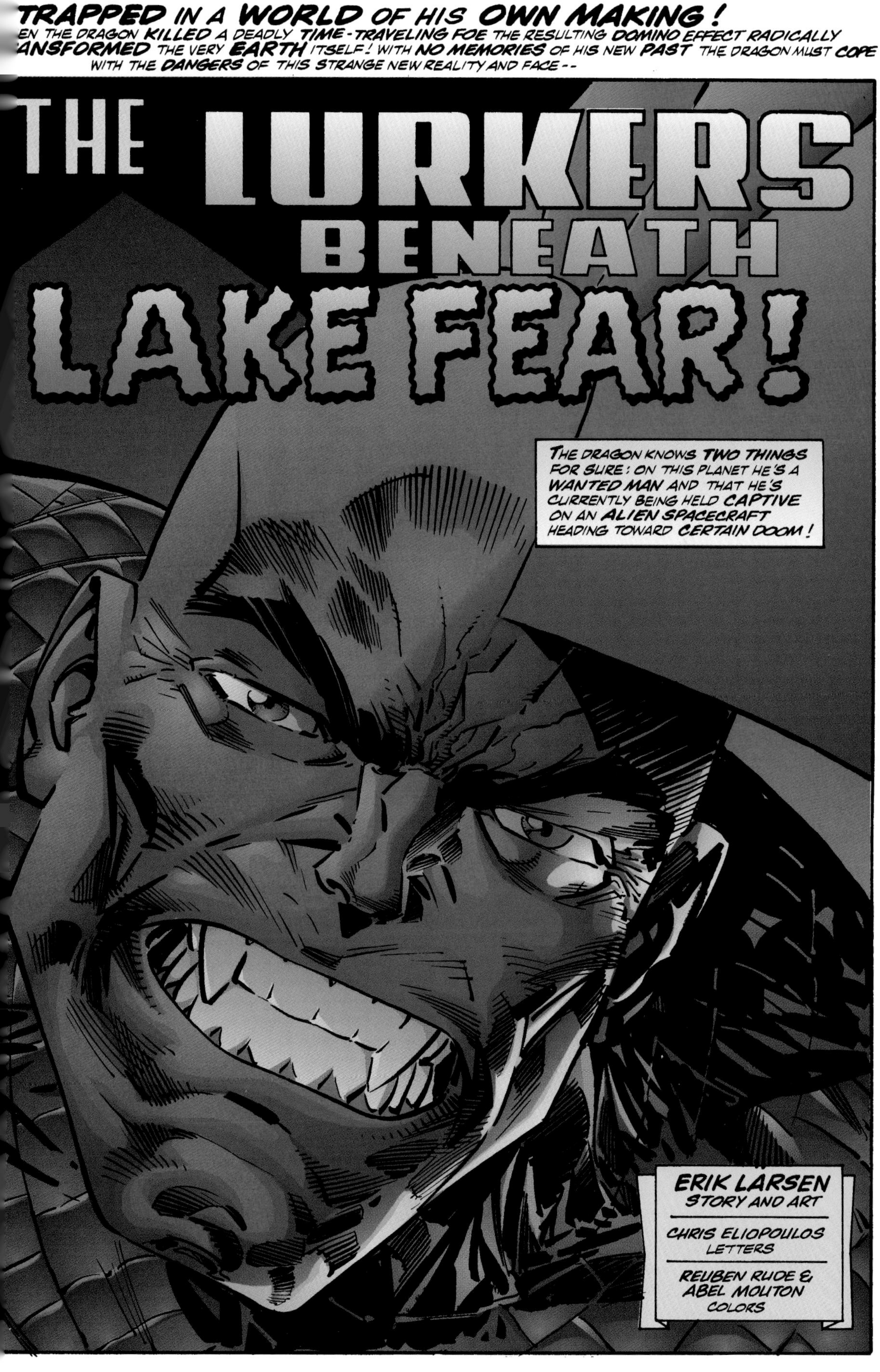
TRAPPED IN A WORLD OF HIS OWN MAKING!
EN THE DRAGON KILLED A DEADLY TIME-TRAVELING FOE THE RESULTING DOMINO EFFECT RADICALLY 'ANSFORMED THE VERY EARTH ITSELF! WITH NO MEMORIES OF HIS NEW PAST THE DRAGON MUST COPE WITH THE DANGERS OF THIS STRANGE NEW REALITY AND FACE--
THE LURKERS BENEATH LAKE FEAR!
THE DRAGON KNOWS TWO THINGS FOR SURE: ON THIS PLANET HE'S A WANTED MAN AND THAT HE'S CURRENTLY BEING HELD CAPTIVE ON AN ALIEN SPACECRAFT HEADING TOWARD CERTAIN DOOM!
ERIK LARSEN STORY AND ART
CHRIS ELIOPOULOS LETTERS
REUBEN RUDE & ABEL MOUTON COLORS

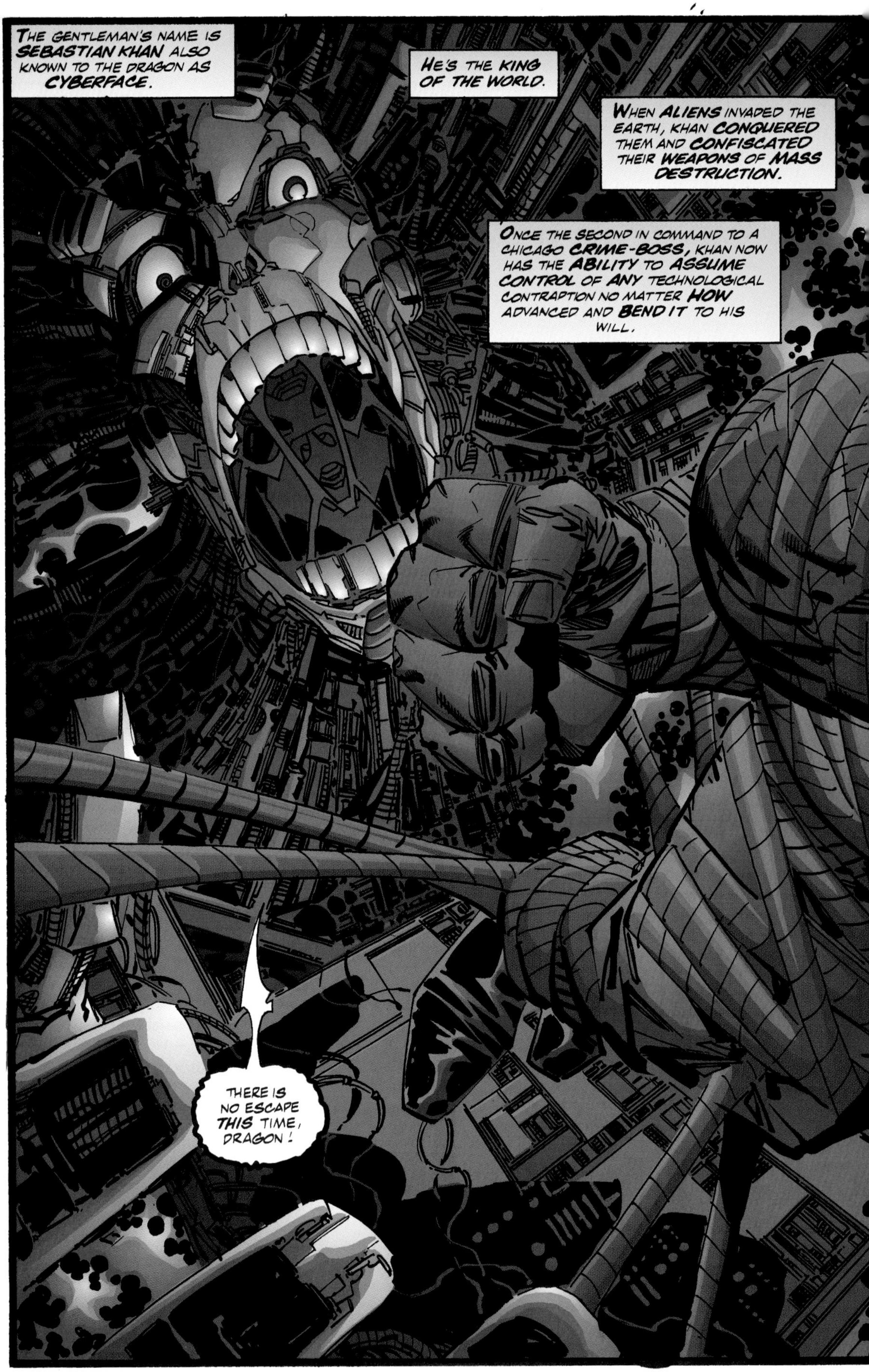
THE GENTLEMAN'S NAME IS SEBASTIAN KHAN ALSO KNOWN TO THE DRAGON AS CYBERFACE.
HE'S THE KING OF THE WORLD.
WHEN ALIENS INVADED THE EARTH, KHAN CONQUERED THEM AND CONFISCATED THEIR WEAPONS OF MASS DESTRUCTION.
ONCE THE SECOND IN COMMAND TO A CHICAGO CRIME-BOSS, KHAN NOW HAS THE ABILITY TO ASSUME CONTROL OF ANY TECHNOLOGICAL CONTRAPTION NO MATTER HOW ADVANCED AND BEND IT TO HIS WILL.
THERE IS NO ESCAPE THIS TIME, DRAGON!

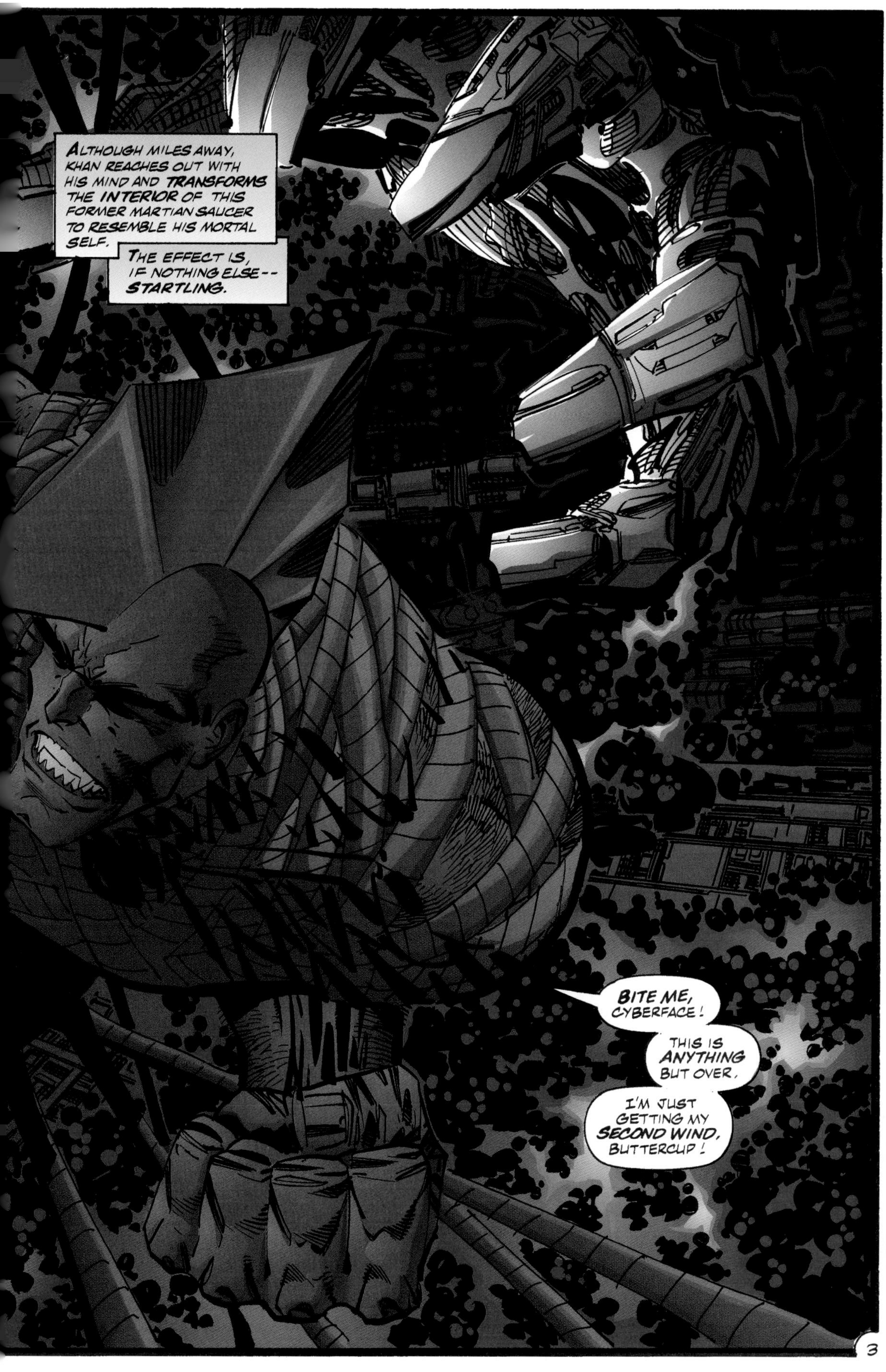
ALTHOUGH MILES AWAY, KHAN REACHES OUT WITH HIS MIND AND TRANSFORMS THE INTERIOR OF THIS FORMER MARTIAN SAUCER TO RESEMBLE HIS MORTAL SELF.
THE EFFECT IS, IF NOTHING ELSE-- STARTLING.
BITE ME, CYBERFACE!
THIS IS ANYTHING BUT OVER.
I'M JUST GETTING MY SECOND WIND, BUTTERCUP!

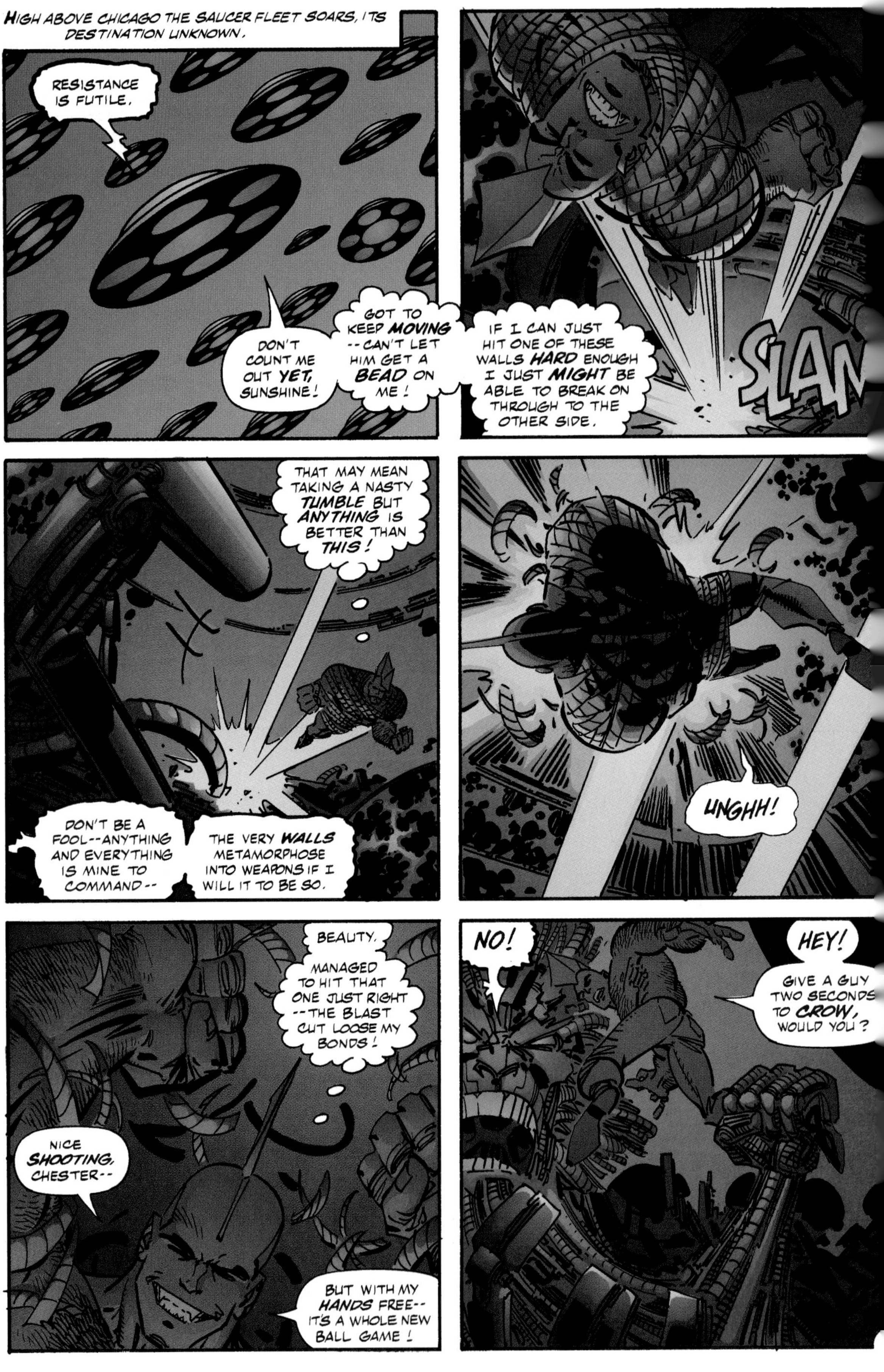
HIGH ABOVE CHICAGO THE SAUCER FLEET SOARS, ITS DESTINATION UNKNOWN.
RESISTANCE IS FUTILE.
DON'T COUNT ME OUT YET, SUNSHINE!
GOT TO KEEP MOVING --CAN'T LET HIM GET A BEAD ON ME!
IF I CAN JUST HIT ONE OF THESE WALLS HARD ENOUGH I JUST MIGHT BE ABLE TO BREAK ON THROUGH TO THE OTHER SIDE.
SLAM
THAT MAY MEAN TAKING A NASTY TUMBLE BUT ANYTHING IS BETTER THAN THIS!
DON'T BE A FOOL--ANYTHING AND EVERYTHING IS MINE TO COMMAND--
THE VERY WALLS METAMORPHOSE INTO WEAPONS IF I WILL IT TO BE SO.
UNGHH!
BEAUTY.
MANAGED TO HIT THAT ONE JUST RIGHT --THE BLAST CUT LOOSE MY BONDS!
NICE SHOOTING, CHESTER--
BUT WITH MY HANDS FREE-- IT'S A WHOLE NEW BALL GAME!
NO!
HEY!
GIVE A GUY TWO SECONDS TO CROW, WOULD YOU?

SKRA-KROOM!

TZAKKA!

ALRIGHT-- *BE* THAT WAY!

ONE CHANCE--

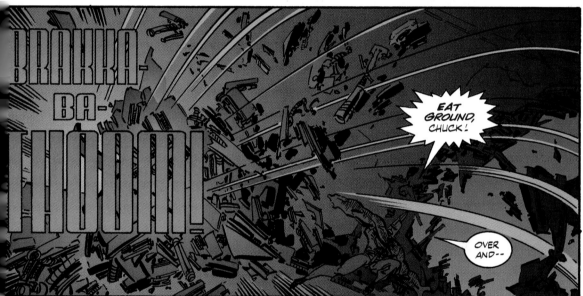

BRAKKA-BA-FHOOM!

EAT GROUND, CHUCK!

OVER AND--

--OUT! YIKES!

I'M PRETTY HIGH UP!

THAT LOOKS LIKE *LAKE MICHIGAN* DOWN THERE--OR ITS EVIL TWIN!

IF I CAN PUSH OFF FROM THIS LOWEST SAUCER JUST RIGHT I *MAY* BE ABLE TO HIT THE WATER WITHOUT GETTING *SPLATTERED* IN THE PROCESS.

5

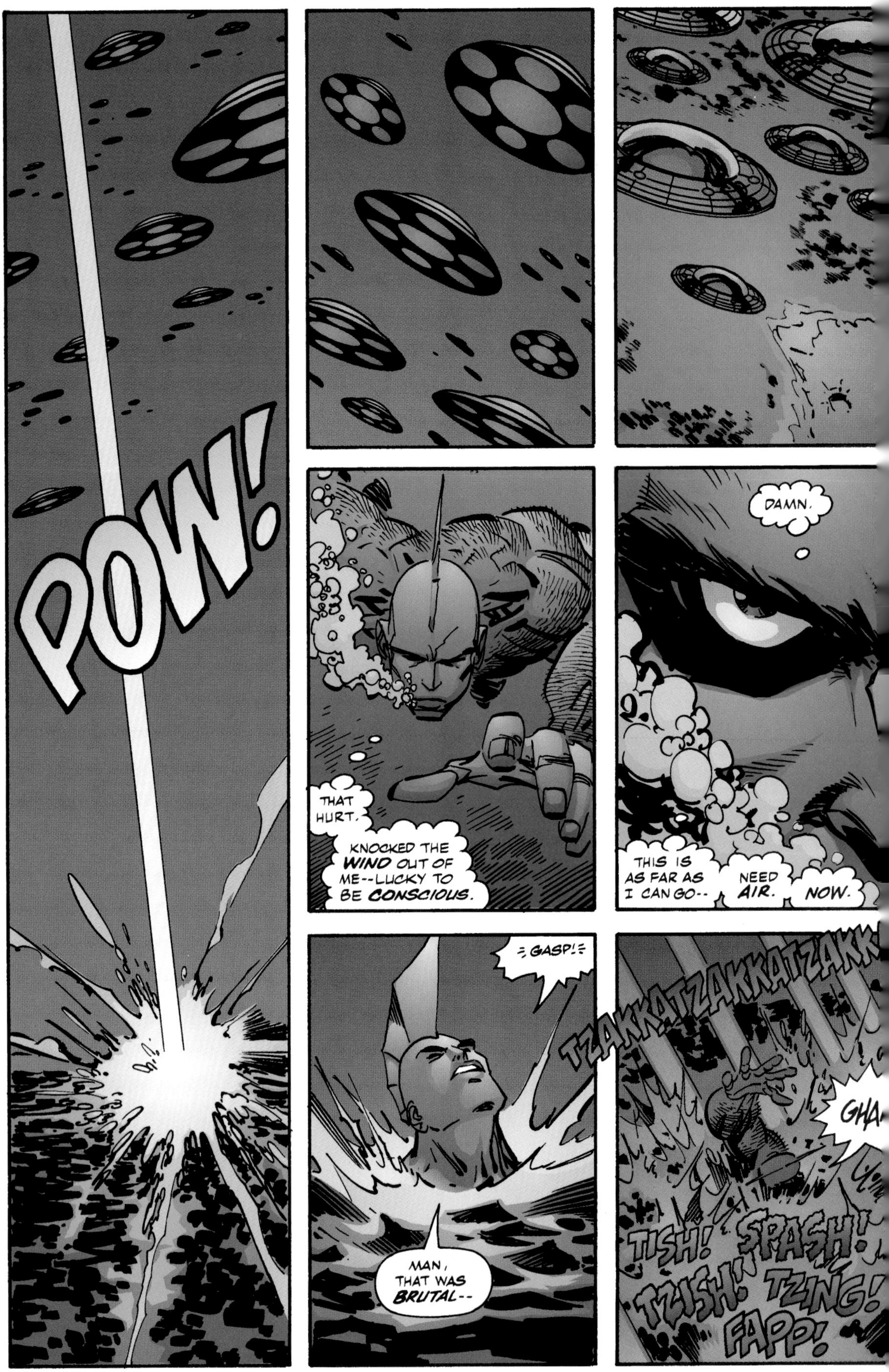
POW!
THAT HURT.
KNOCKED THE WIND OUT OF ME--LUCKY TO BE CONSCIOUS.
DAMN.
THIS IS AS FAR AS I CAN GO--
NEED AIR.
NOW.
GASP!
MAN, THAT WAS BRUTAL--
TZAKKATZAKKATZAKK
TISH! SPASH! TZISH! TZING! FAPP!

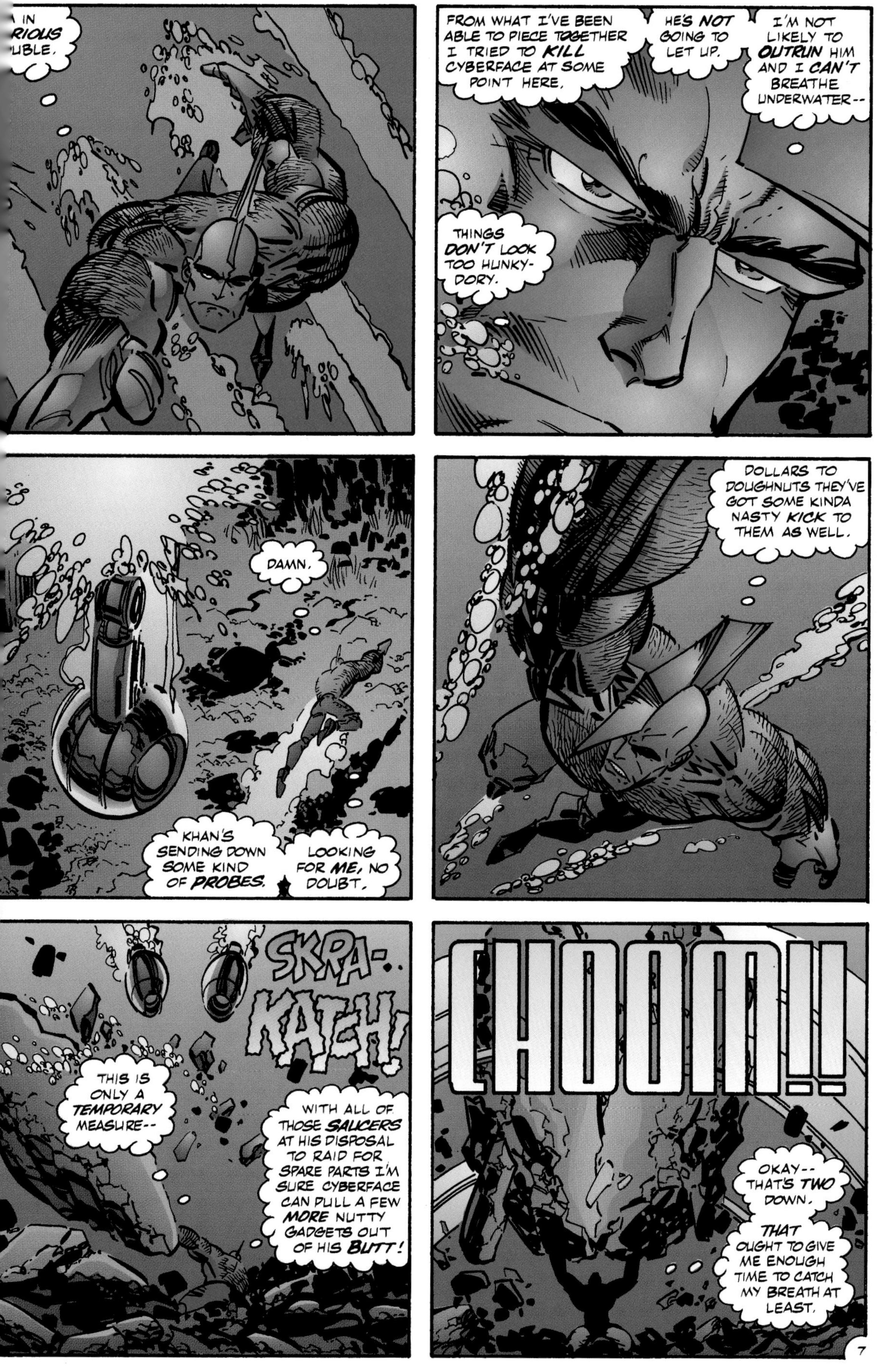

IN
RIOUS
UBLE.
FROM WHAT I'VE BEEN ABLE TO PIECE TOGETHER I TRIED TO KILL CYBERFACE AT SOME POINT HERE.
HE'S NOT GOING TO LET UP.
I'M NOT LIKELY TO OUTRUN HIM AND I CAN'T BREATHE UNDERWATER--
THINGS DON'T LOOK TOO HUNKY-DORY.
DAMN.
KHAN'S SENDING DOWN SOME KIND OF PROBES.
LOOKING FOR ME, NO DOUBT.
DOLLARS TO DOUGHNUTS THEY'VE GOT SOME KINDA NASTY KICK TO THEM AS WELL.
SKRA-KATCH!
THIS IS ONLY A TEMPORARY MEASURE--
WITH ALL OF THOSE SAUCERS AT HIS DISPOSAL TO RAID FOR SPARE PARTS I'M SURE CYBERFACE CAN PULL A FEW MORE NUTTY GADGETS OUT OF HIS BUTT!
CHOOM!!
OKAY-- THAT'S TWO DOWN.
THAT OUGHT TO GIVE ME ENOUGH TIME TO CATCH MY BREATH AT LEAST.

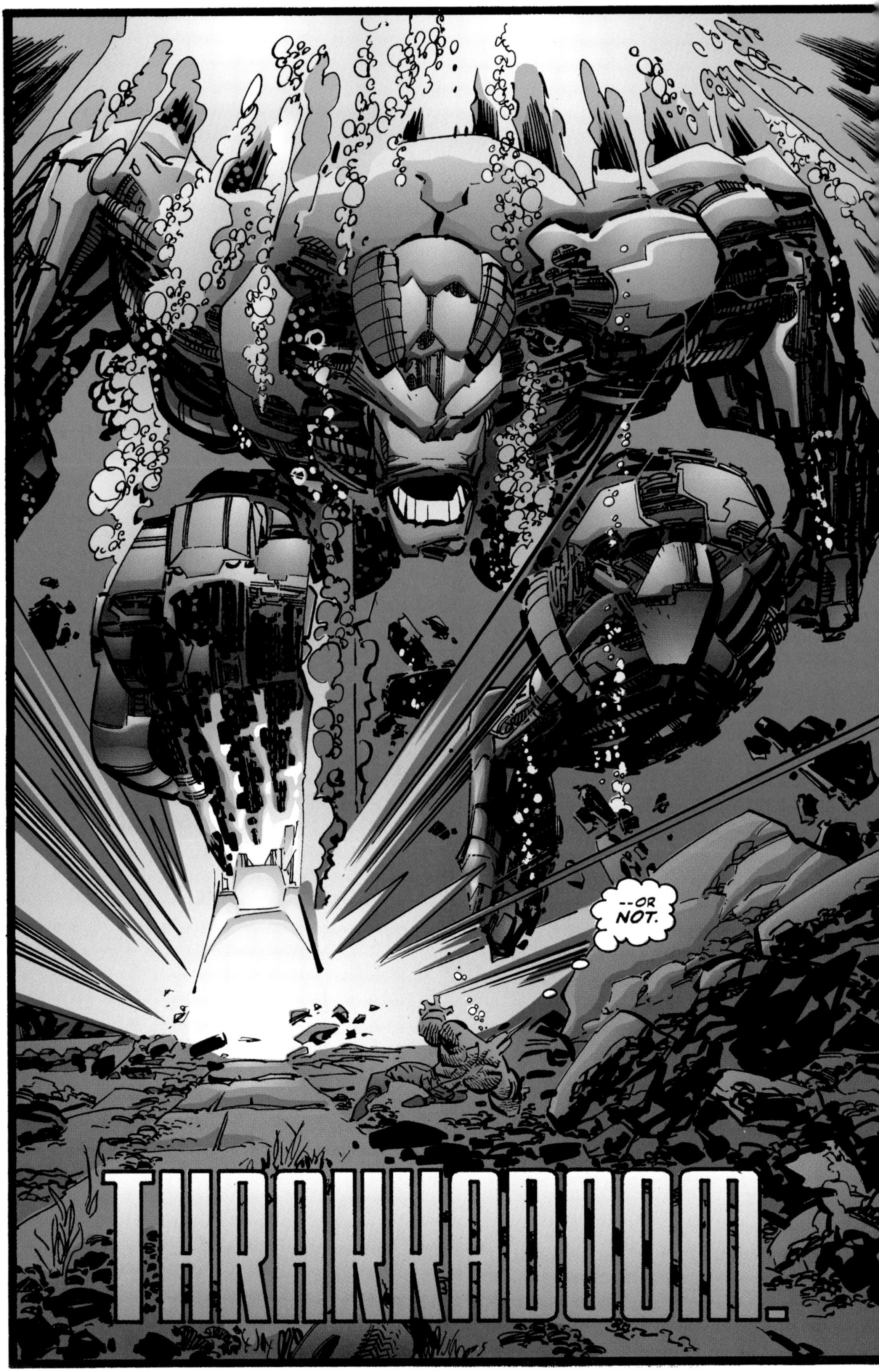
--OR NOT.
THRAKKADOOOM.

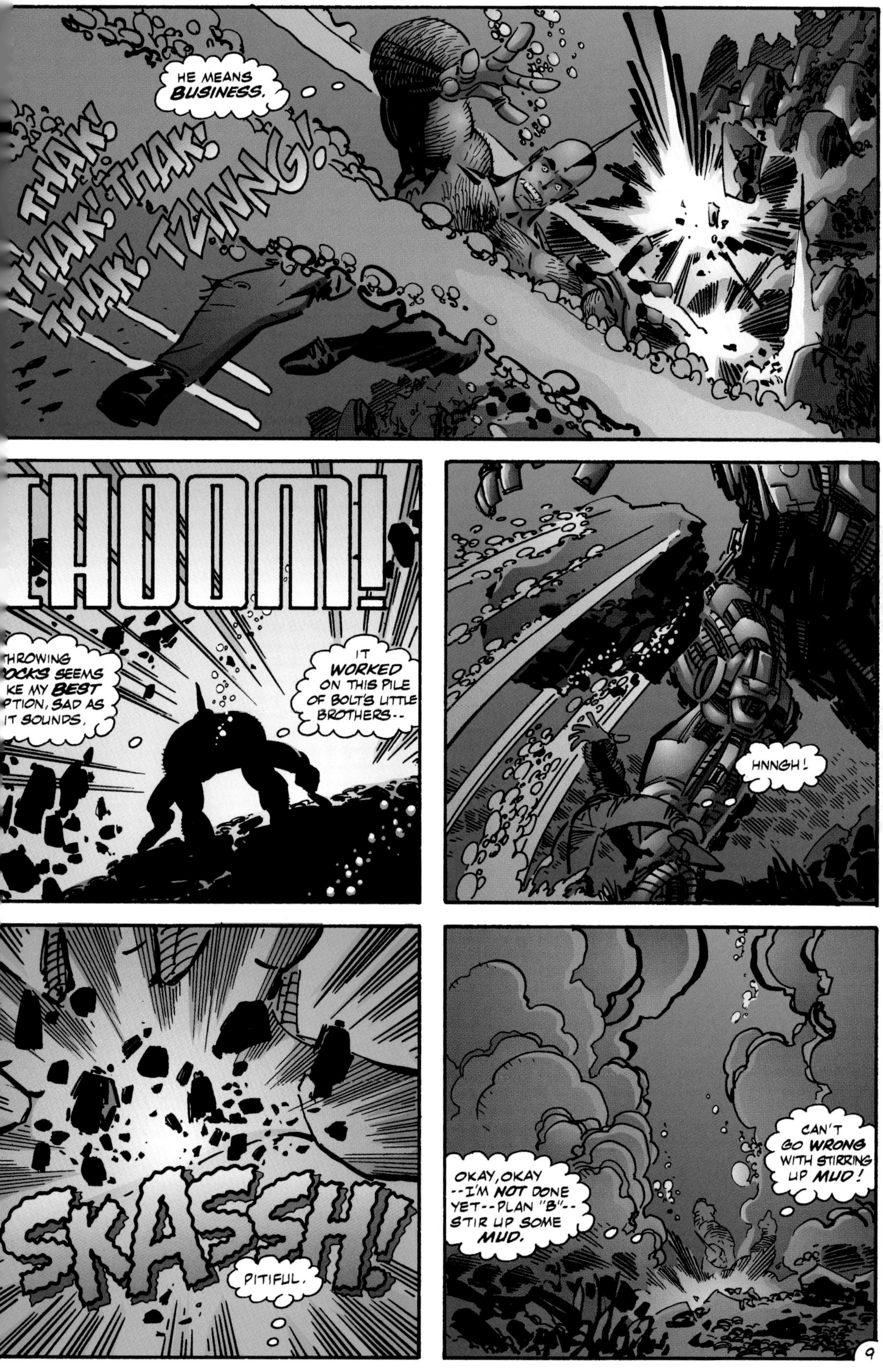
HE MEANS BUSINESS.
THAK! THAK! THAK! THAK! TZINNG!
THOOM!
THROWING ROCKS SEEMS LIKE MY BEST OPTION, SAD AS IT SOUNDS.
IT WORKED ON THIS PILE OF BOLT'S LITTLE BROTHERS--
HNNGH!
SKASSH!
PITIFUL.
OKAY, OKAY --I'M NOT DONE YET--PLAN "B"-- STIR UP SOME MUD.
CAN'T GO WRONG WITH STIRRING UP MUD!

THAT'LL **HAVE** TO DO-- I NEED TO **SUCK** IN ANOTHER THROAT LOAD OF **AIR** BEFORE I PASS OUT.

THERE OUGHT TO BE ENOUGH **CRAP** IN THE WATER TO **CONFUSE** THAT POOR SUCKER'S **SENSORS**--

BUY ME A FEW **SECONDS** IN ORDER TO...

GHAA!

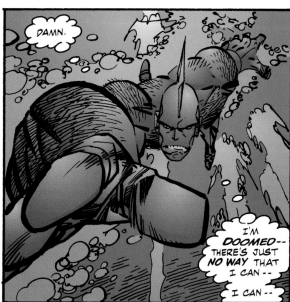

DAMN.

I'M **DOOMED**-- THERE'S JUST **NO WAY** THAT I CAN -- I CAN --

WAIT A MINUTE-- **WAIT** A MINUTE --

I **KNOW** WHERE I AM -- AN OLD **MARTIAN SAUCER** WAS FOUND BURIED SOMEWHERE AROUND HERE BACK IN MY REALITY.

ZAXSSH!
ZAXSSH!

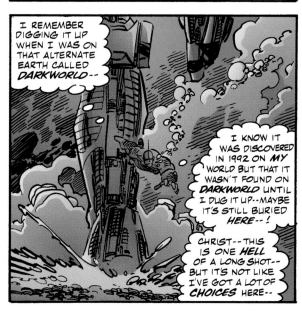

I REMEMBER DIGGING IT UP WHEN I WAS ON THAT ALTERNATE EARTH CALLED **DARKWORLD**--

I KNOW IT WAS DISCOVERED IN 1992 ON **MY** WORLD BUT THAT IT WASN'T FOUND ON **DARKWORLD** UNTIL I DUG IT UP--MAYBE IT'S STILL BURIED **HERE**--!

CHRIST-- THIS IS ONE **HELL** OF A LONG SHOT-- BUT IT'S NOT LIKE I'VE GOT A LOT OF **CHOICES** HERE--

THIS IS I

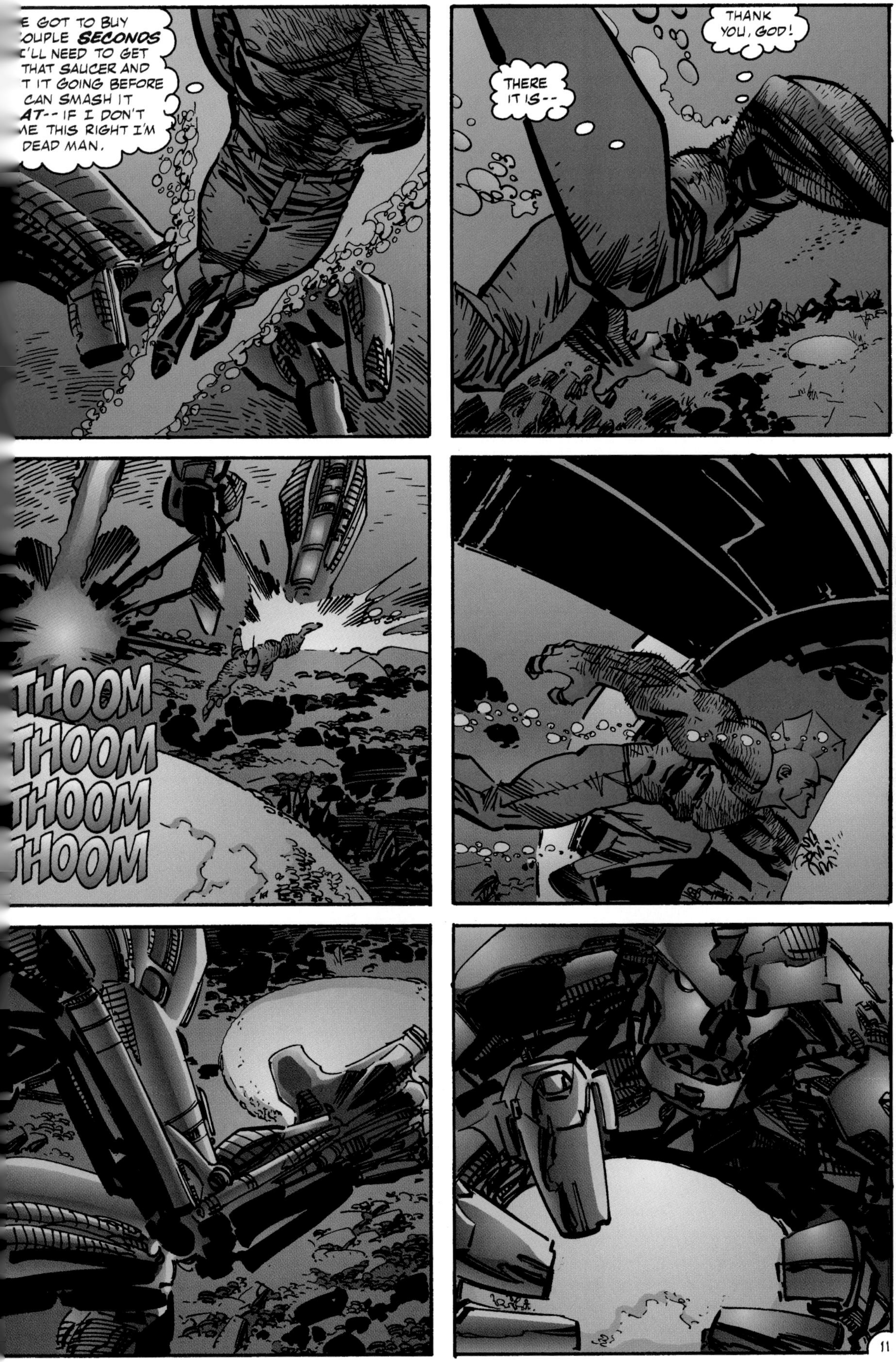
E GOT TO BUY
OUPLE SECONDS
'LL NEED TO GET
THAT SAUCER AND
T IT GOING BEFORE
CAN SMASH IT
AT-- IF I DON'T
ME THIS RIGHT I'M
DEAD MAN.
THERE IT IS--
THANK YOU, GOD!
THOOM
THOOM
THOOM
THOOM

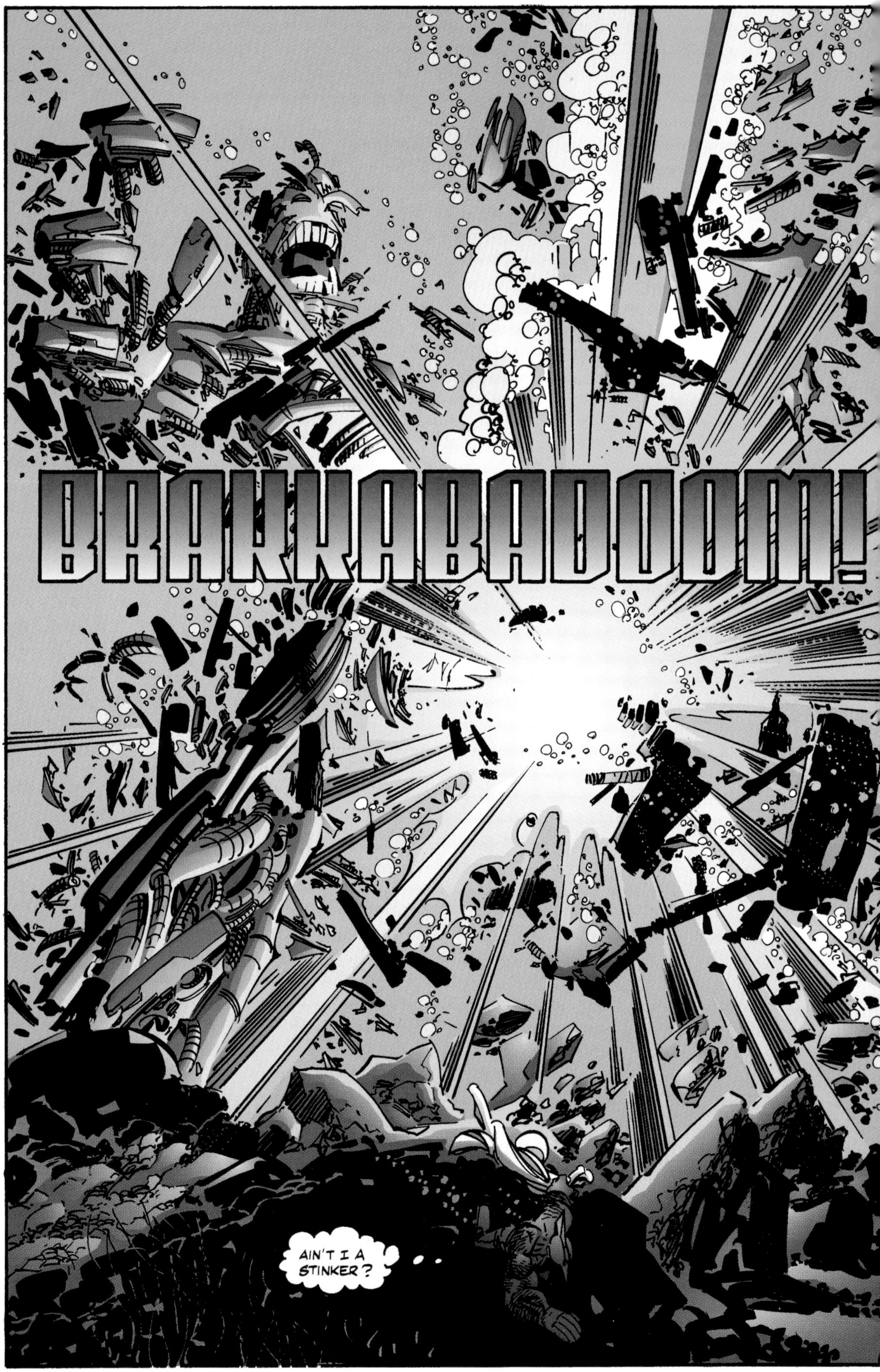
BRAKKABADOOM!
AIN'T I A STINKER?

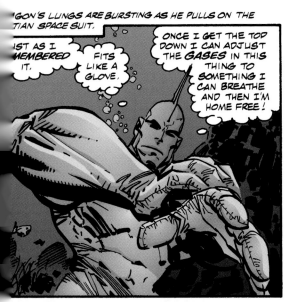

...GON'S LUNGS ARE BURSTING AS HE PULLS ON THE
...TIAN SPACE SUIT.

...ST AS I
...MEMBERED
IT.

FITS
LIKE A
GLOVE.

ONCE I GET THE TOP
DOWN I CAN ADJUST
THE *GASES* IN THIS
THING TO
SOMETHING I
CAN BREATHE
AND THEN I'M
HOME FREE!

AND
DONE.

...'D BETTER
...AKE WAVES--
...T SOME *DISTANCE*
...TWEEN CYBERFACE
AND ME.

HE'LL PULL THAT
SCRAP HEAP INTO
A WORKABLE *ROBOT*
IN JIG TIME.

I OUGHT TO BE ABLE
TO PADDLE MY WAY UP
TO CANADA IN A FEW
HOURS -- I DOUBT
THOSE SAUCERS CAN
COVER THE WHOLE
LAKE!

--AND SINCE CYBERFACE
DOESN'T *KNOW* THAT I
SCRAMBLED OUT AND *UNDER*
THAT SHIP AND GRABBED
MYSELF A SPACE SUIT ON
THE WAY HE'S LIKELY TO
BE SEARCHING THE *WRECKAGE*
FOR PIECES OF ME WHILE
I MAKE MY ESCAPE.

I'D SURE LIKE TO
HEAD BACK TO
CHICAGO BUT IT'S
TOO DAMNED *RISKY*
--HE'D EXPECT ME
TO HEAD THERE.

I CAN
ALWAYS COME
BACK *LATER*
WHEN THE
COAST IS...

...CLEAR...

13

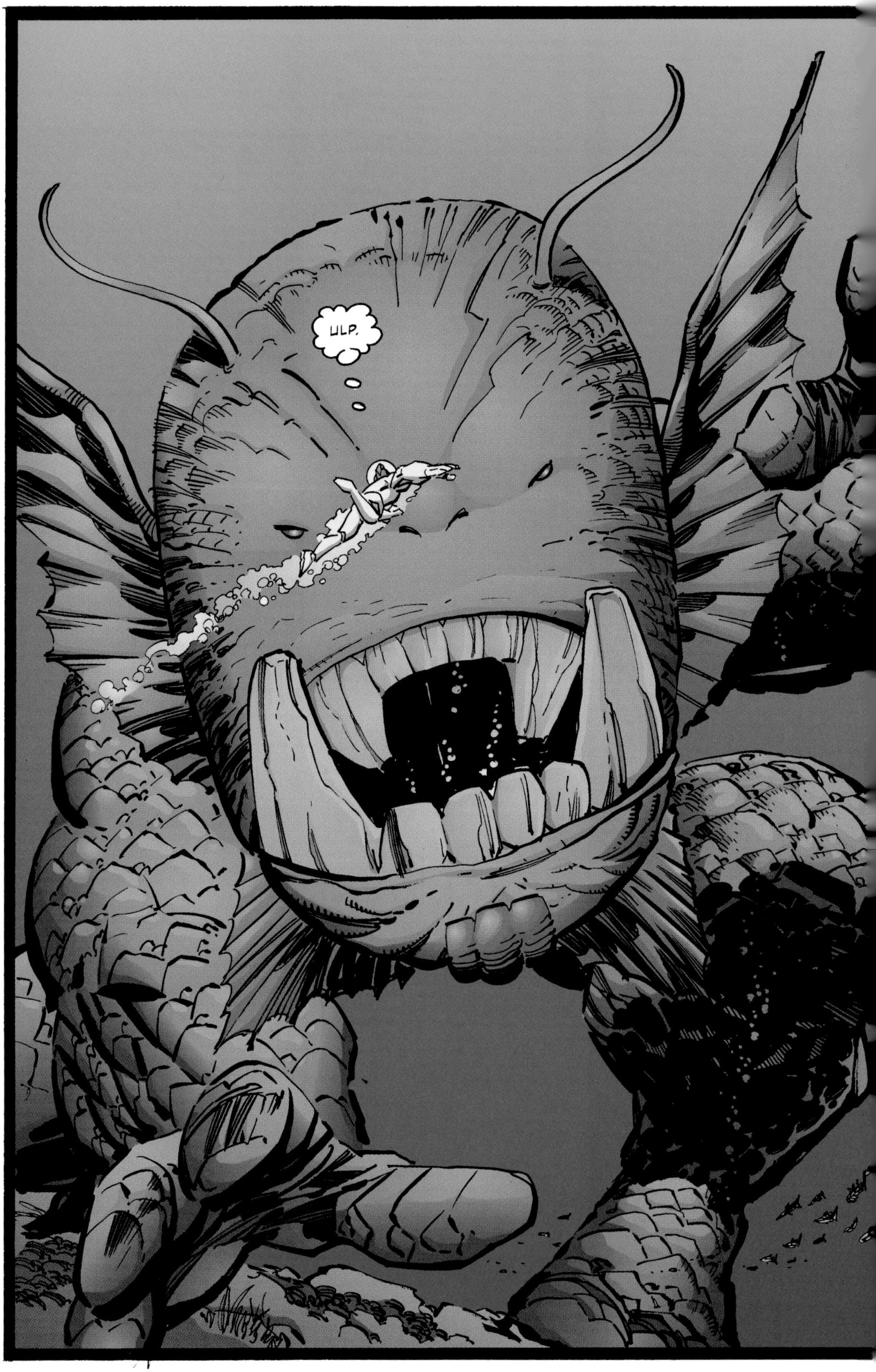
ULP.

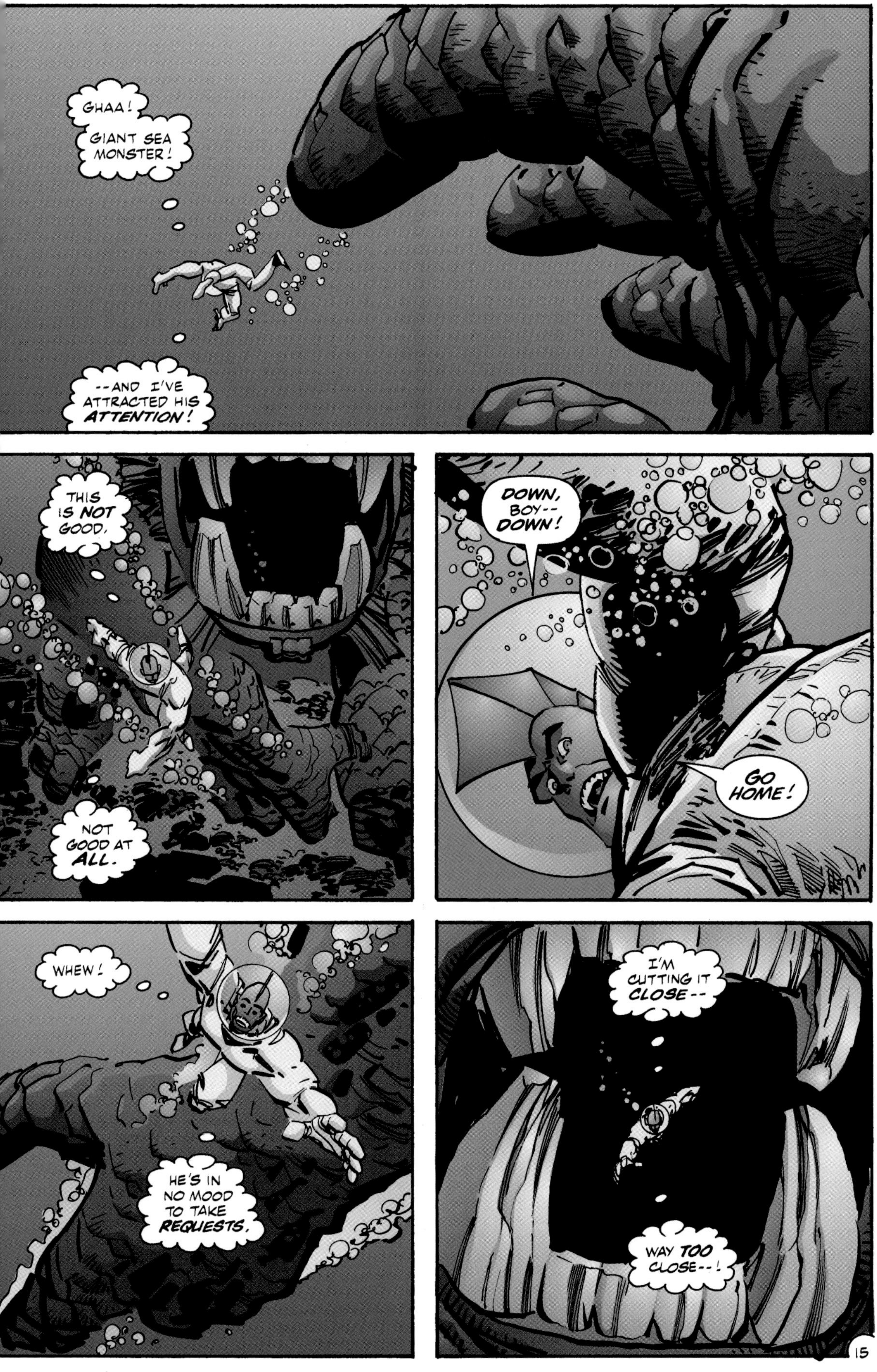
GHAA!
GIANT SEA MONSTER!
--AND I'VE ATTRACTED HIS ATTENTION!
THIS IS NOT GOOD.
NOT GOOD AT ALL.
DOWN, BOY--DOWN!
GO HOME!
WHEW!
HE'S IN NO MOOD TO TAKE REQUESTS.
I'M CUTTING IT CLOSE--
WAY TOO CLOSE--!

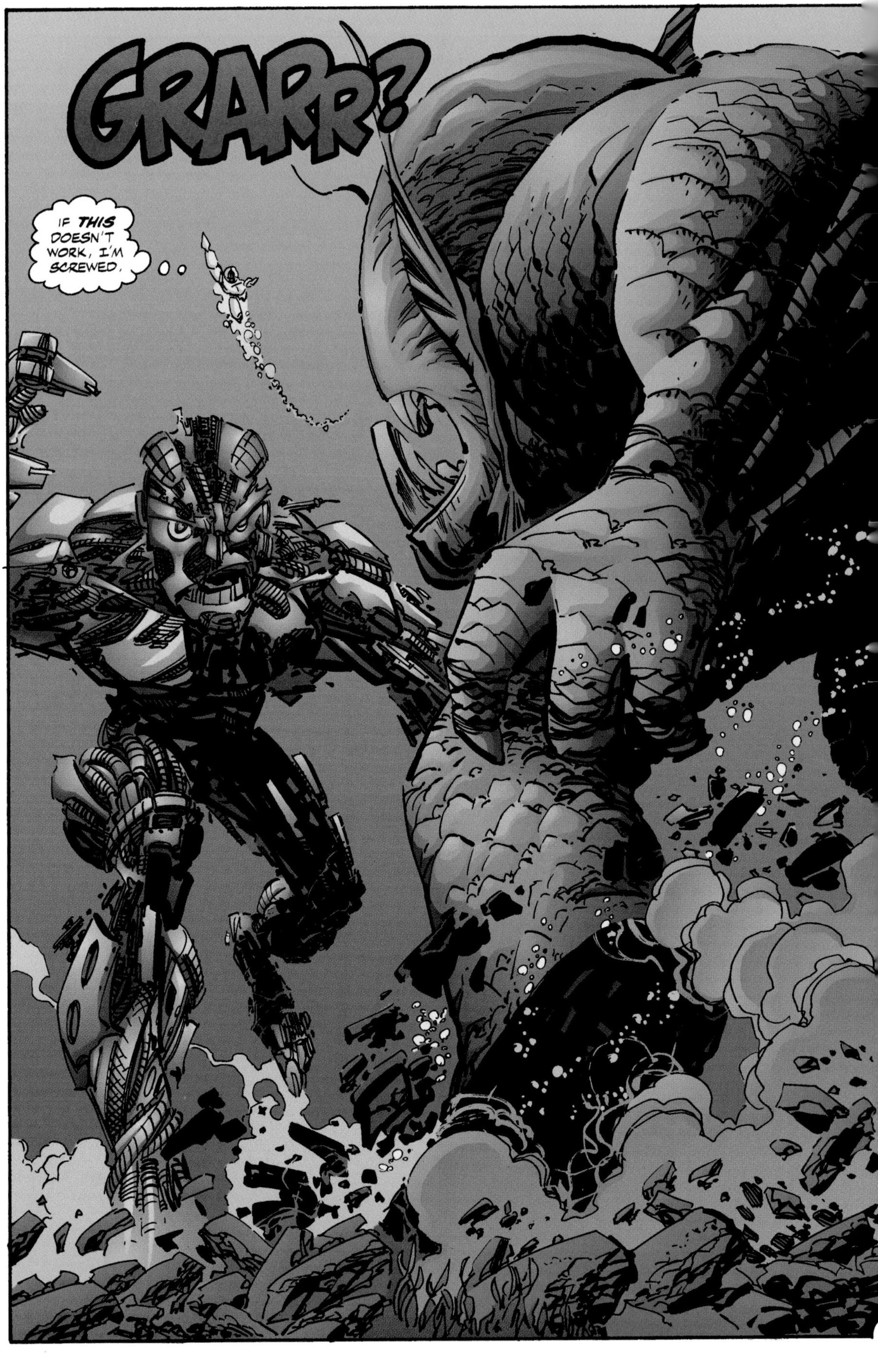
GRARR?
IF THIS DOESN'T WORK, I'M SCREWED.

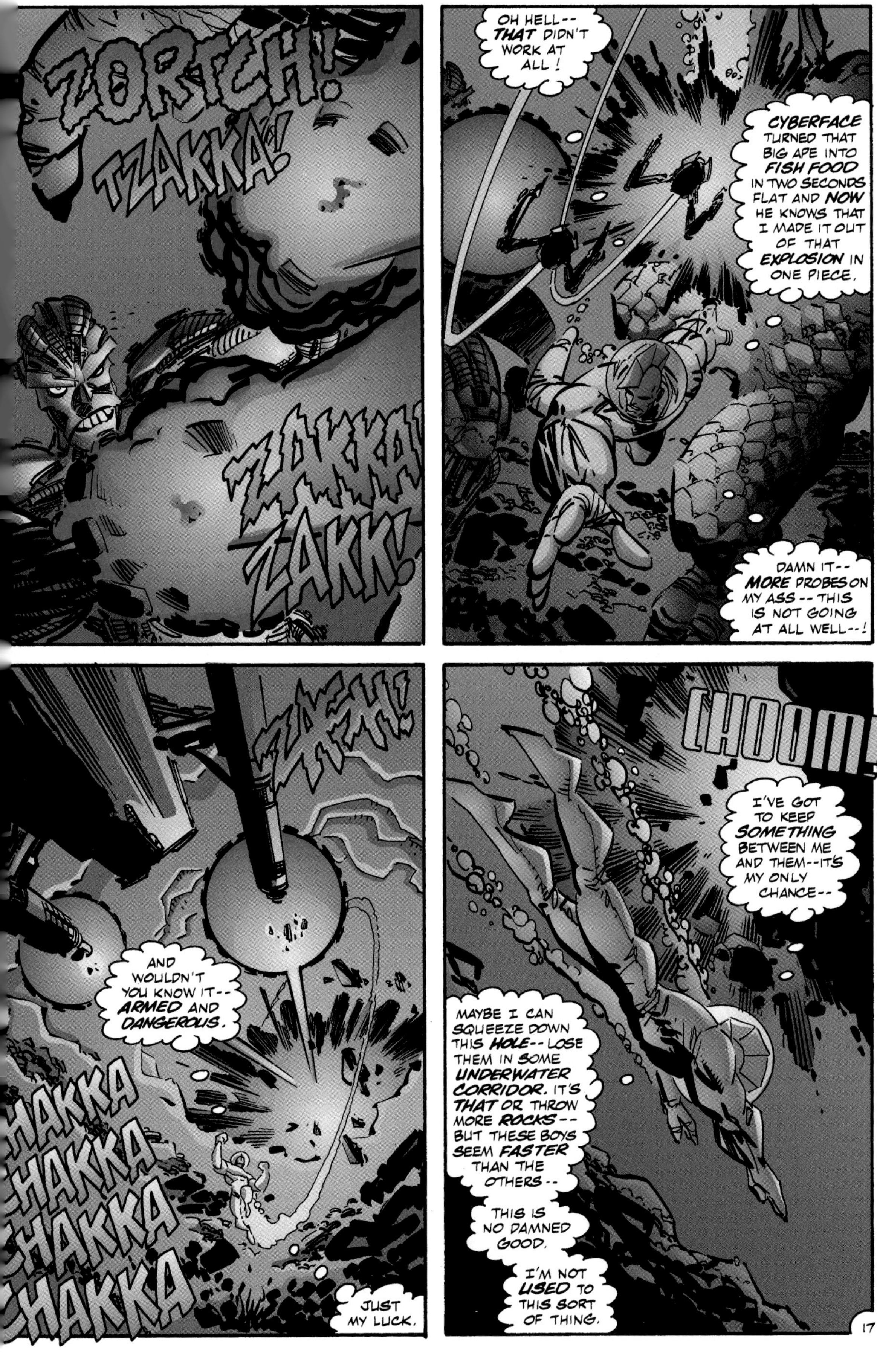
ZORTCH!
TZAKKA!
ZAKKA!
ZAKK!
OH HELL-- THAT DIDN'T WORK AT ALL!
CYBERFACE TURNED THAT BIG APE INTO FISH FOOD IN TWO SECONDS FLAT AND NOW HE KNOWS THAT I MADE IT OUT OF THAT EXPLOSION IN ONE PIECE.
DAMN IT-- MORE PROBES ON MY ASS -- THIS IS NOT GOING AT ALL WELL--!
ZAKKA!
AND WOULDN'T YOU KNOW IT-- ARMED AND DANGEROUS.
CHAKKA CHAKKA CHAKKA CHAKKA
JUST MY LUCK.
CHOOM!
I'VE GOT TO KEEP SOMETHING BETWEEN ME AND THEM--IT'S MY ONLY CHANCE--
MAYBE I CAN SQUEEZE DOWN THIS HOLE-- LOSE THEM IN SOME UNDERWATER CORRIDOR. IT'S THAT OR THROW MORE ROCKS-- BUT THESE BOYS SEEM FASTER THAN THE OTHERS--
THIS IS NO DAMNED GOOD.
I'M NOT USED TO THIS SORT OF THING.

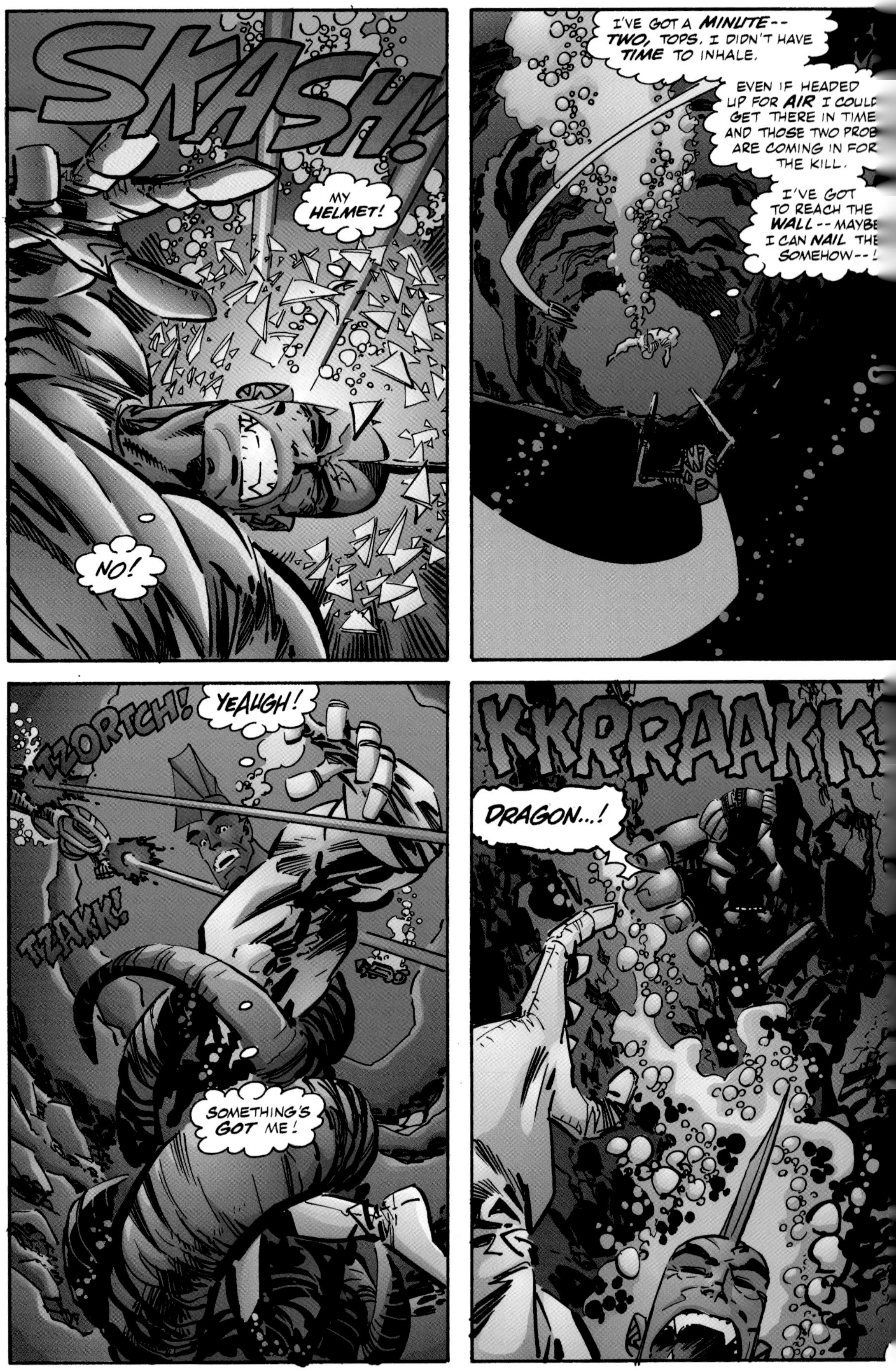
SKASH!
MY HELMET!
NO!
I'VE GOT A MINUTE-- TWO, TOPS, I DIDN'T HAVE TIME TO INHALE.
EVEN IF HEADED UP FOR AIR I COULD GET THERE IN TIME AND THOSE TWO PROB ARE COMING IN FOR THE KILL.
I'VE GOT TO REACH THE WALL -- MAYBE I CAN NAIL THE SOMEHOW-- !
TZORTCH!
YEAUGH!
TZAKK!
SOMETHING'S GOT ME!
KKRRAAKK!
DRAGON...!

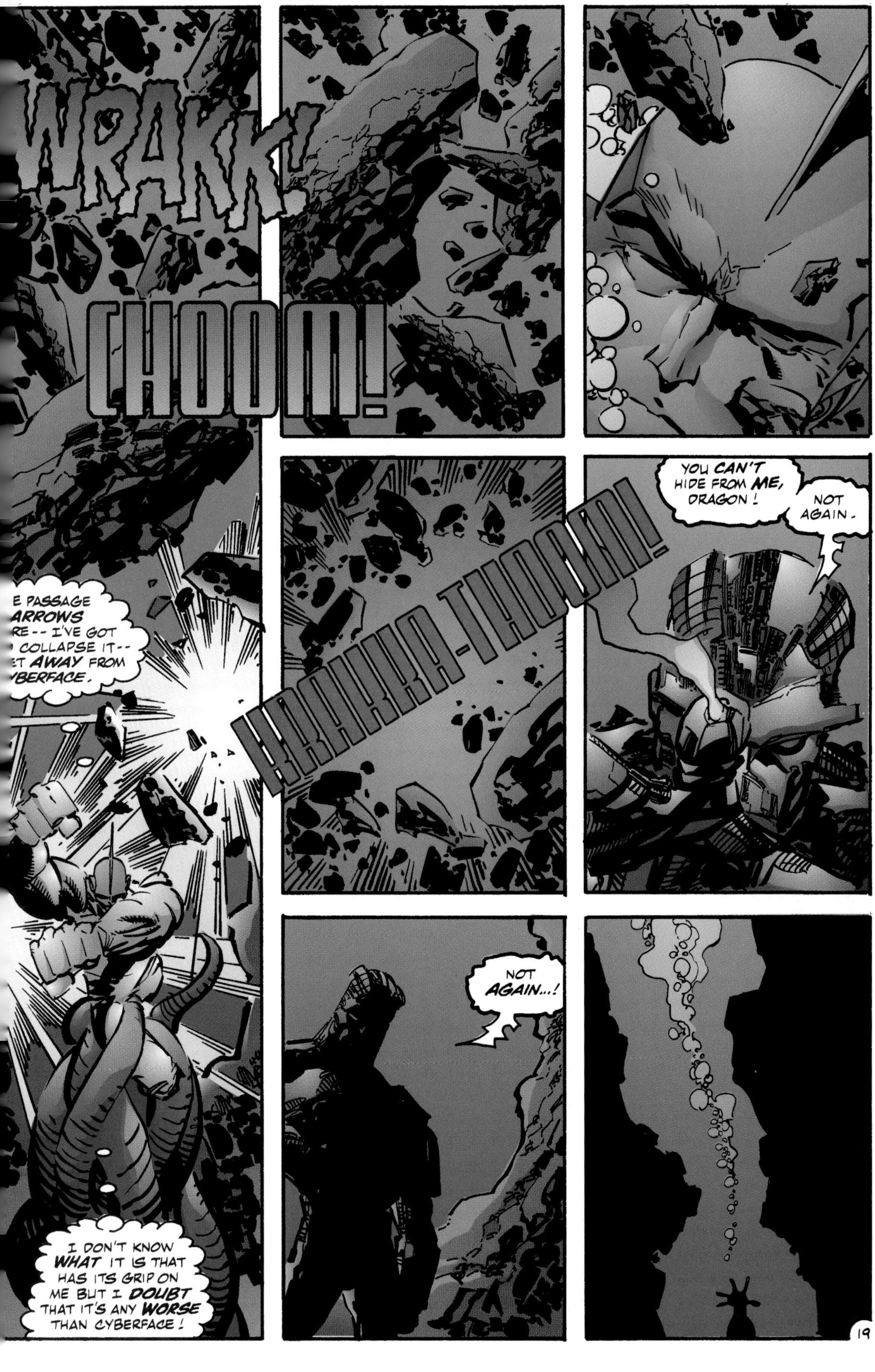
WRAKK!
CHOOM!
E PASSAGE ARROWS RE-- I'VE GOT COLLAPSE IT-- ET AWAY FROM YBERFACE.
I DON'T KNOW WHAT IT IS THAT HAS ITS GRIP ON ME BUT I DOUBT THAT IT'S ANY WORSE THAN CYBERFACE!
KRAKKA-THOOM!
YOU CAN'T HIDE FROM ME, DRAGON!
NOT AGAIN.
NOT AGAIN...!

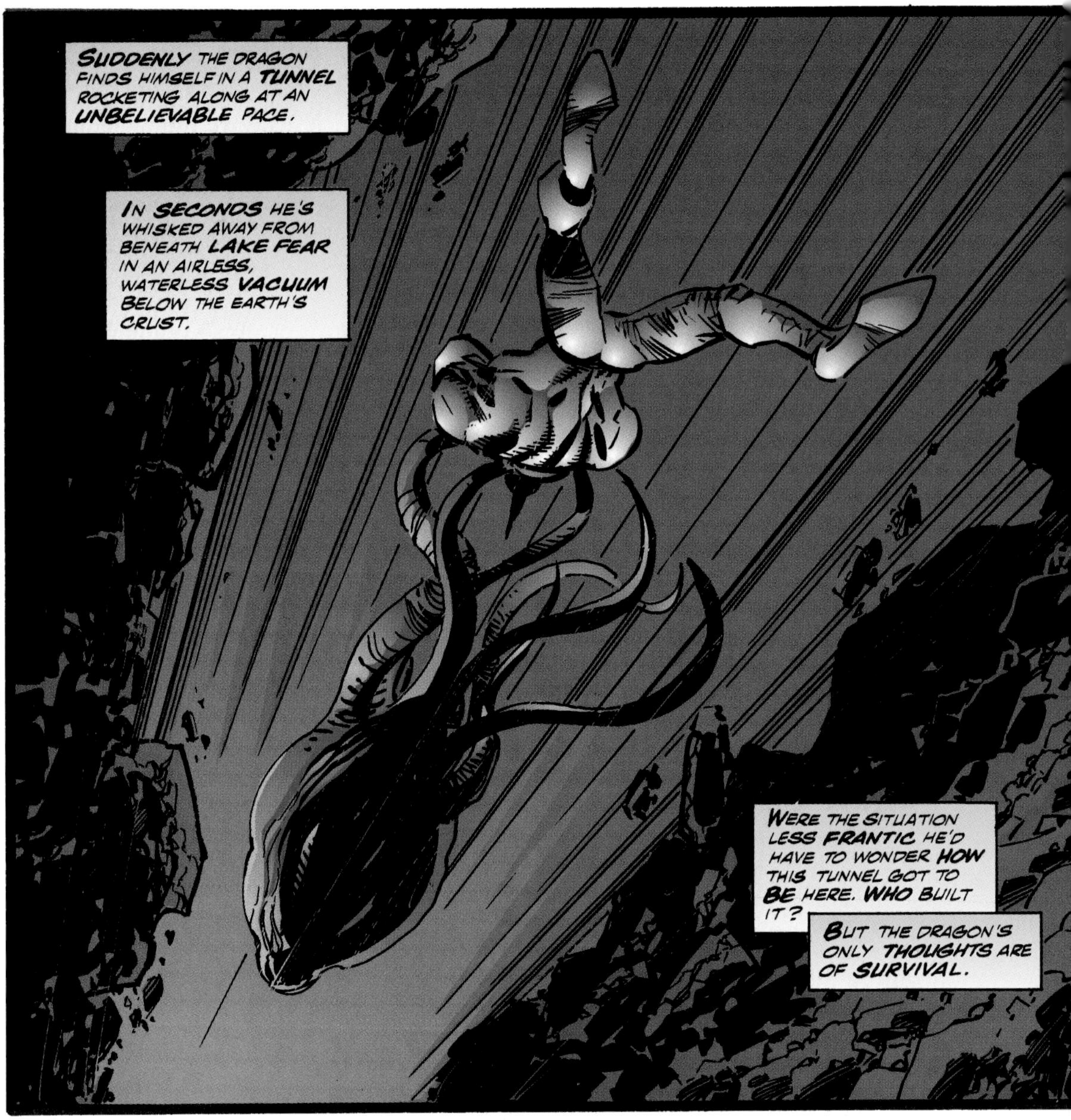
SUDDENLY THE DRAGON FINDS HIMSELF IN A TUNNEL ROCKETING ALONG AT AN UNBELIEVABLE PACE.
IN SECONDS HE'S WHISKED AWAY FROM BENEATH LAKE FEAR IN AN AIRLESS, WATERLESS VACUUM BELOW THE EARTH'S CRUST.
WERE THE SITUATION LESS FRANTIC HE'D HAVE TO WONDER HOW THIS TUNNEL GOT TO BE HERE. WHO BUILT IT?
BUT THE DRAGON'S ONLY THOUGHTS ARE OF SURVIVAL.

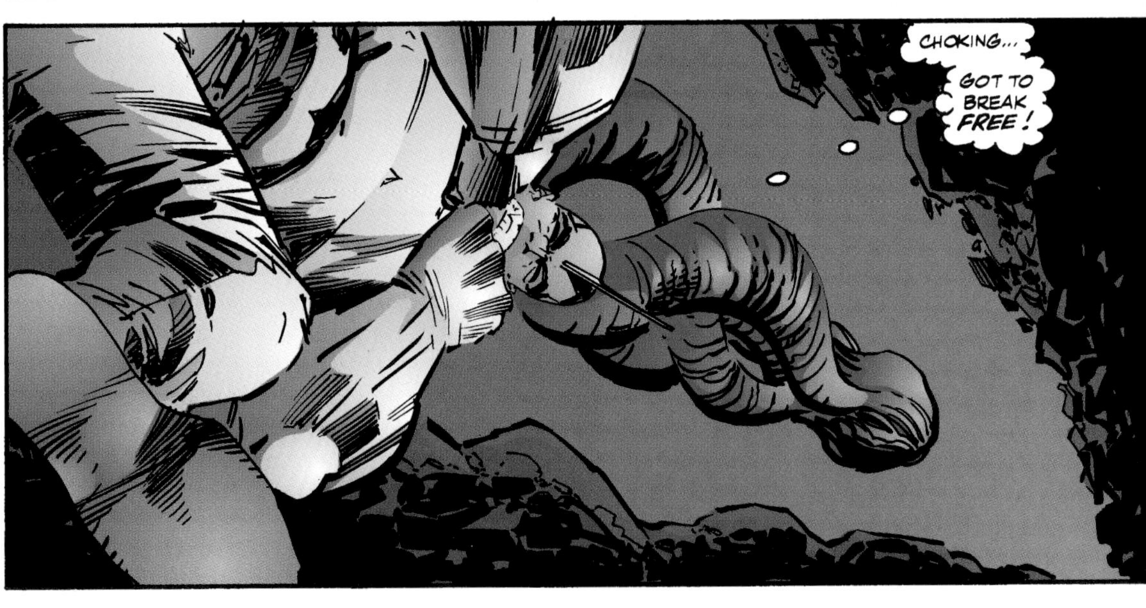
CHOKING...
GOT TO BREAK FREE!

FLAILING **KICK** LOOSENS A WALL OF ROCK.

BRAKKA-CHOOM!

A **WEAPON** PRESENTS ITSELF.

AND THE REPEATED **POUNDING** OF THE DESPERATE **STRANGER** PROVES, AT LAST, TOO GREAT AN **OBSTACLE** FOR THE BEAST TO CONTINUE TO **CLING** TO ITS INTENDED VICTIM.

WRAMM!

BLAM!

WROKK!

CHOOM!

WHEN THE TUNNEL'S **END** HAS BEEN REACHED AND **WATER** IS AGAIN AT HAND, THE BEAST SWIMS AWAY IN PURSUIT OF A LESS **FEISTY** MEAL.

21

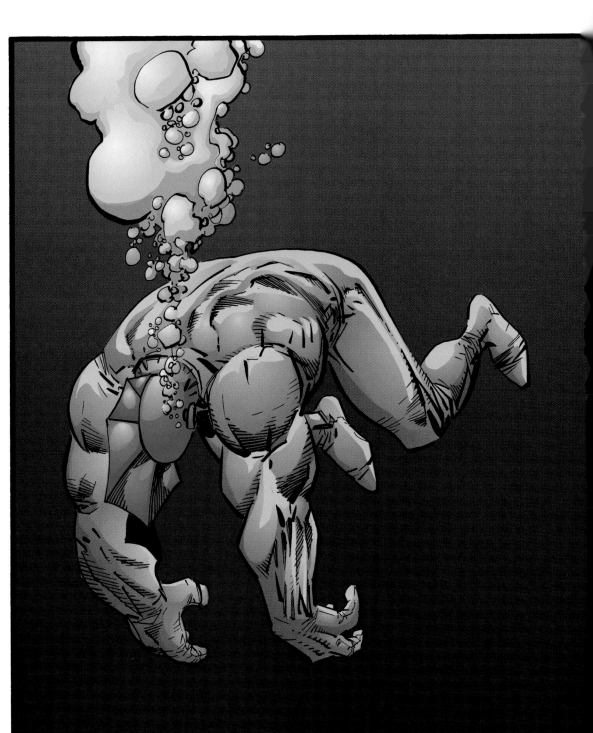

NEXT:
THE LAND
DOWN
UNDER!

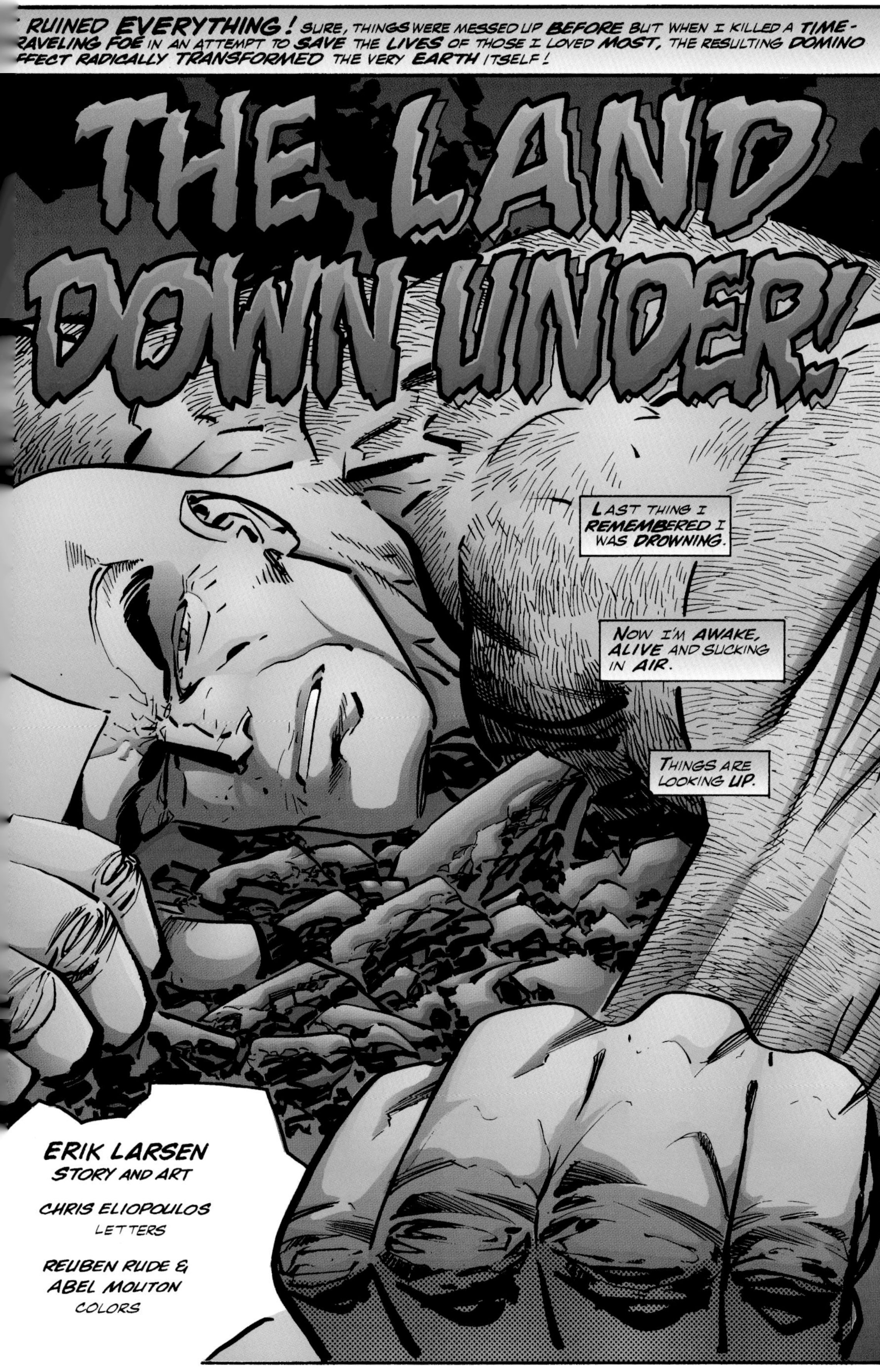

RUINED EVERYTHING! SURE, THINGS WERE MESSED UP BEFORE BUT WHEN I KILLED A TIME-RAVELING FOE IN AN ATTEMPT TO SAVE THE LIVES OF THOSE I LOVED MOST, THE RESULTING DOMINO FFECT RADICALLY TRANSFORMED THE VERY EARTH ITSELF!
THE LAND DOWN UNDER!
LAST THING I REMEMBERED I WAS DROWNING.
NOW I'M AWAKE, ALIVE AND SUCKING IN AIR.
THINGS ARE LOOKING UP.
ERIK LARSEN STORY AND ART
CHRIS ELIOPOULOS LETTERS
REUBEN RUDE & ABEL MOUTON COLORS

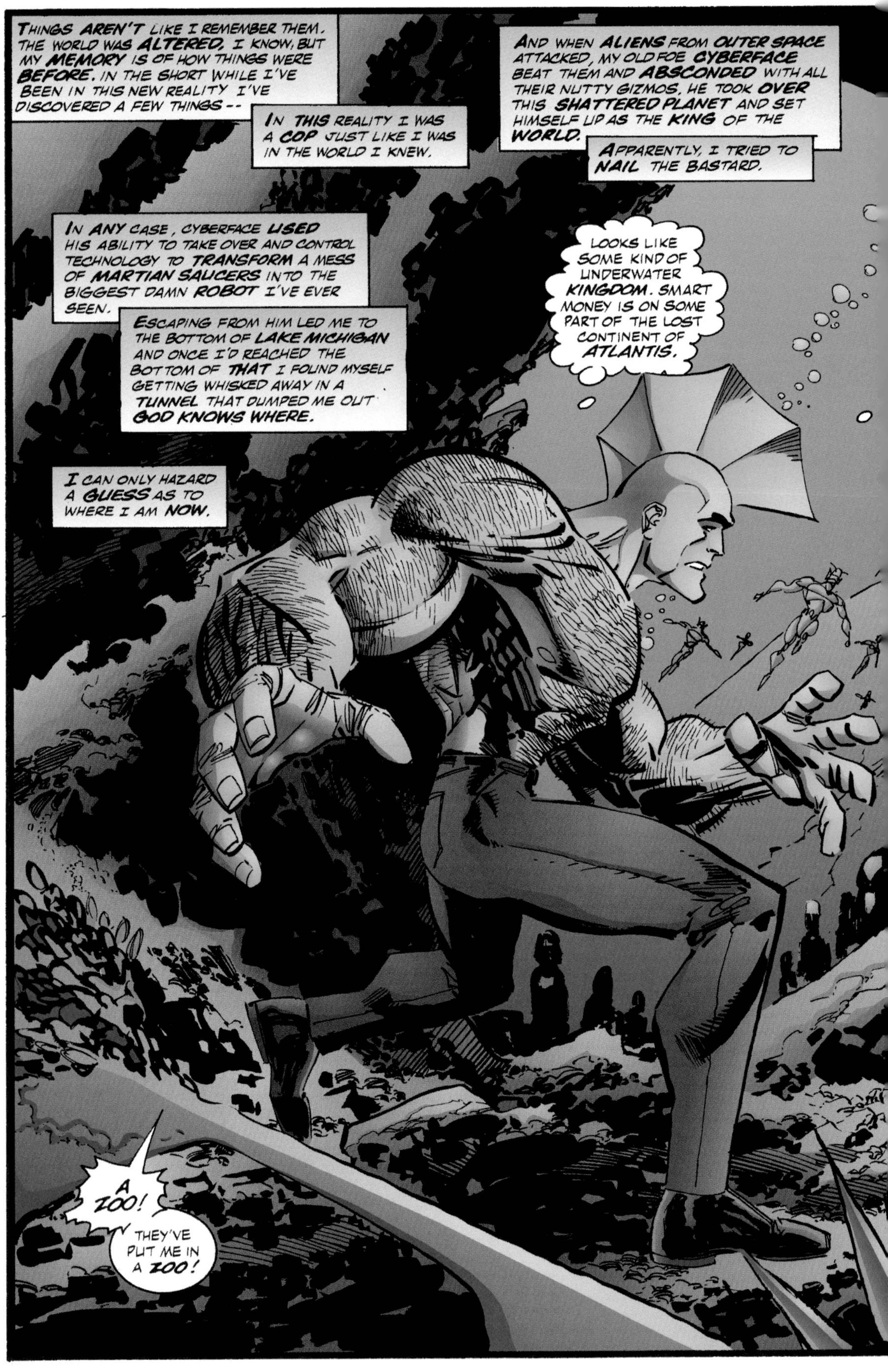
THINGS AREN'T LIKE I REMEMBER THEM. THE WORLD WAS ALTERED, I KNOW, BUT MY MEMORY IS OF HOW THINGS WERE BEFORE. IN THE SHORT WHILE I'VE BEEN IN THIS NEW REALITY I'VE DISCOVERED A FEW THINGS --
IN THIS REALITY I WAS A COP JUST LIKE I WAS IN THE WORLD I KNEW.
AND WHEN ALIENS FROM OUTER SPACE ATTACKED, MY OLD FOE CYBERFACE BEAT THEM AND ABSCONDED WITH ALL THEIR NUTTY GIZMOS. HE TOOK OVER THIS SHATTERED PLANET AND SET HIMSELF UP AS THE KING OF THE WORLD.
APPARENTLY, I TRIED TO NAIL THE BASTARD.
IN ANY CASE, CYBERFACE USED HIS ABILITY TO TAKE OVER AND CONTROL TECHNOLOGY TO TRANSFORM A MESS OF MARTIAN SAUCERS INTO THE BIGGEST DAMN ROBOT I'VE EVER SEEN.
ESCAPING FROM HIM LED ME TO THE BOTTOM OF LAKE MICHIGAN AND ONCE I'D REACHED THE BOTTOM OF THAT I FOUND MYSELF GETTING WHISKED AWAY IN A TUNNEL THAT DUMPED ME OUT GOD KNOWS WHERE.
LOOKS LIKE SOME KIND OF UNDERWATER KINGDOM. SMART MONEY IS ON SOME PART OF THE LOST CONTINENT OF ATLANTIS.
I CAN ONLY HAZARD A GUESS AS TO WHERE I AM NOW.
A ZOO!
THEY'VE PUT ME IN A ZOO!

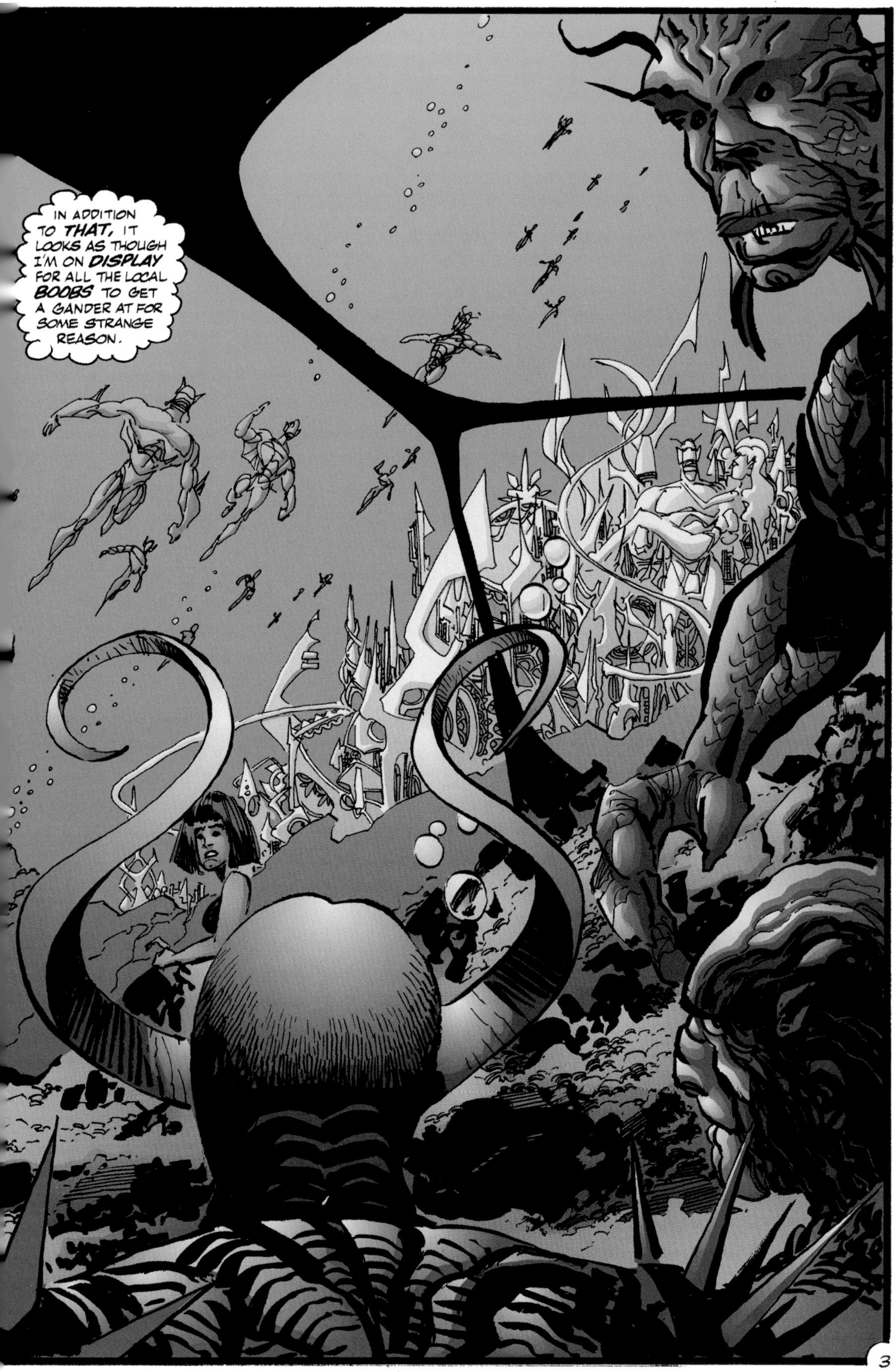
IN ADDITION TO THAT, IT LOOKS AS THOUGH I'M ON DISPLAY FOR ALL THE LOCAL BOOBS TO GET A GANDER AT FOR SOME STRANGE REASON.

THINGS COULD BE *WORSE.*

AT LEAST I'M STILL *ALIVE.*

I'LL ENTER *THAT* LITTLE NUGGET INTO THE "PLUS" COLUMN.

WHAT ARE *YOU* LOOKING AT?

YOU ARE *AWAKE.* YOU SPEAK *ENGLISH.*

GOOD, GOOD.

PLEASE-- SIT DOWN, RELAX.

WE MEAN YOU NO *HARM.*

THANKS FOR SAVING MY LIFE, I GUESS.

TELL ME -- WHAT *SPECIES* ARE YOU? *WHERE* DO YOU *COME* FROM?

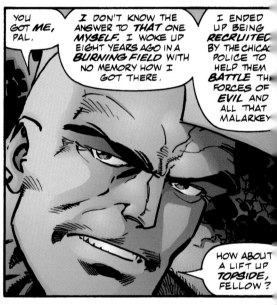

YOU GOT *ME,* PAL.

I DON'T KNOW THE ANSWER TO *THAT* ONE *MYSELF.* I WOKE UP EIGHT YEARS AGO IN A *BURNING FIELD* WITH NO MEMORY HOW I GOT THERE.

I ENDED UP BEING *RECRUITED* BY THE CHICAGO POLICE TO HELP THEM *BATTLE* THE FORCES OF *EVIL* AND ALL THAT MALARKEY.

HOW ABOUT A LIFT UP *TOPSIDE,* FELLOW?

I AM AFRAID THAT SUCH A THING IS *NOT* POSSIBLE. NOW THAT YOU HAVE BECOME *AWARE* OF US THERE CAN BE *NO* RETURNING FROM WHENCE YOU CAME.

OH, *COME* NOW.

YOU DON'T *EXPECT* ME TO JUST *SIT HERE* ON MY *FATASS* FOR THE REST OF MY LIFE, DO YOU?

YOU HAVE NO OTHER *CHOICE,* SURFACE-DWELLER, SAVE *DEATH.*

BEAUTIFUL.

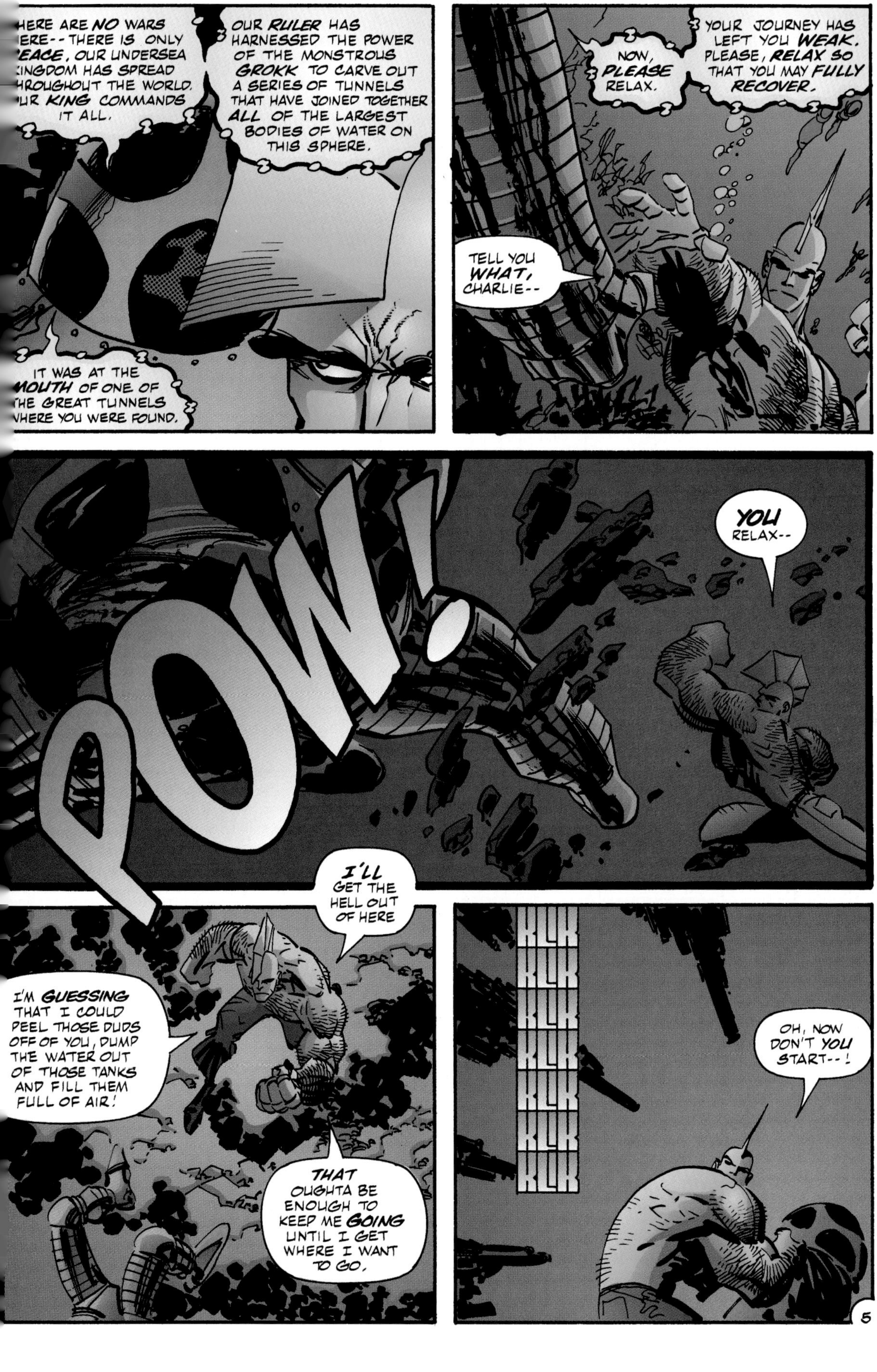

HERE ARE NO WARS ERE-- THERE IS ONLY PEACE. OUR UNDERSEA KINGDOM HAS SPREAD THROUGHOUT THE WORLD. OUR KING COMMANDS IT ALL.
OUR RULER HAS HARNESSED THE POWER OF THE MONSTROUS GROKK TO CARVE OUT A SERIES OF TUNNELS THAT HAVE JOINED TOGETHER ALL OF THE LARGEST BODIES OF WATER ON THIS SPHERE.
IT WAS AT THE MOUTH OF ONE OF THE GREAT TUNNELS WHERE YOU WERE FOUND.
NOW, PLEASE RELAX.
YOUR JOURNEY HAS LEFT YOU WEAK. PLEASE, RELAX SO THAT YOU MAY FULLY RECOVER.
TELL YOU WHAT, CHARLIE--
POW!
YOU RELAX--
I'LL GET THE HELL OUT OF HERE
I'M GUESSING THAT I COULD PEEL THOSE DUDS OFF OF YOU, DUMP THE WATER OUT OF THOSE TANKS AND FILL THEM FULL OF AIR!
THAT OUGHTA BE ENOUGH TO KEEP ME GOING UNTIL I GET WHERE I WANT TO GO.
KLIK KLIK KLIK KLIK KLIK KLIK KLIK
OH, NOW DON'T YOU START--!

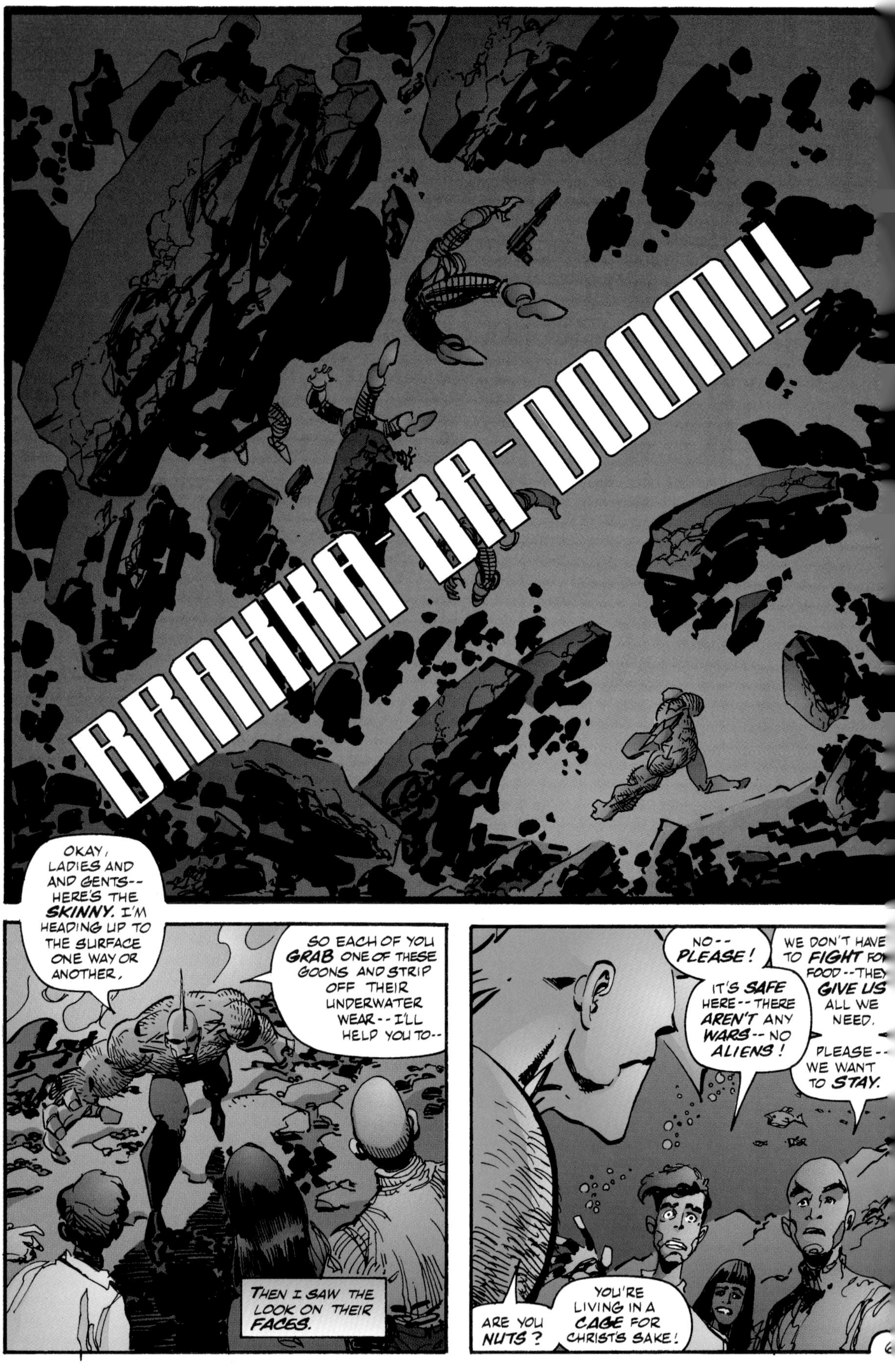
BRAKKA-BA-DOOM!!
OKAY, LADIES AND AND GENTS-- HERE'S THE SKINNY. I'M HEADING UP TO THE SURFACE ONE WAY OR ANOTHER,
SO EACH OF YOU GRAB ONE OF THESE GOONS AND STRIP OFF THEIR UNDERWATER WEAR-- I'LL HELP YOU TO--
THEN I SAW THE LOOK ON THEIR FACES.
NO-- PLEASE!
IT'S SAFE HERE-- THERE AREN'T ANY WARS-- NO ALIENS!
WE DON'T HAVE TO FIGHT FO FOOD--THEY GIVE US ALL WE NEED.
PLEASE-- WE WANT TO STAY.
ARE YOU NUTS?
YOU'RE LIVING IN A CAGE FOR CHRIST'S SAKE!

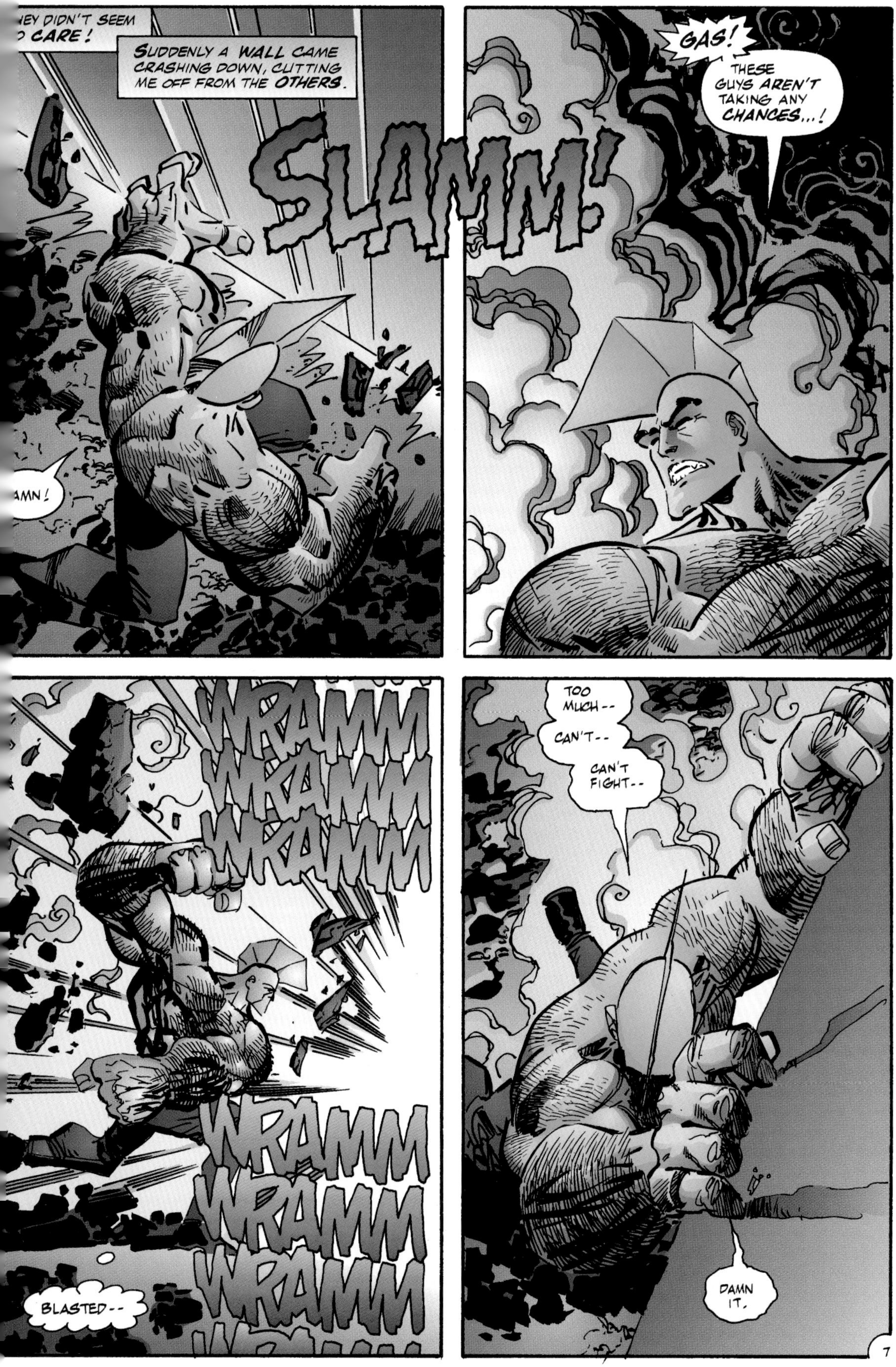

...HEY DIDN'T SEEM
...O CARE!
SUDDENLY A WALL CAME CRASHING DOWN, CUTTING ME OFF FROM THE OTHERS.
SLAMM!
...AMN!
GAS!
THESE GUYS AREN'T TAKING ANY CHANCES...!
WRAMM WRAMM WRAMM
WRAMM WRAMM WRAMM
BLASTED--
TOO MUCH--
CAN'T--
CAN'T FIGHT--
DAMN IT.

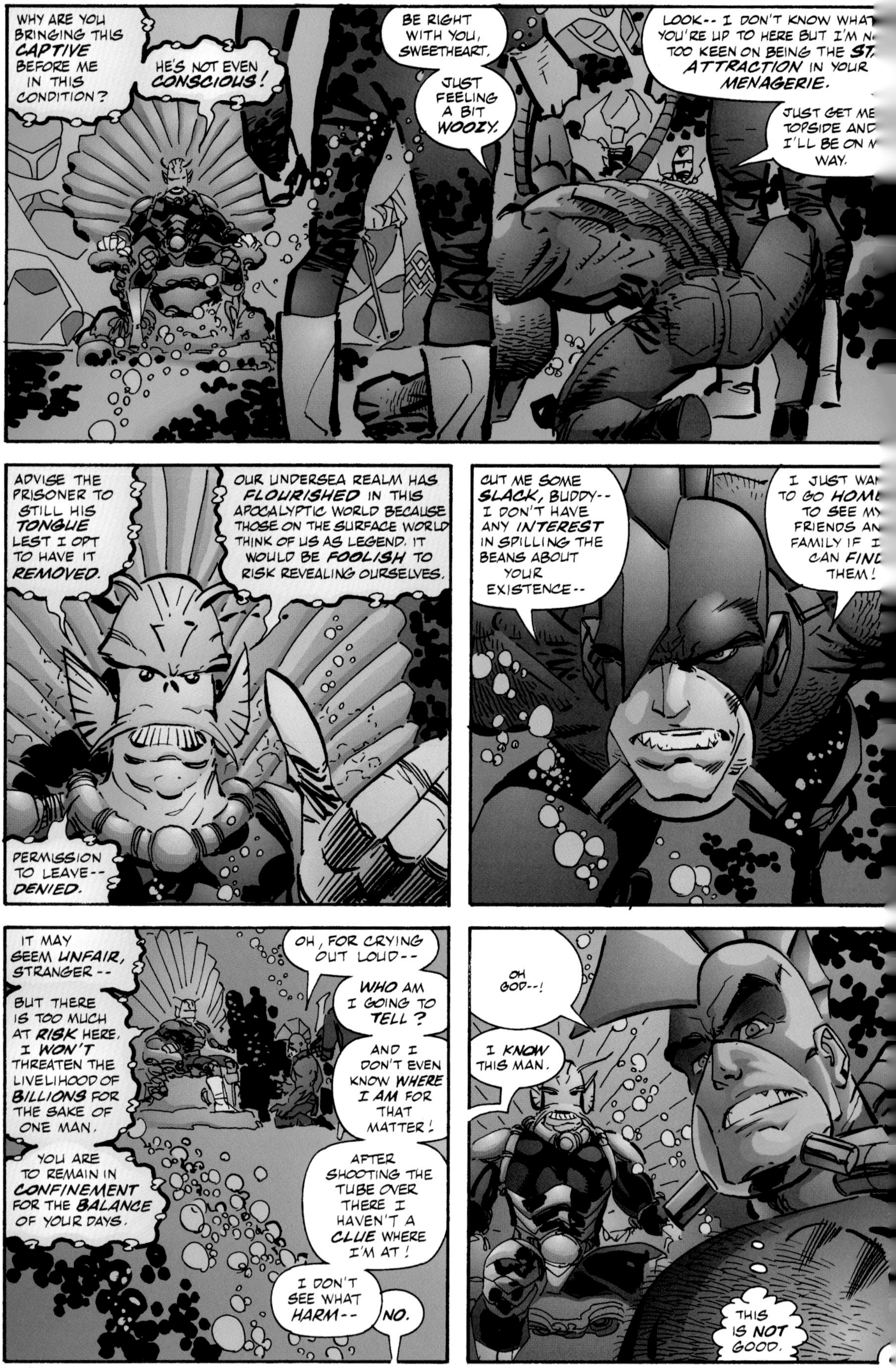
WHY ARE YOU BRINGING THIS CAPTIVE BEFORE ME IN THIS CONDITION?
HE'S NOT EVEN CONSCIOUS!
BE RIGHT WITH YOU, SWEETHEART.
JUST FEELING A BIT WOOZY.
LOOK-- I DON'T KNOW WHAT YOU'RE UP TO HERE BUT I'M NOT TOO KEEN ON BEING THE STAR ATTRACTION IN YOUR MENAGERIE.
JUST GET ME TOPSIDE AND I'LL BE ON MY WAY.
ADVISE THE PRISONER TO STILL HIS TONGUE LEST I OPT TO HAVE IT REMOVED.
OUR UNDERSEA REALM HAS FLOURISHED IN THIS APOCALYPTIC WORLD BECAUSE THOSE ON THE SURFACE WORLD THINK OF US AS LEGEND. IT WOULD BE FOOLISH TO RISK REVEALING OURSELVES.
PERMISSION TO LEAVE-- DENIED.
CUT ME SOME SLACK, BUDDY-- I DON'T HAVE ANY INTEREST IN SPILLING THE BEANS ABOUT YOUR EXISTENCE--
I JUST WANT TO GO HOME TO SEE MY FRIENDS AND FAMILY IF I CAN FIND THEM!
IT MAY SEEM UNFAIR, STRANGER--
BUT THERE IS TOO MUCH AT RISK HERE. I WON'T THREATEN THE LIVELIHOOD OF BILLIONS FOR THE SAKE OF ONE MAN.
YOU ARE TO REMAIN IN CONFINEMENT FOR THE BALANCE OF YOUR DAYS.
OH, FOR CRYING OUT LOUD--
WHO AM I GOING TO TELL?
AND I DON'T EVEN KNOW WHERE I AM FOR THAT MATTER!
AFTER SHOOTING THE TUBE OVER THERE I HAVEN'T A CLUE WHERE I'M AT!
I DON'T SEE WHAT HARM--
NO.
OH GOD--!
I KNOW THIS MAN.
THIS IS NOT GOOD.

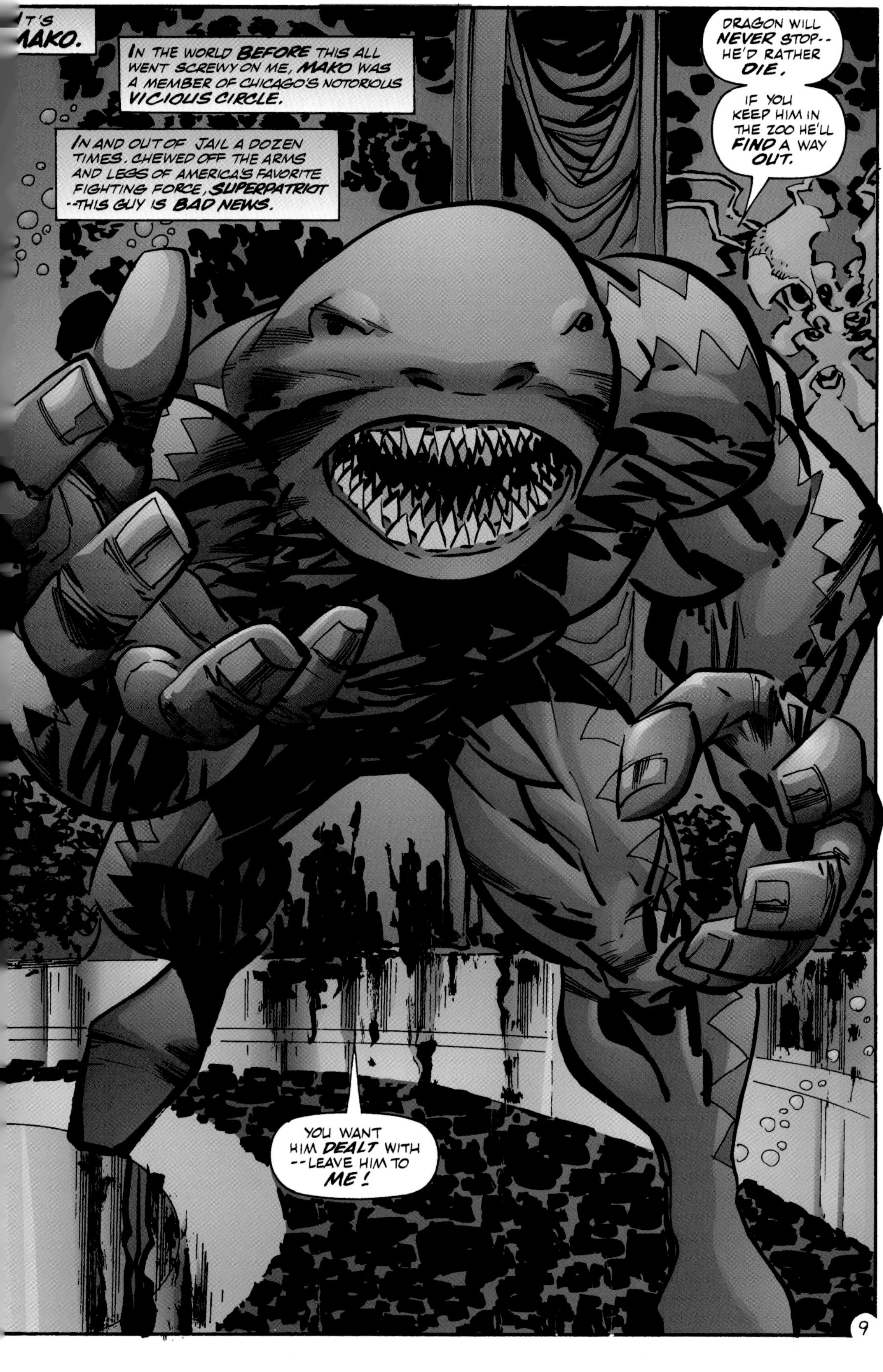
IT'S MAKO.
IN THE WORLD BEFORE THIS ALL WENT SCREWY ON ME, MAKO WAS A MEMBER OF CHICAGO'S NOTORIOUS VICIOUS CIRCLE.
IN AND OUT OF JAIL A DOZEN TIMES. CHEWED OFF THE ARMS AND LEGS OF AMERICA'S FAVORITE FIGHTING FORCE, SUPERPATRIOT --THIS GUY IS BAD NEWS.
DRAGON WILL NEVER STOP-- HE'D RATHER DIE.
IF YOU KEEP HIM IN THE ZOO HE'LL FIND A WAY OUT.
YOU WANT HIM DEALT WITH --LEAVE HIM TO ME!

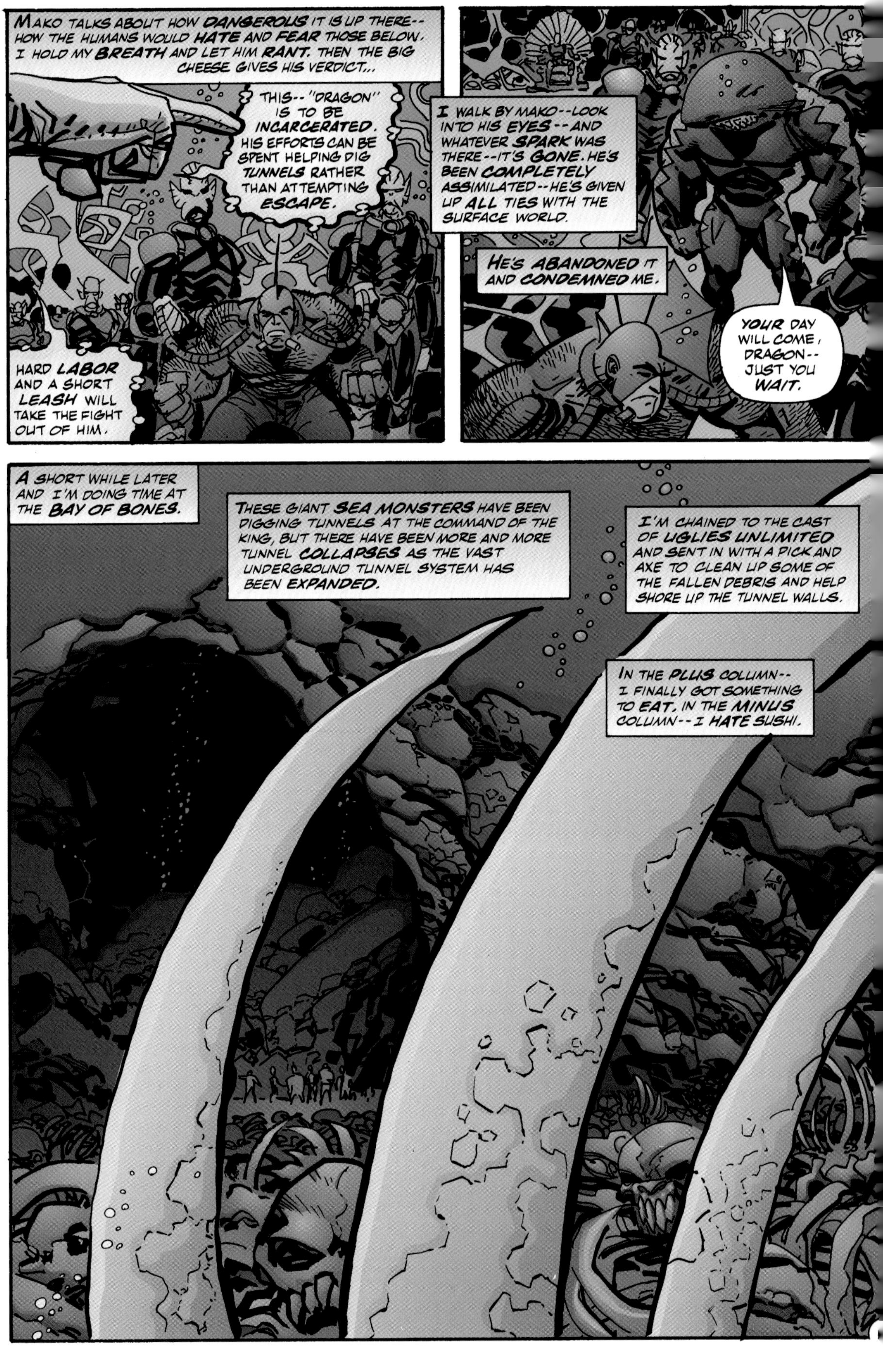
MAKO TALKS ABOUT HOW DANGEROUS IT IS UP THERE-- HOW THE HUMANS WOULD HATE AND FEAR THOSE BELOW. I HOLD MY BREATH AND LET HIM RANT. THEN THE BIG CHEESE GIVES HIS VERDICT...
THIS-- "DRAGON" IS TO BE INCARCERATED. HIS EFFORTS CAN BE SPENT HELPING DIG TUNNELS RATHER THAN ATTEMPTING ESCAPE.
HARD LABOR AND A SHORT LEASH WILL TAKE THE FIGHT OUT OF HIM.
I WALK BY MAKO--LOOK INTO HIS EYES--AND WHATEVER SPARK WAS THERE--IT'S GONE. HE'S BEEN COMPLETELY ASSIMILATED--HE'S GIVEN UP ALL TIES WITH THE SURFACE WORLD.
HE'S ABANDONED IT AND CONDEMNED ME.
YOUR DAY WILL COME, DRAGON-- JUST YOU WAIT.
A SHORT WHILE LATER AND I'M DOING TIME AT THE BAY OF BONES.
THESE GIANT SEA MONSTERS HAVE BEEN DIGGING TUNNELS AT THE COMMAND OF THE KING, BUT THERE HAVE BEEN MORE AND MORE TUNNEL COLLAPSES AS THE VAST UNDERGROUND TUNNEL SYSTEM HAS BEEN EXPANDED.
I'M CHAINED TO THE CAST OF UGLIES UNLIMITED AND SENT IN WITH A PICK AND AXE TO CLEAN UP SOME OF THE FALLEN DEBRIS AND HELP SHORE UP THE TUNNEL WALLS.
IN THE PLUS COLUMN-- I FINALLY GOT SOMETHING TO EAT. IN THE MINUS COLUMN--I HATE SUSHI.

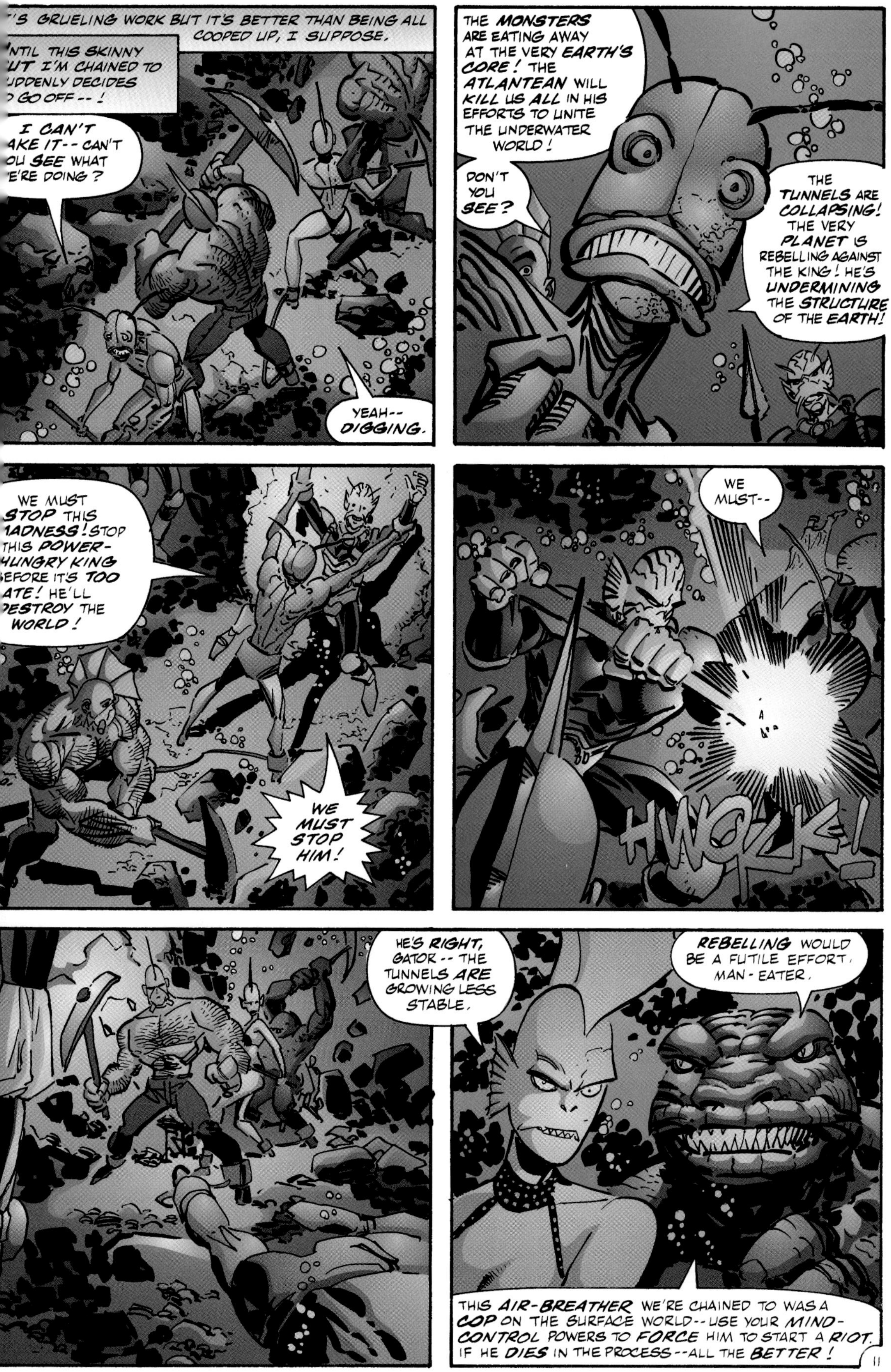

'S GRUELING WORK BUT IT'S BETTER THAN BEING ALL COOPED UP, I SUPPOSE.
NTIL THIS SKINNY UT I'M CHAINED TO UDDENLY DECIDES O GO OFF -- !
I CAN'T AKE IT -- CAN'T OU SEE WHAT E'RE DOING?
YEAH -- DIGGING.
THE MONSTERS ARE EATING AWAY AT THE VERY EARTH'S CORE! THE ATLANTEAN WILL KILL US ALL IN HIS EFFORTS TO UNITE THE UNDERWATER WORLD!
DON'T YOU SEE?
THE TUNNELS ARE COLLAPSING! THE VERY PLANET IS REBELLING AGAINST THE KING! HE'S UNDERMINING THE STRUCTURE OF THE EARTH!
WE MUST STOP THIS ADNESS! STOP THIS POWER-HUNGRY KING EFORE IT'S TOO ATE! HE'LL DESTROY THE WORLD!
WE MUST STOP HIM!
WE MUST--
HWOLK!
HE'S RIGHT, GATOR -- THE TUNNELS ARE GROWING LESS STABLE.
REBELLING WOULD BE A FUTILE EFFORT, MAN-EATER.
THIS AIR-BREATHER WE'RE CHAINED TO WAS A COP ON THE SURFACE WORLD -- USE YOUR MIND-CONTROL POWERS TO FORCE HIM TO START A RIOT. IF HE DIES IN THE PROCESS -- ALL THE BETTER!

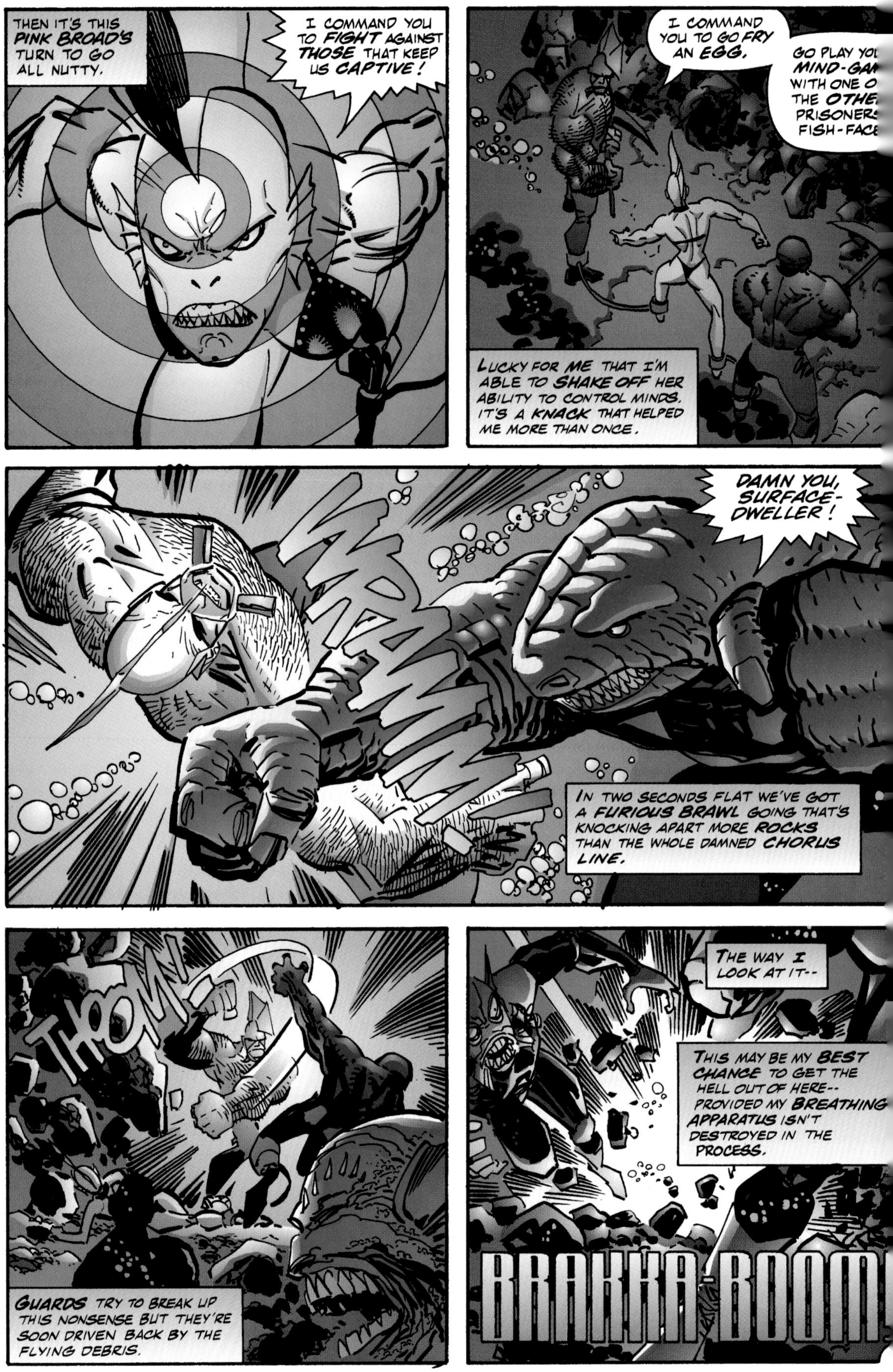

THEN IT'S THIS PINK BROAD'S TURN TO GO ALL NUTTY.
I COMMAND YOU TO FIGHT AGAINST THOSE THAT KEEP US CAPTIVE!
I COMMAND YOU TO GO FRY AN EGG.
GO PLAY YOU MIND-GAM WITH ONE O THE OTHE PRISONERS FISH-FACE
LUCKY FOR ME THAT I'M ABLE TO SHAKE OFF HER ABILITY TO CONTROL MINDS. IT'S A KNACK THAT HELPED ME MORE THAN ONCE.
DAMN YOU, SURFACE-DWELLER!
IN TWO SECONDS FLAT WE'VE GOT A FURIOUS BRAWL GOING THAT'S KNOCKING APART MORE ROCKS THAN THE WHOLE DAMNED CHORUS LINE.
THOOM!
GUARDS TRY TO BREAK UP THIS NONSENSE BUT THEY'RE SOON DRIVEN BACK BY THE FLYING DEBRIS.
THE WAY I LOOK AT IT--
THIS MAY BE MY BEST CHANCE TO GET THE HELL OUT OF HERE-- PROVIDED MY BREATHING APPARATUS ISN'T DESTROYED IN THE PROCESS.
BRAKKA-BOOM

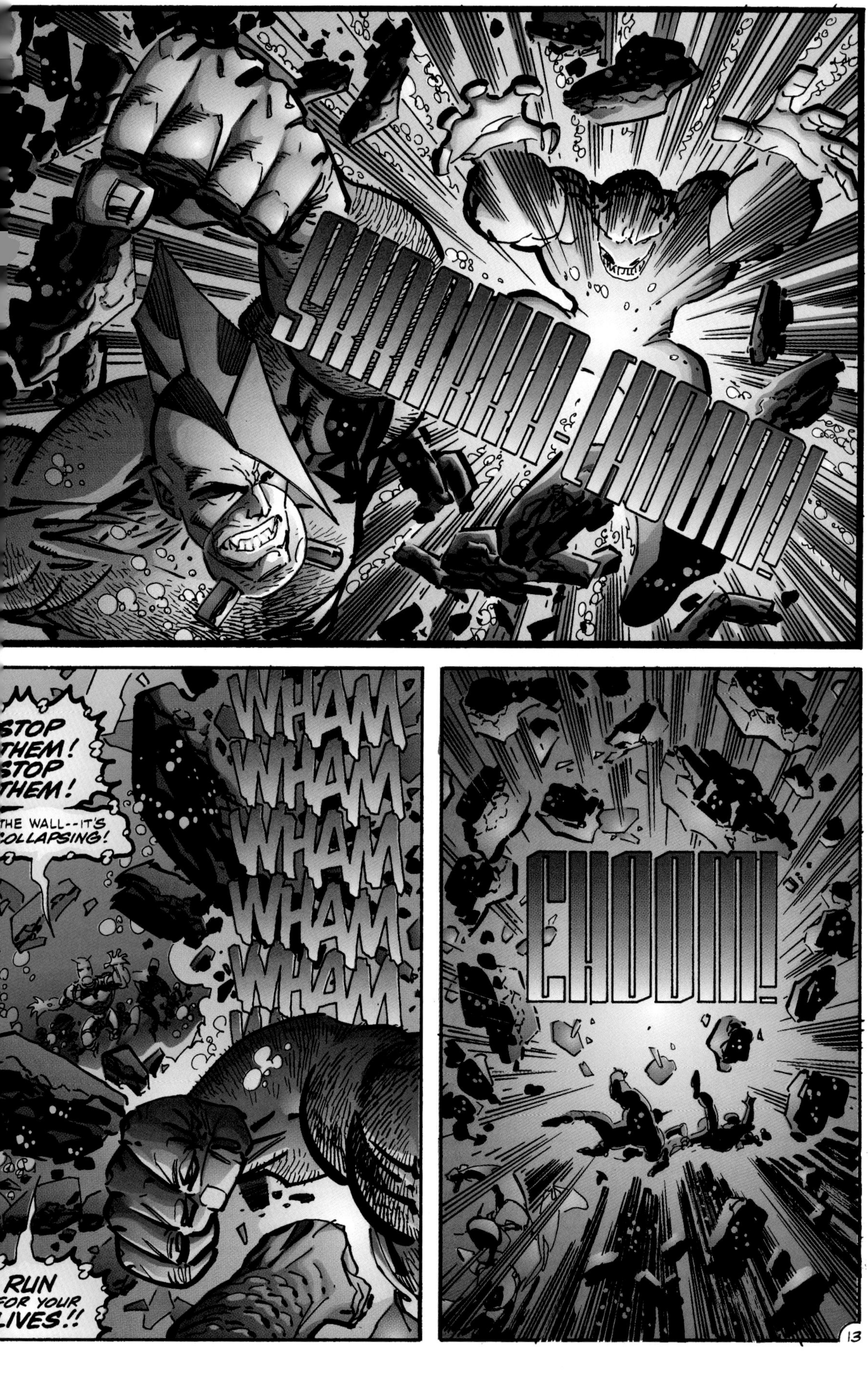
SHHHKKKKK-CHOOM!
WHAM
WHAM
WHAM
WHAM
WHAM
STOP THEM! STOP THEM!
THE WALL--IT'S COLLAPSING!
RUN FOR YOUR LIVES!!
CHOOM!

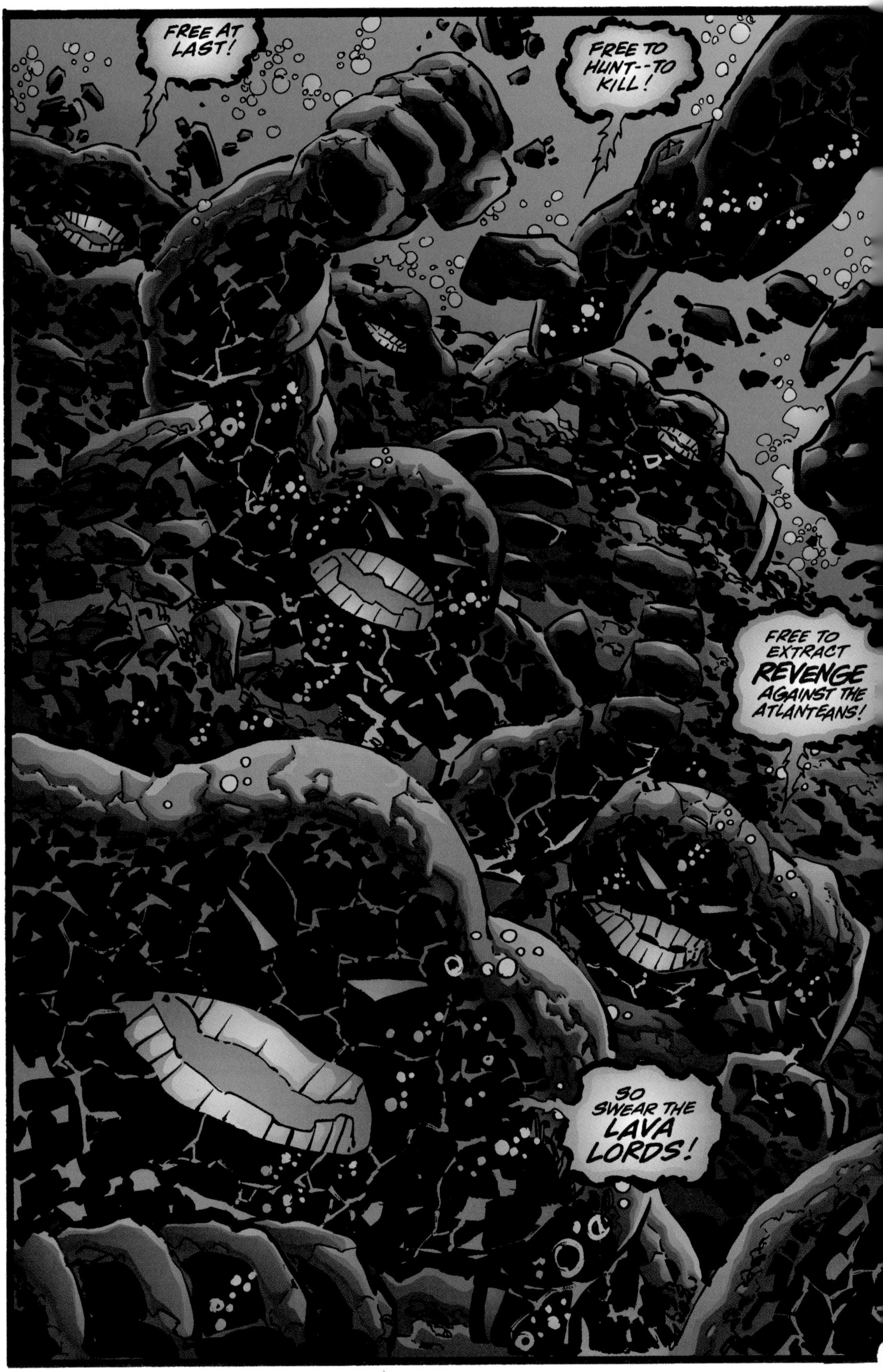
FREE AT LAST!
FREE TO HUNT--TO KILL!
FREE TO EXTRACT REVENGE AGAINST THE ATLANTEANS!
SO SWEAR THE LAVA LORDS!

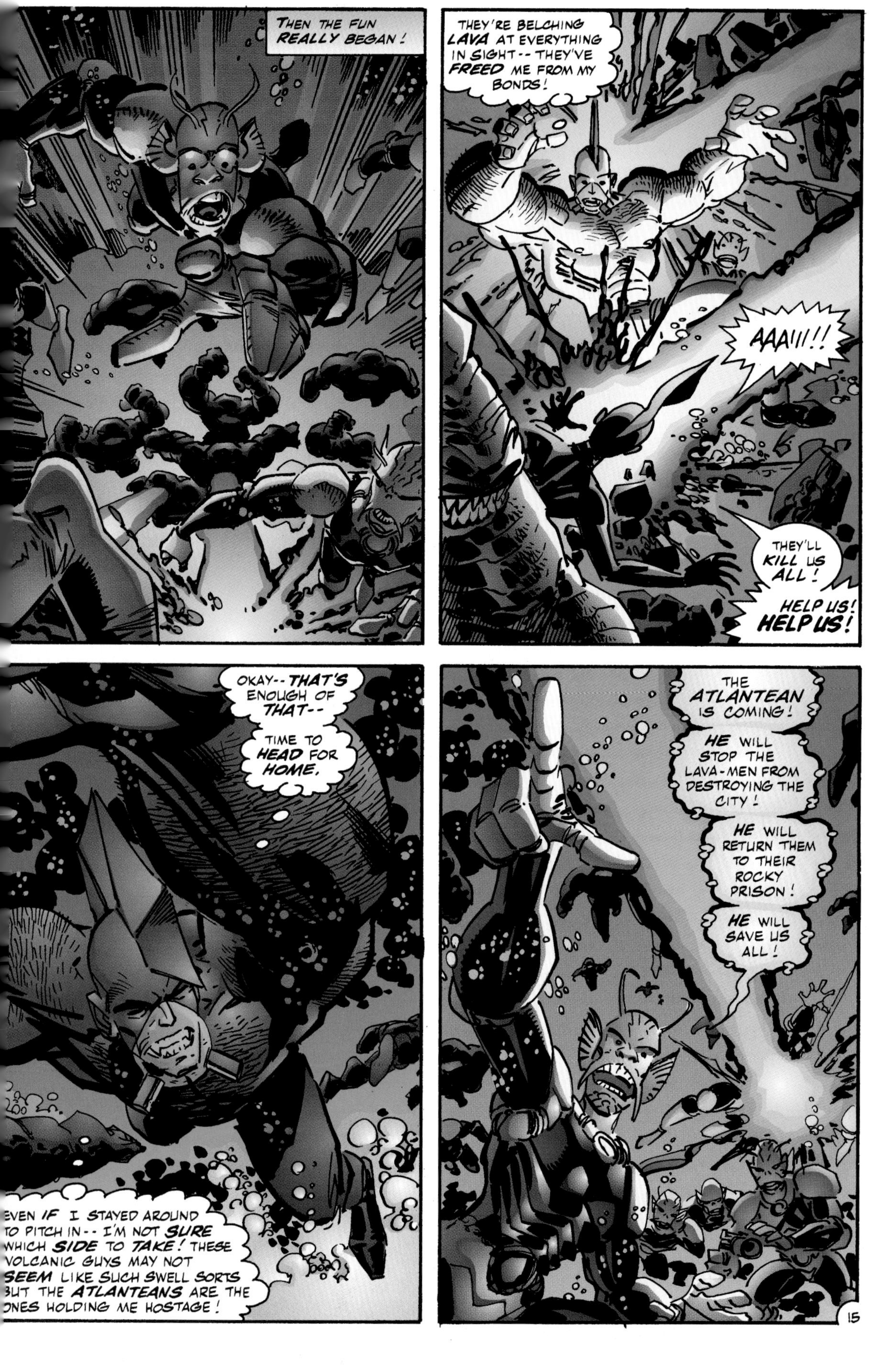
THEN THE FUN REALLY BEGAN!
THEY'RE BELCHING LAVA AT EVERYTHING IN SIGHT -- THEY'VE FREED ME FROM MY BONDS!
AAAIII!!
THEY'LL KILL US ALL!
HELP US! HELP US!
OKAY -- THAT'S ENOUGH OF THAT --
TIME TO HEAD FOR HOME.
EVEN IF I STAYED AROUND TO PITCH IN -- I'M NOT SURE WHICH SIDE TO TAKE! THESE VOLCANIC GUYS MAY NOT SEEM LIKE SUCH SWELL SORTS BUT THE ATLANTEANS ARE THE ONES HOLDING ME HOSTAGE!
THE ATLANTEAN IS COMING!
HE WILL STOP THE LAVA-MEN FROM DESTROYING THE CITY!
HE WILL RETURN THEM TO THEIR ROCKY PRISON!
HE WILL SAVE US ALL!

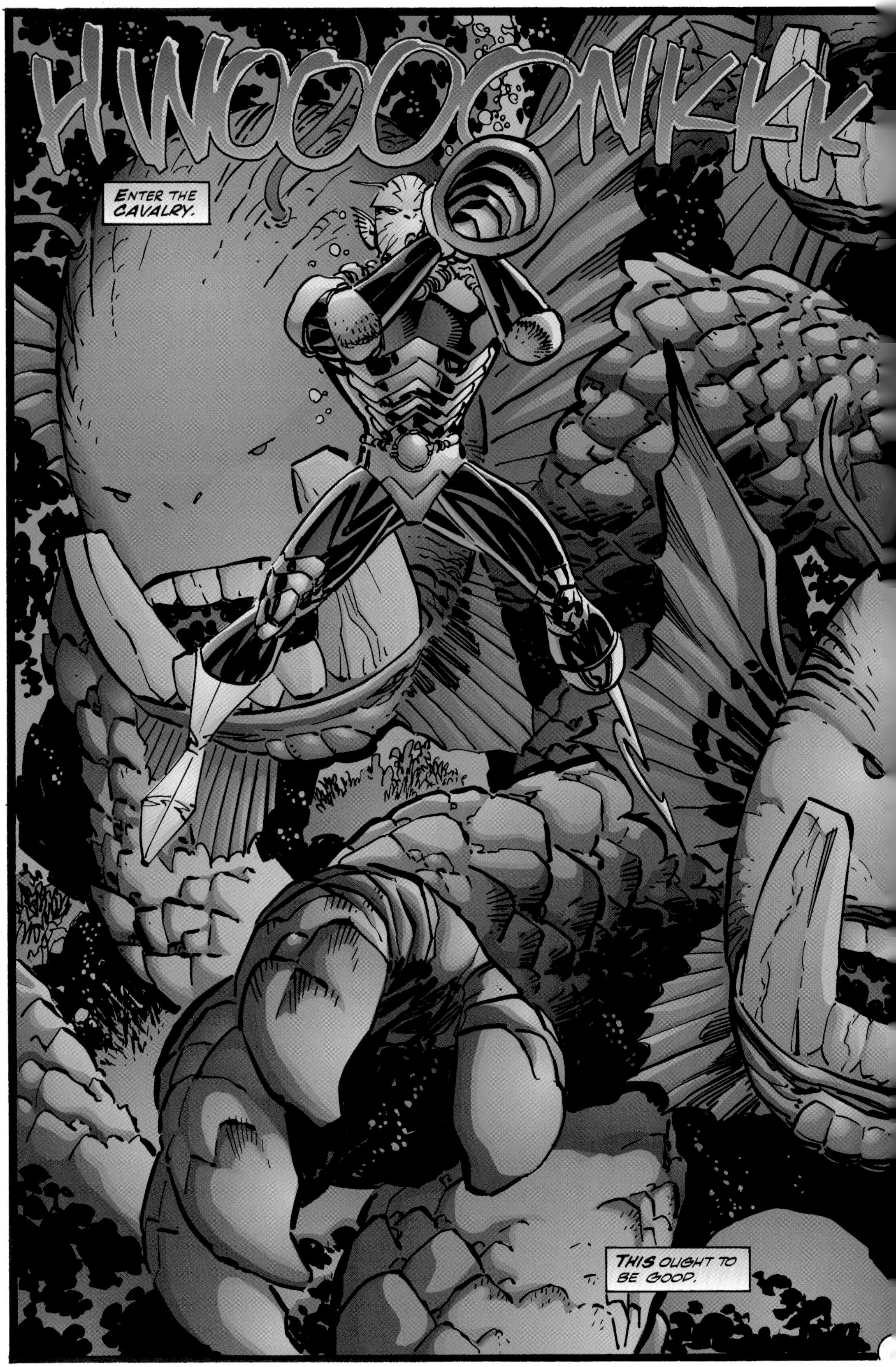
HWOOOONKKK
ENTER THE CAVALRY.
THIS OUGHT TO BE GOOD.

WOO-HOO!

GO GET 'EM, GUY!

WHATEVER IT TAKES TO KEEP YOU OCCUPIED WHILE I HIGHTAIL IT OUT OF HERE IS FINE BY ME.

GHAA!

IT'S MAKO--

AND HE'S SWIMMING RIGHT AT ME--!

DODGED-- JUST IN TIME--

BUT THIS GUY'S MORE SHARK THAN MAN-- HE'LL CIRCLE BACK AND BE ON MY ASS BEFORE I CAN GET TEN FEET!

17

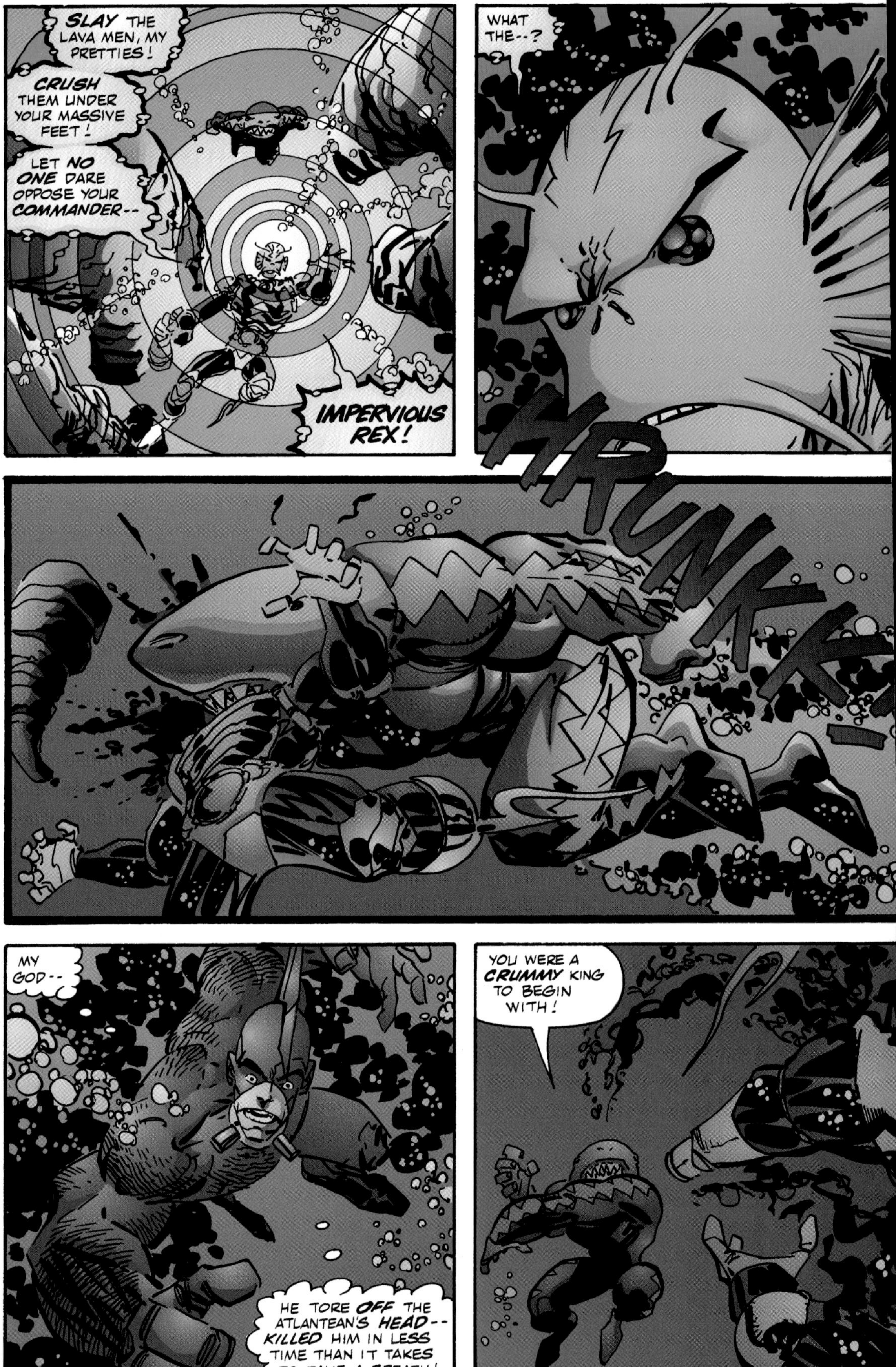
SLAY THE LAVA MEN, MY PRETTIES!
CRUSH THEM UNDER YOUR MASSIVE FEET!
LET NO ONE DARE OPPOSE YOUR COMMANDER--
IMPERVIOUS REX!
WHAT THE--?
HRUNKK
MY GOD--
HE TORE OFF THE ATLANTEAN'S HEAD-- KILLED HIM IN LESS TIME THAN IT TAKES TO TAKE A BREATH!
YOU WERE A CRUMMY KING TO BEGIN WITH!

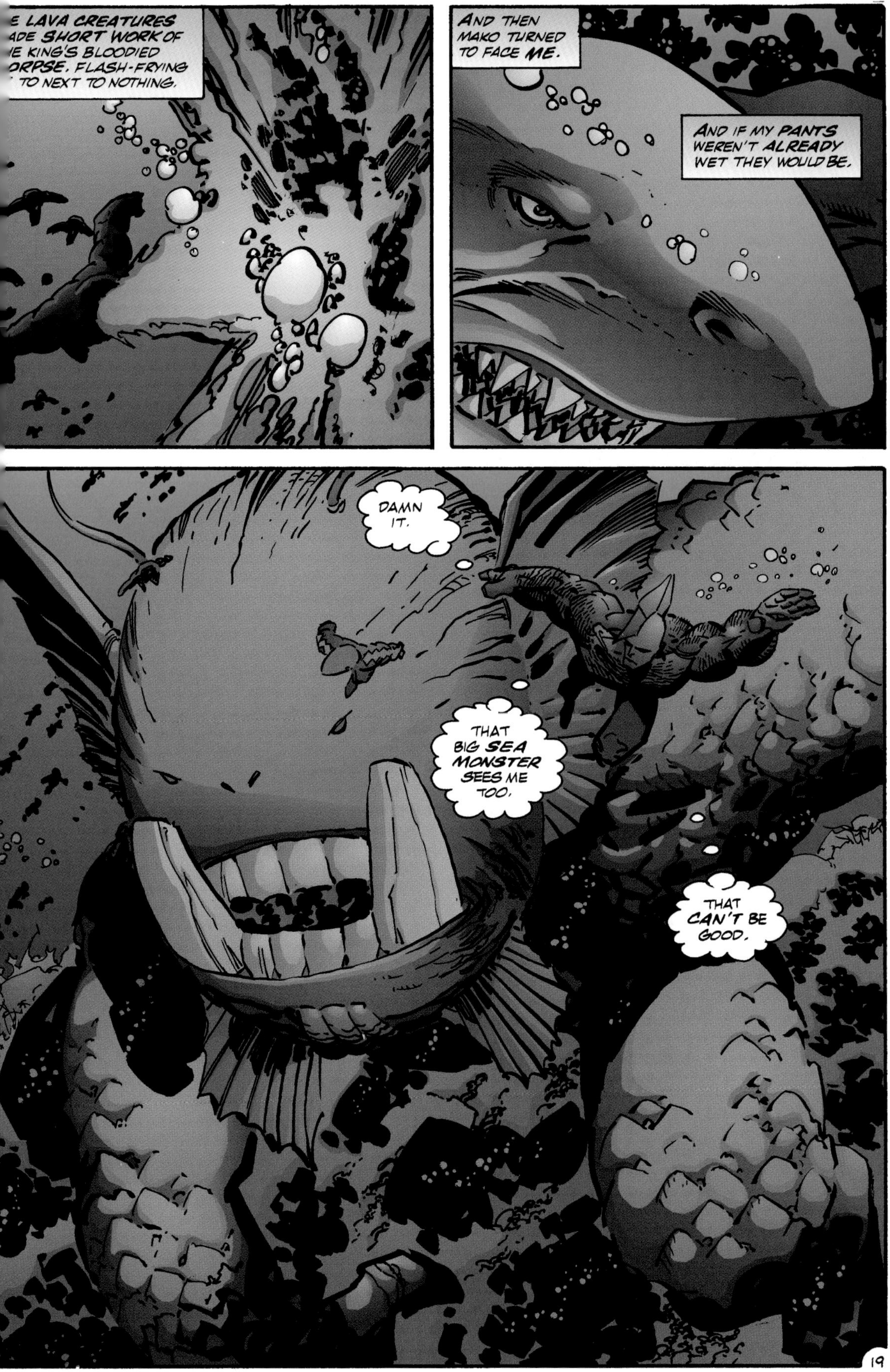

E LAVA CREATURES ADE SHORT WORK OF E KING'S BLOODIED ORPSE, FLASH-FRYING T TO NEXT TO NOTHING.
AND THEN MAKO TURNED TO FACE ME.
AND IF MY PANTS WEREN'T ALREADY WET THEY WOULD BE.
DAMN IT.
THAT BIG SEA MONSTER SEES ME TOO.
THAT CAN'T BE GOOD.

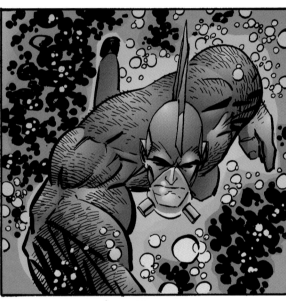

?

THE HELL...?

I'M ALONE-- THE CREATURE AND MAKO ARE GONE.

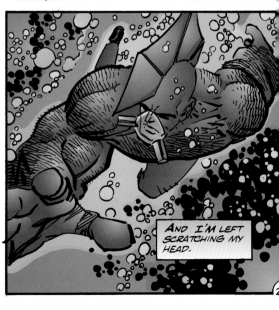

AND I'M LEFT SCRATCHING MY HEAD.

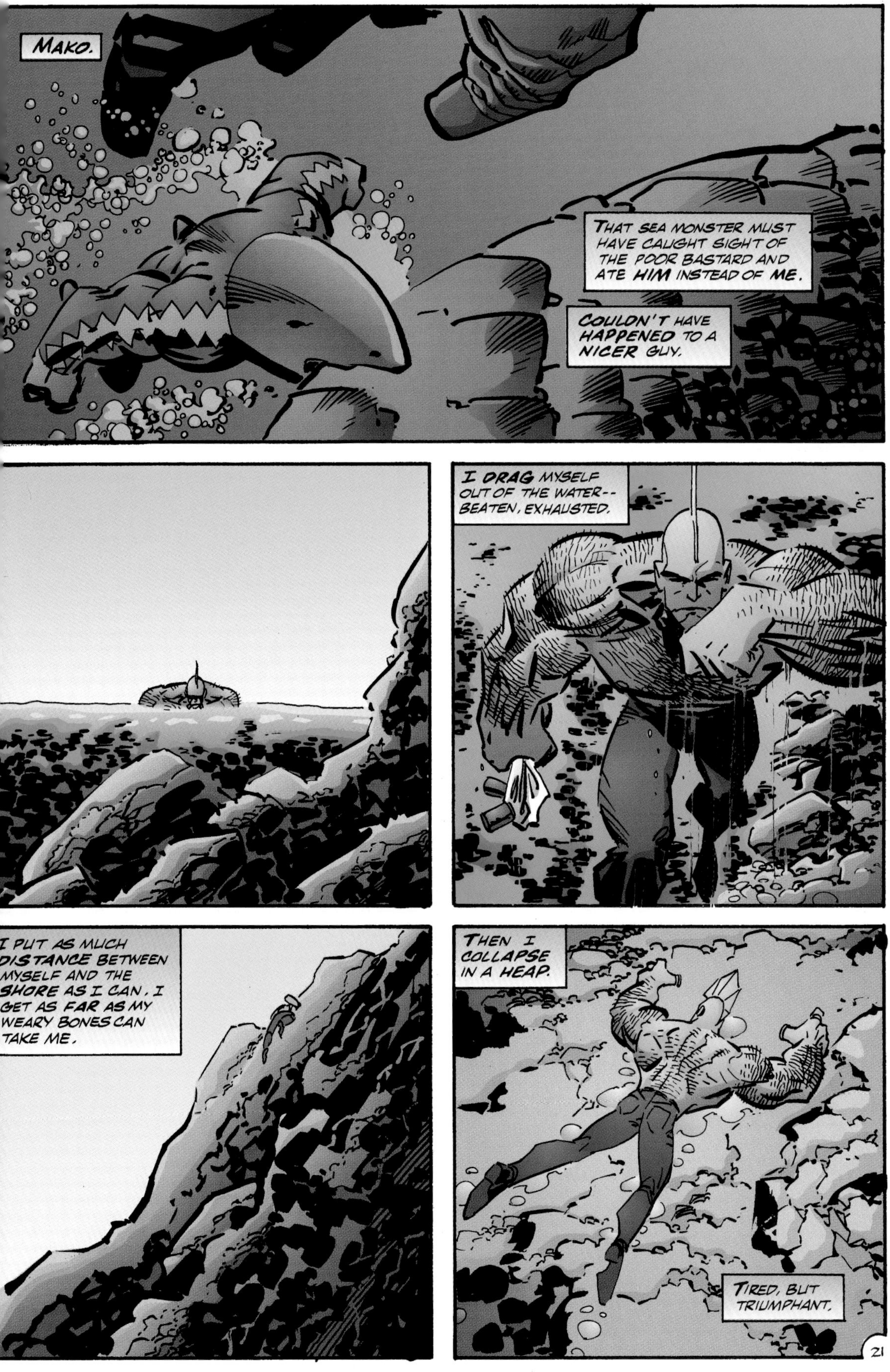
MAKO.
THAT SEA MONSTER MUST HAVE CAUGHT SIGHT OF THE POOR BASTARD AND ATE HIM INSTEAD OF ME.
COULDN'T HAVE HAPPENED TO A NICER GUY.
I DRAG MYSELF OUT OF THE WATER-- BEATEN, EXHAUSTED.
I PUT AS MUCH DISTANCE BETWEEN MYSELF AND THE SHORE AS I CAN. I GET AS FAR AS MY WEARY BONES CAN TAKE ME.
THEN I COLLAPSE IN A HEAP.
TIRED, BUT TRIUMPHANT.

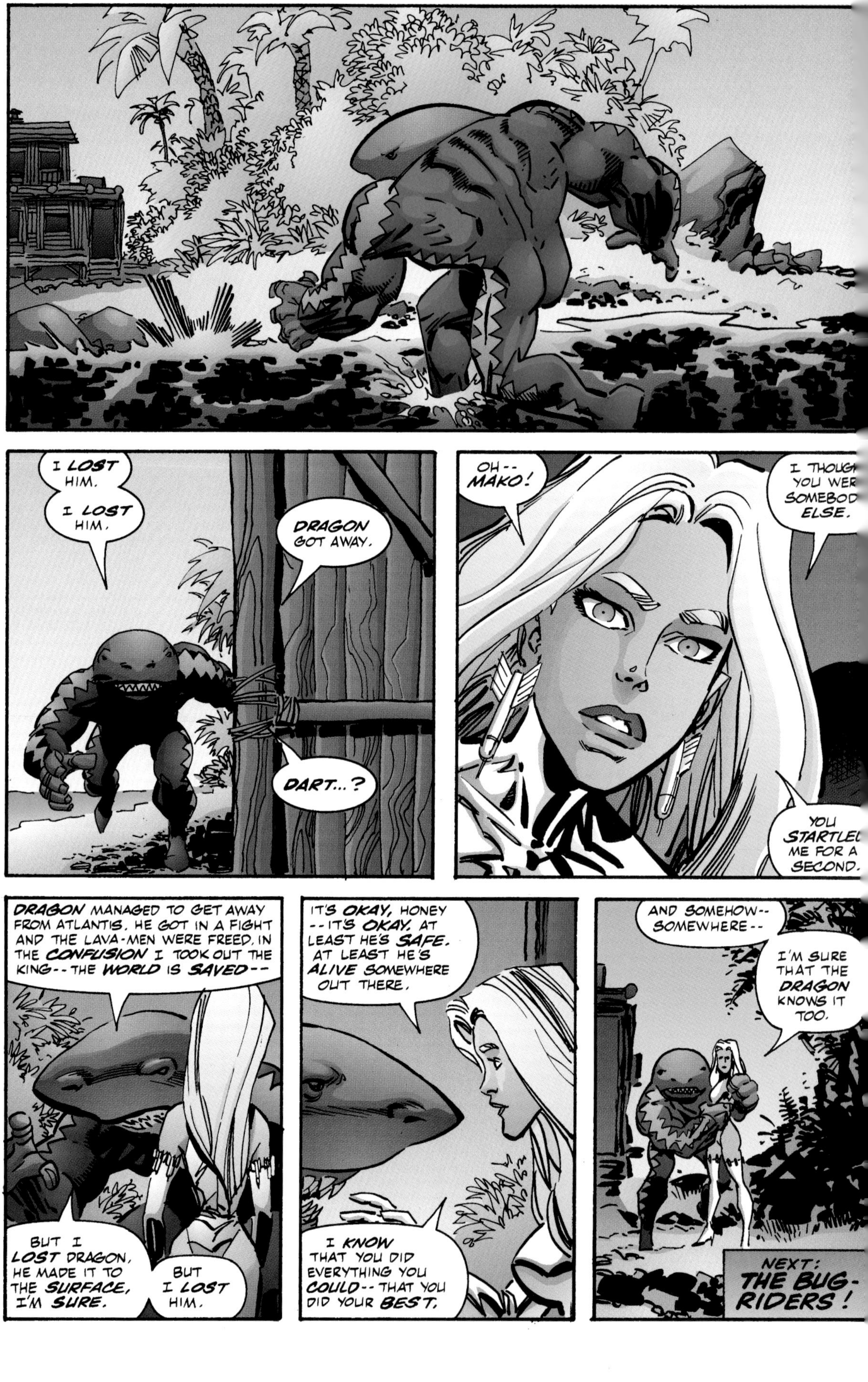
I LOST HIM. I LOST HIM.
DRAGON GOT AWAY.
DART...?
OH-- MAKO!
I THOUG YOU WER SOMEBOD ELSE.
YOU STARTLE ME FOR A SECOND.
DRAGON MANAGED TO GET AWAY FROM ATLANTIS. HE GOT IN A FIGHT AND THE LAVA-MEN WERE FREED. IN THE CONFUSION I TOOK OUT THE KING--THE WORLD IS SAVED--
BUT I LOST DRAGON. HE MADE IT TO THE SURFACE, I'M SURE.
BUT I LOST HIM.
IT'S OKAY, HONEY --IT'S OKAY. AT LEAST HE'S SAFE. AT LEAST HE'S ALIVE SOMEWHERE OUT THERE.
I KNOW THAT YOU DID EVERYTHING YOU COULD--THAT YOU DID YOUR BEST.
AND SOMEHOW-- SOMEWHERE--
I'M SURE THAT THE DRAGON KNOWS IT TOO.
NEXT: THE BUG-RIDERS!

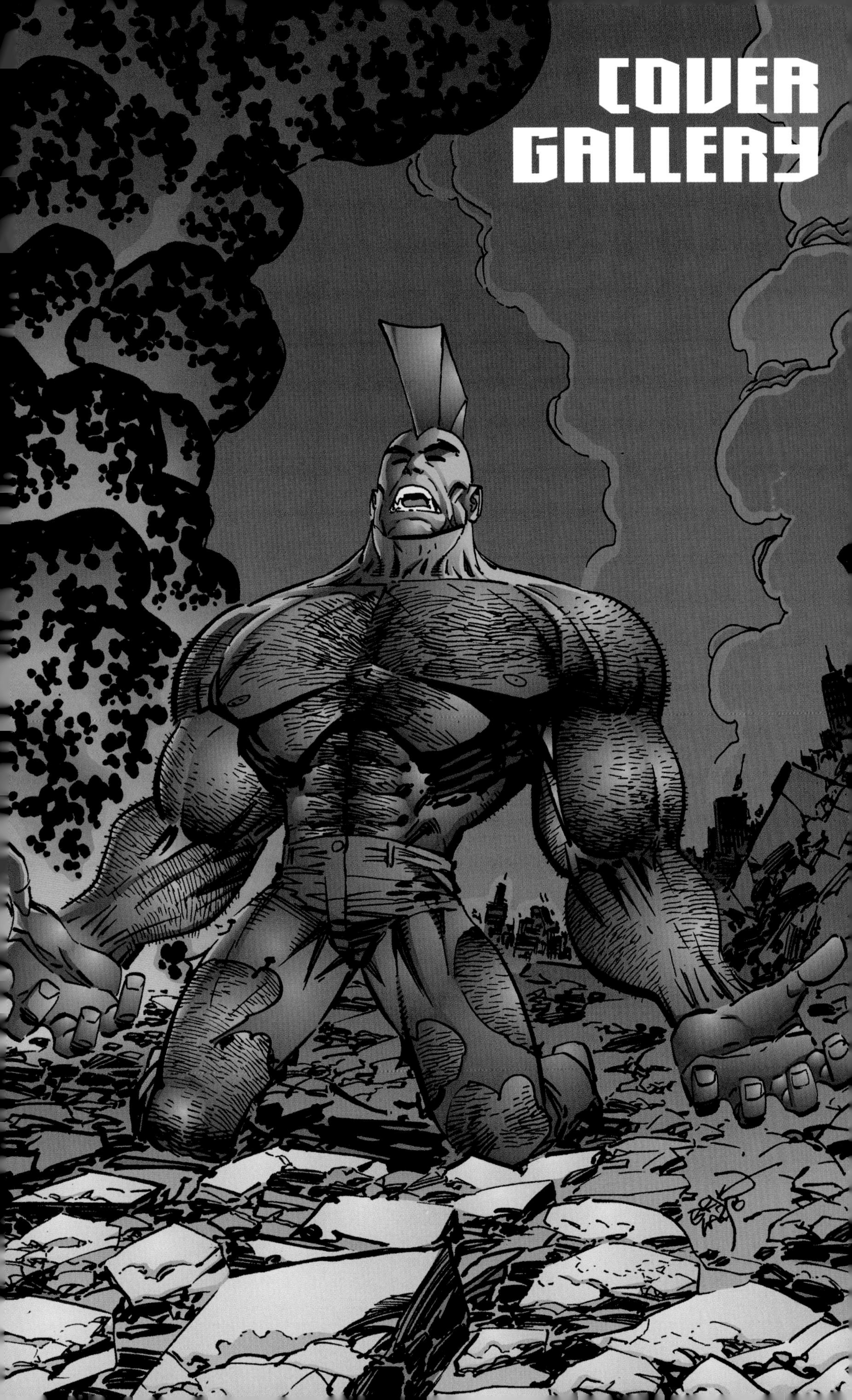
COVER
GALLERY

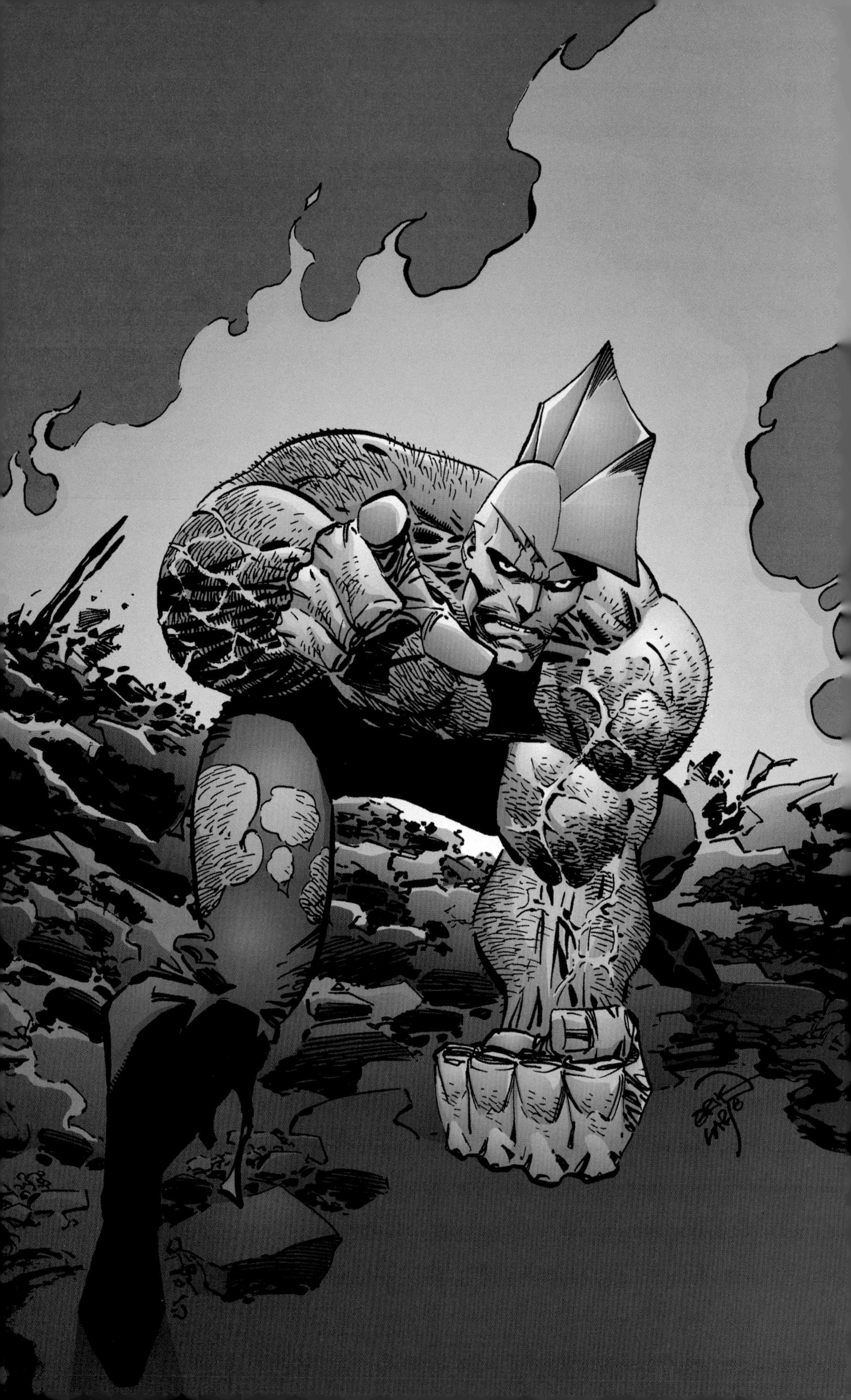

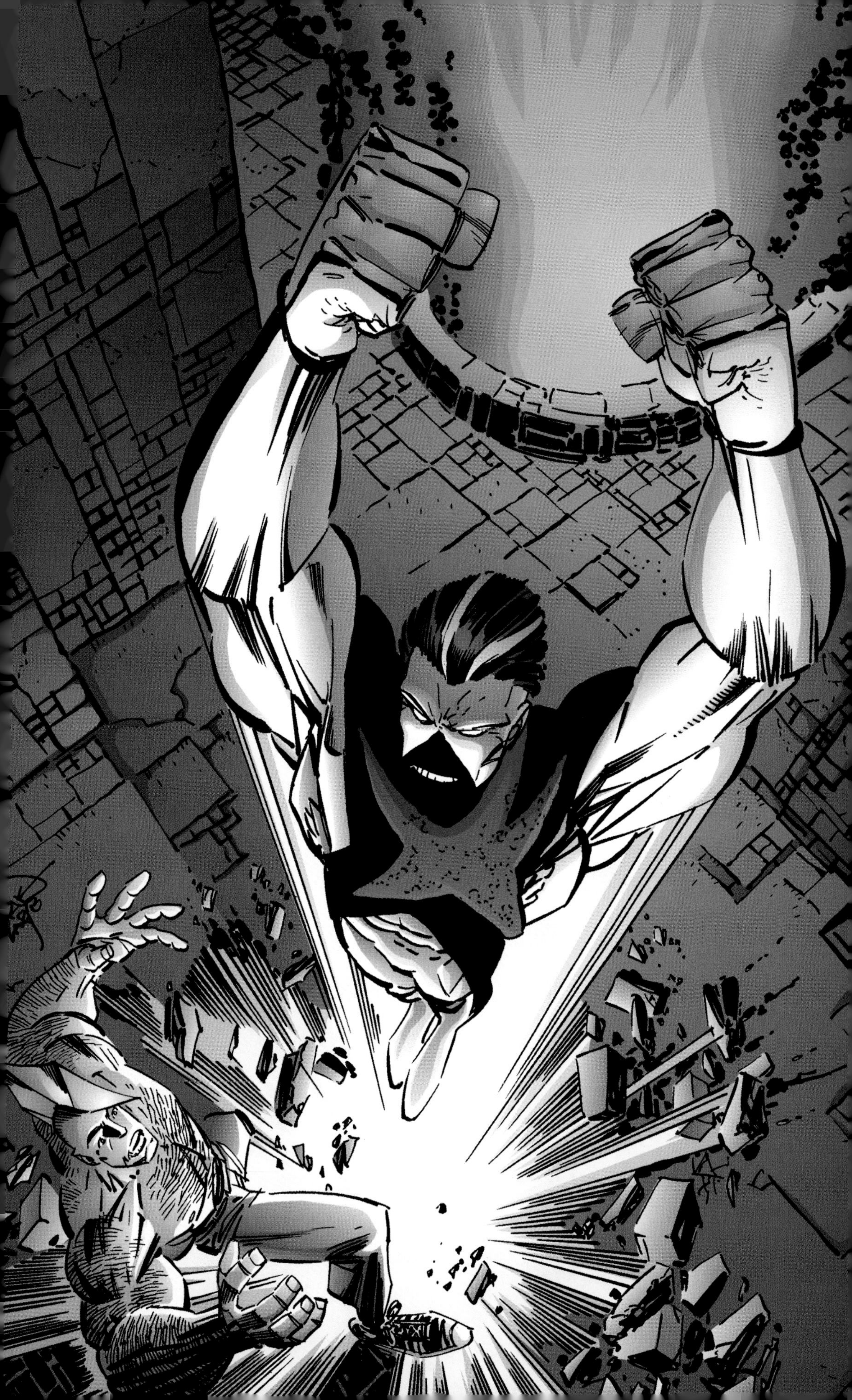

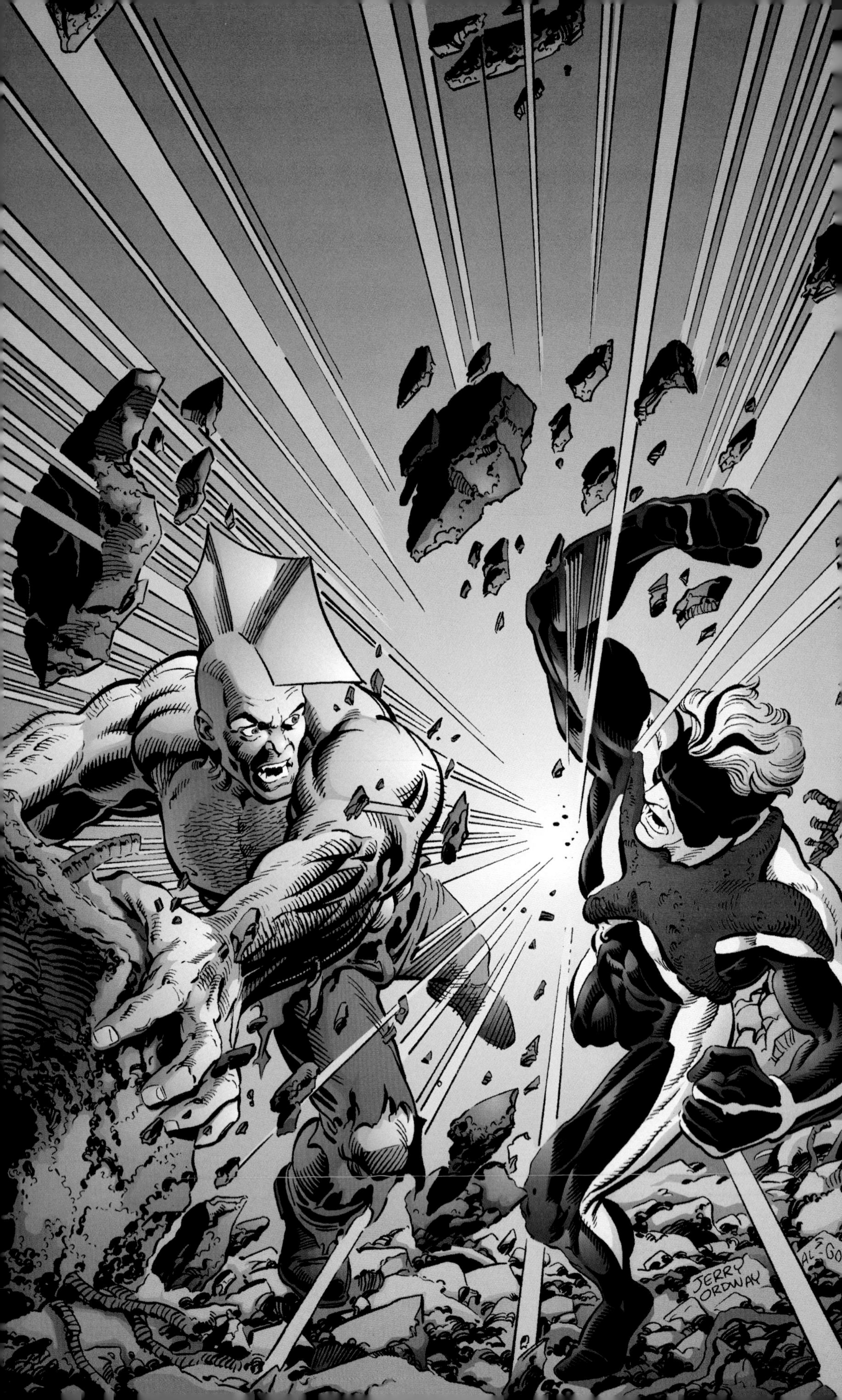
JERRY ORDWAY

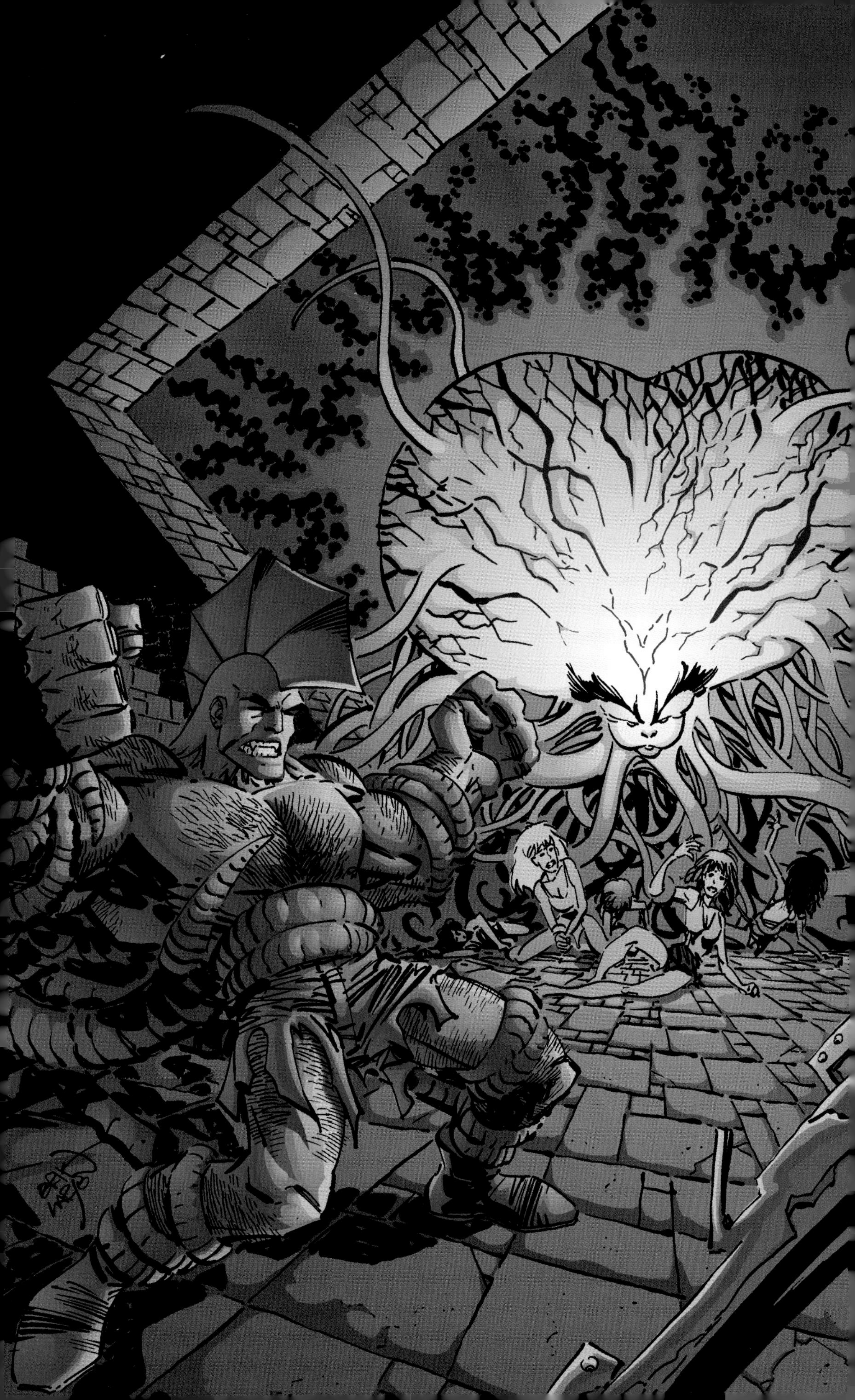

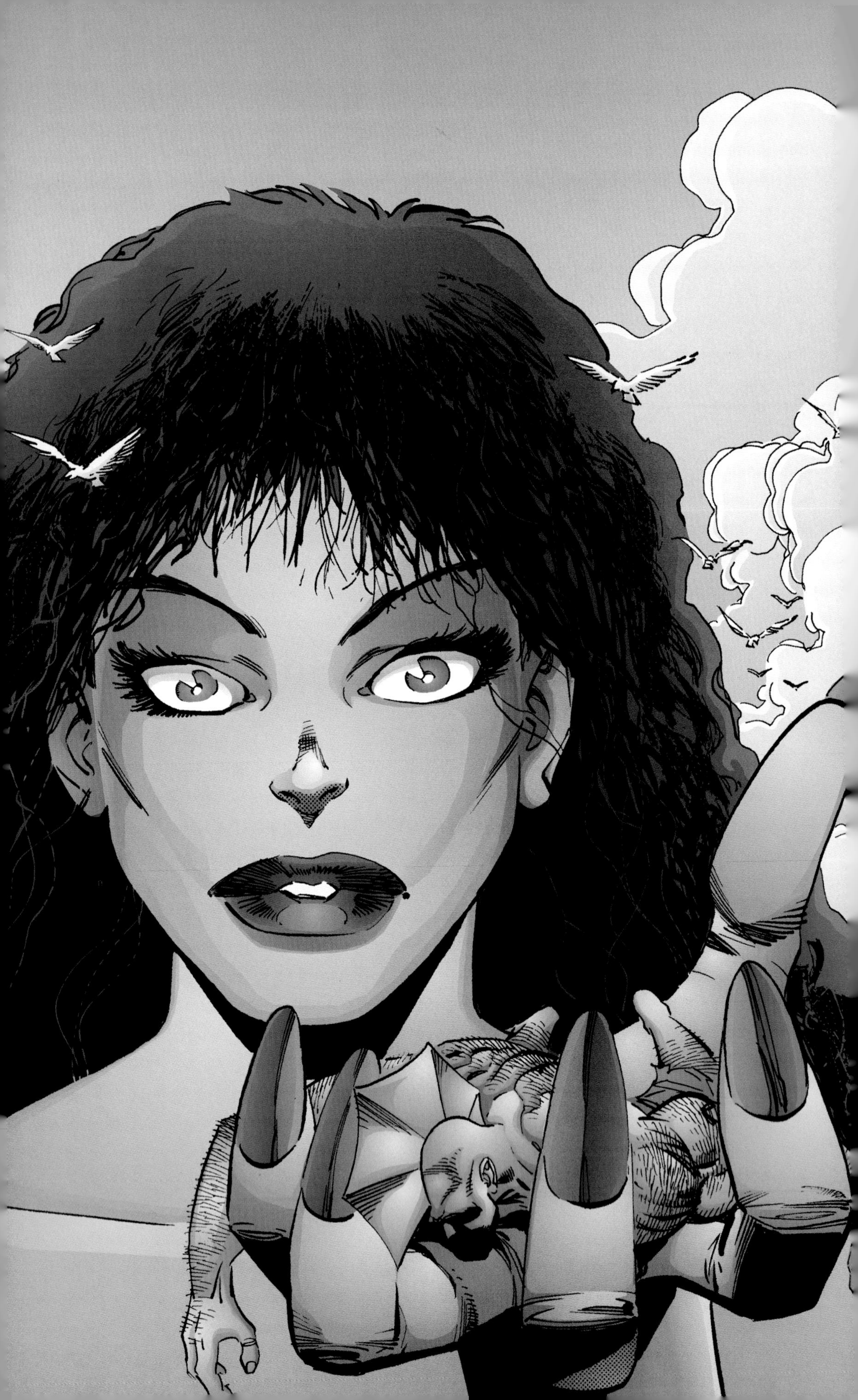

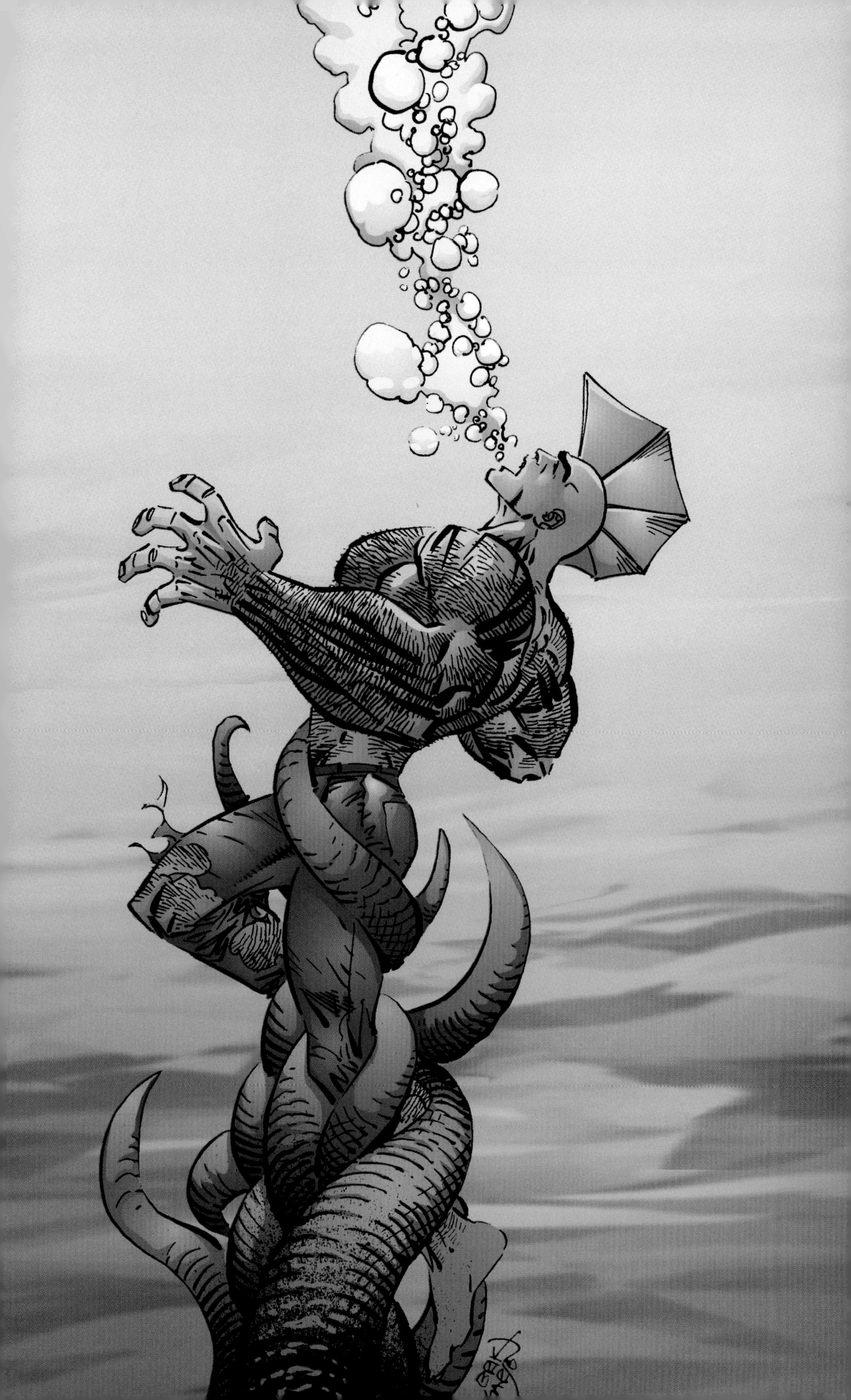

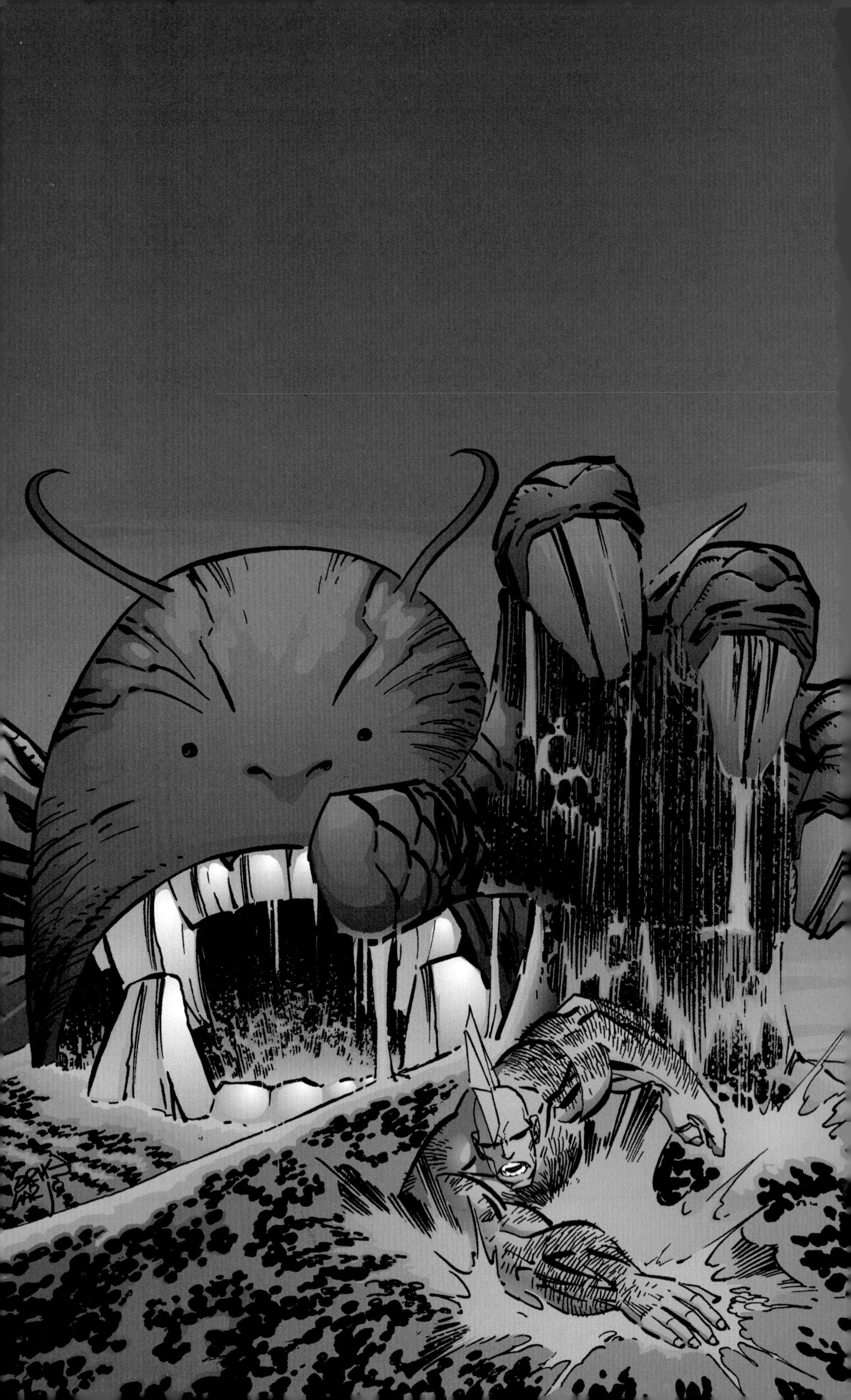